Building Enterprise Blockchain Solutions on AWS

A Developer's Guide to Build, Deploy, and Managed Apps Using Ethereum, Hyperledger Fabric, and AWS Blockchain

---

Murughan Palaniachari

www.bpbonline.com

FIRST EDITION 2021

Copyright © BPB Publications, India

ISBN: 978-93-90684-434

LIMITS OF LIABILITY AND DISCLAIMER OF WARRANTY

Distributors:

BPB PUBLICATIONS
20, Ansari Road, Darya Ganj
New Delhi-110002
Ph: 23254990/23254991

DECCAN AGENCIES
4-3-329, Bank Street,
Hyderabad-500195
Ph: 24756967/24756400

MICRO MEDIA
Shop No. 5, Mahendra Chambers,
150 DN Rd. Next to Capital Cinema,
V.T. (C.S.T.) Station, MUMBAI-400 001
Ph: 22078296/22078297

BPB BOOK CENTRE
376 Old Lajpat Rai Market,
Delhi-110006
Ph: 23861747

To View Complete
BPB Publications Catalogue
Scan the QR Code:

Published by Manish Jain for BPB Publications, 20 Ansari Road, Darya Ganj, New Delhi-110002 and Printed by him at Repro India Ltd, Mumbai

www.bpbonline.com

Dedicated to

My beloved twin babies,
Mishi
Nivin

&

My wife Karishma

About the Author

Murughan Palaniachari is a developer, speaker, blogger, trainer, DevOps, and Blockchain expert.

He has 14+ years of software development and operations experience in multiple technology stacks, including C#, Javascript, NodeJS, Java, Python, and Blockchain. He has expertise in Blockchain, Ethereum, Solidity, Hyperledger Fabric, and Cryptocurrency. He is an expert in building Enterprise Blockchain solutions using Ethereum, Hyperledger Fabric, and Stellar.

He is an organizer of TAC (Technical Agility Conference), meetup organizer of Blockchain, DevOps, and Cloud.

About the Reviewer

Mrugesh Patel is a strategic thinker and entrepreneur at heart. He can still write code with the best of them, and also understand what makes a product and business great.

He is passionate about building talented, healthy, and motivated engineering organizations and leading them to accomplish extraordinary things. He cares deeply about organizational health and principled leadership, as these are the greatest drivers for any team to harness its maximum potential.

He believes success is far more achievable, and with fun, when one has a healthy, engaged, and talented workforce led by leaders with unquestionable integrity and full transparency.

He considers himself fortunate that he has been a part of some noteworthy engineering teams, and built, and led some great ones too. He values strong relationships and builds high performing teams that are built on trust.

Currently, he is an Engineering Manager as well as a Technical founder in Tech Startups. He has more than 16+ years of experience in Software Development with various technologies, including AWS and Blockchain. He has been part of a successful startup from stealth mode to successful exit and well-established MNC companies.

Acknowledgement

There are a few people I want to thank for the continued and ongoing support that they have given me during the writing of this book. First and foremost, I would like to thank my wife (Karishma G H) for continuously encouraging me to write this book — I could have never completed it without her support.

I am grateful to the course and the companies which provided me with support throughout the learning process of Building Enterprise Blockchain solutions on AWS. Thank you for all the hidden support provided. I gratefully acknowledge Mr. Mrugesh Patel for a technical review of this book.

My gratitude also goes to the team at BPB Publications for being supportive enough to provide me with time to finish the first part of the book and also allow me to publish the book in multiple parts. Image processing, being a vast and very active area of research, was impossible to deep-dive into different class of problems in a single book without making it too voluminous.

Preface

This book covers the practical implementation of blockchain applications across Healthcare, Banking, and Finance. It contains a step-by-step guide to building dApps with Hyperledger Fabric and Ethereum, writing smart contracts with Solidity and nodejs chain code, and deploying and managing scalable private blockchain network on AWS Blockchain.

This book is divided into 12 chapters. They cover Blockchain overview, AWS Blockchain offerings, Amazon Quantum Ledger Database, Hyperledger Fabric, AWS Managed Blockchain, Nodejs chain code, Ethereum, Solidity smart contract language, and AWS Blockchain templates. The details are listed as follows:

Chapter 1 will cover what a blockchain is, why a blockchain, Issues with Web2.0 and centralized infrastructure, features of a blockchain, how a blockchain works, consensus mechanism algorithms, public blockchain, private and permissioned blockchain, criteria to choose a blockchain, and blockchain use-cases.

Chapter 2 will cover the problems with self-hosting a blockchain network, understanding of an Amazon managed blockchain, AWS blockchain templates, Amazon Quantum Ledger Database, advantages of using AWS blockchain services, when to use these services, and who is using AWS blockchain services.

Chapter 3 will cover the understanding of a record keeping system, auditing in a bank, deep diving into QLDB, working of QLDB, and building a record keeping database with QLDB for banking auditing.

Chapter 4 will cover Hyperledger Fabric overview, features of Hyperledger Fabric, when to use Hyperledger Fabric, Hyperledger Fabric architecture, Hyperledger Fabric workflow, Hyperledger Fabric models, Hyperledger Fabric network components, Hyperledger Fabric consensus, and application transaction flow.

Chapter 5 will cover deep dive into Amazon managed blockchain, understanding of the healthcare supply chain, current challenges in the healthcare supply chain, blockchain in the healthcare supply chain, stages in building a healthcare supply chain system with blockchain Hyperledger Fabric, and building the Hyperledger Fabric network for the healthcare supply chain.

Chapter 6 will cover the understanding of a chaincode, chaincode lifecycle, understanding the Fabric Node.js SDK, identifying the chaincode functions for the healthcare supply chain project, writing the healthcare chaincode with the Node.js SDK, installing and instantiating the healthcare chaincode on the peer, querying the healthcare chaincode functions, invoking the healthcare chaincode functions, creating the API with Express.js to interact with the chaincode, and designing the UI with Angular to interact with the chaincode through the API.

Chapter 7 will cover inviting a member to join the Fabric network, configuring a Fabric network to add a new member, creating a peer node for a new member, creating a Fabric client node for a new member, installing and instantiating chaincode, and running the chaincode.

Chapter 8 will cover the Ethereum platform, Ethereum Virtual Machine, Ethereum accounts, Ether denominations, Gas and Ether, transactions in the Ethereum blockchain, Ethereum network, Ethereum test network, and Ethereum main network.

Chapter 9 will cover the AWS blockchain templates for Ethereum, Deployment options – ECS and Docker-local, create a VPC and Subnets, security groups, an IAM role, a Bastion host, provision private Ethereum network, connect to the EthStats and EthExplorer, and the Ethereum network through MetaMask wallet.

Chapter 10 will cover what a smart contract is, how smart contract works within Ethereum, Solidity — language to write a smart contract, Solidity compiler, Solidity files, structure of a contract, data types, functions, modifiers, conditional statements, loops, constructors, inheritance, polymorphism, abstract contract, interface, libraries, exceptions, events, and logging.

Chapter 11 will cover what an asset management is, what are assets, challenges with asset tracking in the real world, asset tracker use case, local Blockchain network with Ganache Truffle framework, Web3.js, identify participants in the asset tracker application, create a participant contract and an asset contract, build an asset tracker smart contract with Solidity, and deploy an AssetTracker smart contact to AWS Ethereum private network.

Chapter 12 will cover writing a unit test for smart contracts, using web3.js to interact with smart contracts, invoke smart contracts through the UI, and execute smart contracts against the AWS Ethereum private blockchain.

Downloading the code bundle and coloured images:

Please follow the link to download the
Code Bundle and the *Coloured Images* of the book:

https://rebrand.ly/b222d7

Errata

We take immense pride in our work at BPB Publications and follow best practices to ensure the accuracy of our content to provide with an indulging reading experience to our subscribers. Our readers are our mirrors, and we use their inputs to reflect and improve upon human errors, if any, that may have occurred during the publishing processes involved. To let us maintain the quality and help us reach out to any readers who might be having difficulties due to any unforeseen errors, please write to us at :

errata@bpbonline.com

Your support, suggestions and feedbacks are highly appreciated by the BPB Publications' Family.

Did you know that BPB offers eBook versions of every book published, with PDF and ePub files available? You can upgrade to the eBook version at www.bpbonline.com and as a print book customer, you are entitled to a discount on the eBook copy. Get in touch with us at :

business@bpbonline.com for more details.

At **www.bpbonline.com**, you can also read a collection of free technical articles, sign up for a range of free newsletters, and receive exclusive discounts and offers on BPB books and eBooks.

BPB is searching for authors like you

If you're interested in becoming an author for BPB, please visit **www.bpbonline.com** and apply today. We have worked with thousands of developers and tech professionals, just like you, to help them share their insight with the global tech community. You can make a general application, apply for a specific hot topic that we are recruiting an author for, or submit your own idea.

The code bundle for the book is also hosted on GitHub at **https://github. com/bpbpublications/Building-Enterprise-Blockchain-Solutions-on-AWS**. In case there's an update to the code, it will be updated on the existing GitHub repository.

We also have other code bundles from our rich catalog of books and videos available at **https://github.com/bpbpublications**. Check them out!

PIRACY

If you come across any illegal copies of our works in any form on the internet, we would be grateful if you would provide us with the location address or website name. Please contact us at **business@bpbonline.com** with a link to the material.

If you are interested in becoming an author

If there is a topic that you have expertise in, and you are interested in either writing or contributing to a book, please visit **www.bpbonline.com**.

REVIEWS

Please leave a review. Once you have read and used this book, why not leave a review on the site that you purchased it from? Potential readers can then see and use your unbiased opinion to make purchase decisions, we at BPB can understand what you think about our products, and our authors can see your feedback on their book. Thank you!

For more information about BPB, please visit **www.bpbonline.com**.

Table of Contents

CHAPTER 1

An Introduction to a Blockchain

We have top technologies to modernize the way we operate, but we haven't had any technology in the past that could bring trust to the system. Traditional applications are centralized in nature, where the operating company owns and controls the application data and behavior. Data stored in these centralized servers could be hacked, deleted, or modified, which makes centralized applications to be non-trustable.

A blockchain is a peer-to-peer distributed, secured, shared, immutable ledger, and decentralized technology that brings trust to the system. A blockchain is the future of the Internet and will revolutionize the way businesses are operating.

Structure

In this chapter, we will discuss the following topics:

- What is a blockchain?
- Why a blockchain?
- Issues with Web2.0 and centralized infrastructure
- Features of a blockchain
- How a blockchain works
- Consensus mechanism algorithms

- Public blockchain
- Private and permissioned blockchain
- Criteria to choose a blockchain
- Blockchain use-cases

Objectives

After studying this unit, you should be able to:

- Understand the concept of a blockchain
- Understand how a blockchain works
- Discuss the types of blockchain
- Identify blockchain use-cases

Challenges with the traditional centralized infrastructure

Applications like Facebook, Gmail, Twitter, or any banking and ecommerce applications we use on a daily basis runs on a centralized infrastructure that means these applications have complete control over application data and application behavior.

Because of this centralized nature, if data is compromised by a hacker, then our data is at risk. Also, application data can be tampered by hackers or authority organizations. This leads us to not trust the system. For example, when you send an email, it is processed by the central authority and stored in the database. Email service providers have control over your data, and they can use the data for their promotions.

Let's look at some of the challenges being faced by applications hosted on a centralized infrastructure:

- **Centralized power**: Day-to-day applications we use are central in nature, and the operating company has complete control over the application behavior and data.

- **Lack of trust and integrity**: The data stored in centralized systems can be tampered anytime by the system owners or hackers, which leaves us to work within a non-trustable environment, spending a lot of money with agreements, and paying for a third party like a bank to manage the trust between the parties.

- **Lack of traceability**: It is unable to track the province of any asset like high-value goods (Rolex, Diamond, Gold, and so on.), supply chain, healthcare, and government. In the supply chain, when a consumer finds the food is contaminated, we don't have any trusted process to find out the root cause as hundreds of parties are involved in the entire system starting from the producer to the consumer. Each one maintains their own central digital database, or even worse, maintains data in a non-digital format or do not maintain any data at all.

- **Lack of visibility**: Data is not transparent across the business. For instance, in the transportation and logistics industry, when a consumer sends the parcel, it takes days or weeks to reach the destination. While it's in the transition period, the consumer can't get the right information on the state of their parcel. For example, if the parcel is a perishable item, then is that parcel being maintained at the right temperature and humidity, or when will the end user receive the product. All these pieces of information are not visible to everyone or to relevant parties.

- **Fraud and data tampering**: Since the data is controlled by the central authority, they can tamper the data. Business legal agreements are managed through paper or something else which is not as much transparent and traceable, which opens the door for fraud.

- **High operating cost**: We spend a lot of money and time to secure servers and data from hackers. There is a high cost to maintain the authenticity of data as many intermediate, manual work, and paperwork are involved in a business.

- **Middlemen**: Too many middlemen are involved in the business. In agriculture, for example, the farmer often gets paid only a little percentage of money that the consumer pays. Most of the money goes to the middlemen and there is no peer-to-peer business.

Now that we've seen some of the challenges of the existing infrastructure, let's look at how a blockchain could eliminate or reduce the preceding problems.

What is a blockchain?

A blockchain is a shared ledger which records transactions in a block in an append-only manner. A blockchain is maintained by a peer-to-peer distributed system within the decentralized infrastructure, which is secured by the cryptographic hashing mechanism and with the support of smart contracts, effective collaboration, and cooperation between organizations and individuals.

Let's look at some features of a blockchain.

Cryptographically secured

A blockchain maintains all the events/transactions in the immutable ledger in a linear, chronological order with details like block number, nonce – unique number added by miners, block hash – unique identifier, previous block hash – unique identifier of the previous block, encrypted transaction/message, timestamp, Merkle, and transaction list.

Sets of transactions are stored in a block with the cryptographic hash key, and the blocks are connected to the previous block with cryptographic hashing which forms an immutable chain of blocks.

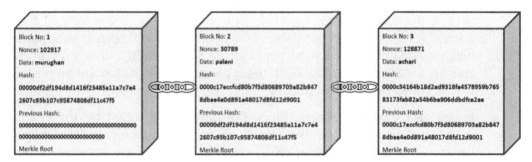

Figure 1.1: *Cryptographically secured*

Immutability is achieved through a cryptographically secured process called **hashing**. Hashing takes in input data and creates 64 random characters as output digital signatures. Whether it's a single character or full Wikipedia content, it always generates 64 random characters as the **Hash key**. Even for a small change in the input, it creates an altogether different hash. There is no way to figure out the input with the output hash key. The algorithm used here is SHA-256.

Immutability

Data stored in a blockchain is an unalterable history of transactions. If data needs to be updated, then a new block gets added instead of deleting the old data. As the blocks are linked with the previous hash, data tampering will lead to breaking the entire chain. This feature of immutability makes it easy for auditing and traceability purpose.

Figure 1.2: Immutability

In the preceding image, we can see that tampering data in the second block leads to breaking the entire blockchain from the second block. This is proof that someone is trying to tamper the data.

Distributed ledger

A blockchain stores data in a distributed manner wherein data is replicated and shared across multiple parties globally in a peer-to-peer network and synchronized with the latest data without any central point of control.

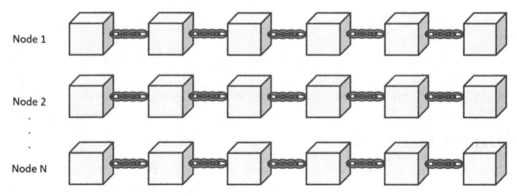

Figure 1.3: Distributed ledger

In the preceding diagram, we can see nodes such as Node 1, Node 2 till Node N which maintains the replicated copy of the ledger.

Decentralized

A blockchain is a completely decentralized network of nodes, unlike the case of traditional companies where everything is stored centrally. This way it eliminates the central point of control and gives control back to the user or other parties in the network. Also, rather than relying on the central party to handle the security, a blockchain uses consensus to validate the correctness of data that goes into a blockchain by making use of the data that is replicated across multiple nodes. For the same reason, it also eliminates the problem of a single node failure.

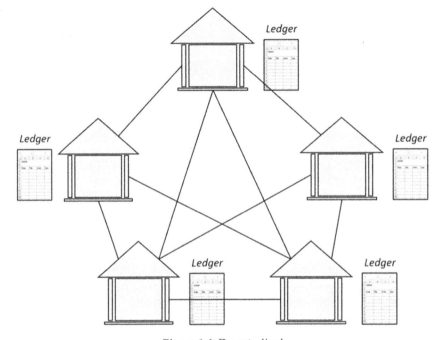

Figure 1.4: Decentralized

In the preceding diagram, we can see that data is decentralized and all the five organizations have the replicated copy of the ledger any time a new block gets created. All the nodes will be synchronized with the latest data.

Smart contract

With the release of the second generation blockchain, Ethereum introduces the concept of **Smart Contract**. In the traditional system, we manage business contracts with paper and some third-party bank or government legal agreement to transact.

Smart contracts revolutionize the way we run a business. All the business rules are coded as a program and deployed into the blockchain which gets executed based on the event. Because of this immutability concept, a smart contract can't be overwritten. For example: In the case of a supply chain, where multiple parties involved to run a business, we write/code all the agreements as smart contracts. Smart contract has events/business logic which gets executed when particular conditions are met. In the Ethereum blockchain, we use the solidity language to write smart contracts. These smart contracts are validated and executed in the Ethereum virtual machine by the public. In a private and permissioned ledger **Hyperledger Fabric,** we call it chaincode and it can be written in Golang, Node.js, and Java.

How a blockchain works

In the blockchain decentralized world, a request is processed by peer-to-peer distributed nodes instead of a central authority. Anyone can host the node and process the request in a public blockchain. Once the request is processed, the new block gets created with the transaction details and replicated across the network.

The following diagram depicts how requests/transactions are processed in the public (permission less) blockchain:

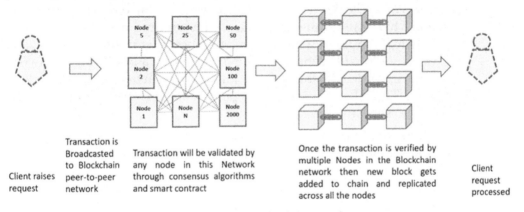

Figure 1.5: How a blockchain works

The following steps take place when any transaction is requested to a blockchain:

1. A client raises a transaction which is digitally signed to provide the proof of ownership.

2. The client transaction will be broadcasted to the decentralized peer-to-peer networks, which are basically computers across the globe. This peer-to-peer network can be permission less such as public, permissioned, or private.

3. In a public blockchain, miners verify the transactions using the cryptographic algorithm called **Proof-of-Work** or **Proof-of-Stake**.

4. Miners solve the difficult puzzle and send the mined blocks to their peers.

5. In the permissioned blockchain, the node validates the client request against the smart contract and through the consensus mechanism.

6. Peer nodes validate and accept the verification.

7. Once multiple nodes verify the transactions, the longest chain will be selected as a new block and added to the blockchain.

8. This new block gets replicated and the data is synchronized across all the nodes in the network.

9. A client request is processed and gets confirmed.

Consensus mechanism algorithms

We understand that data in a blockchain is immutable and trustable. Since multiple parties are involved in the system, we need to ensure that the reliable data goes inside the blockchain where all the parties validate and agree to the process. In the blockchain network, trust is achieved through consensus using consensus algorithms.

The following are some of consensus mechanism algorithms:

- **Proof of Work (PoW):** This was introduced by bitcoin. The process of generating blocks with the proofs known as **mining** and the individuals that participate in the mining process are known as **miners**. Miners solve an extremely difficult cryptographic puzzle to add a block to the network. Miners get rewarded for this activity. Bitcoin and Ethereum run on the PoW algorithm. This algorithm is very compute-intense and consumes more electricity to solve the puzzle.

- **Proof of Stake (PoS):** To avoid high electricity consumption, Proof-of-Stake consensus was introduced, wherein nodes would participate in the network by pledging cryptocurrency as stake. Validators have selected a combination of random selection and amount of cryptocurrency they own. In this situation, only rich will have more advantage, so to avoid this situation, different selection methods are used like randomize block selection, coin age-based selection, and delegated proof-of-stake.

- **Proof of Authority (PoA):** PoA is a modified version of PoS where instead of staking with crypto currency wealth of node, the validator's identity performs the role of the stake. Consensus algorithms are evolving.

There are some more algorithms like **Proof of Importance**, **Proof of Elapsed Time**, **Proof of Deposit**, **Federated Consensus**, and more coming in the future.

Public blockchain

A public blockchain is a decentralized network where anyone from anywhere can join and run a node, read, and write data to a blockchain. Client requests are processed by public nodes.

The following are some of public blockchains:

Bitcoin

Bitcoin was the first generation public blockchain that was introduced by a person or group with an anonymous name called *Satoshi Nakamoto*. Bitcoin is a peer-to-peer electronic cash system that uses the PoW consensus algorithm which proved to the world that payments can be made without any central authority like a bank in between.

Ethereum

Later in the year 2013, a programmer called *Vitalik Buterin* wanted to build a platform that could be used beyond financial use cases like the ownership of fungible and non-fungible items, controlling digital assets through code having business rules, and for more use cases.

Ethereum is a blockchain platform with a built-in full-fledged Turing-complete programming language to build and deploy any decentralized applications simply by writing the logic in a few lines of code as a smart contract. Ether is the cryptocurrency of Ethereum, and it allows us to create our own cryptocurrency token to complete ICO for startups.

With the Ethereum platform, you can build decentralized applications. Here are some of the applications built on a public blockchain like Ethereum, EOS, and Tron. Check this link to see all the apps **https://dappradar.com/.**

Current challenges with a public blockchain

More than 1800 decentralized apps are running on the public blockchain and still many apps are getting built. A lot of research is happening to improvise the public blockchain.

The following are the current challenges of a public blockchain:

- Low performance
- Scalability issue
- Limited privacy and confidentiality
- Storage constraint
- Unsustainable consensus mechanisms
- Lack of governance and standards
- Quantum computing threat
- Not suitable for enterprises where privacy and confidentiality are needed

Because of preceding challenges, we cannot use a public blockchain for all use-cases.

Private and permissioned blockchain

A private and permissioned blockchain is the same as a public blockchain with one major difference that only known entities can join and transact in the network. This identity defines who can access and do what on the network. A private blockchain is used when any institution or business wants to build secured, immutable, and decentralized internal applications for auditing. A permissioned blockchain is used when multiple parties are involved that are working on the same goal/interest, for example, supply chain, healthcare, agriculture, and others.

Some of the private and permissioned blockchains are **Hyperledger Fabric**, **Hyperledger Burrow**, **Hyperledger Grid**, **Hyperledger Indy**, **Hyperledger Iroha**, and **Hyperledger Sawtooth**. In this book, we will explore Hyperledger Fabric.

Hyperledger Fabric is an open source Linux foundation blockchain framework with over 35 organizations and nearly 200 developers contributing to Fabric. Hyperledger Fabric is the framework for business blockchain applications that enable privacy and confidentiality of transactions and are highly modular and have configurable architecture with high transaction throughput performance.

Public versus a private blockchain

Let us understand the difference between a public (permissionless) and private (permissioned) blockchain to help you choose the right blockchain for specific use cases.

	Public Blockchain - Ethereum	Private Blockchain - Hyperledger Fabric
Blockchain	Platform	Framework
Governance	Ethereum is developed by a worldwide team of passionate developers	Linux Foundation
Network	Public and Permissioned	Private and Permissioned
Consensus Mechanism	PoW	Pluggable Consensus
Currency	Ether	None
Smart Contract	Solidity	Golang, Java, Node.js
When to choose	If the transactions are public	If the transactions needs privacy, confidentiality and identity.

Figure 1.6: Public versus private blockchain

In the preceding image, we can see some of the differences between a public (permissionless) and private (permissioned) blockchain.

Blockchain use-cases

A blockchain is a revolution that promises to bring trust within the system through the shared ledger, decentralized technology, smart contract, and cryptography. Many entrepreneurs are analyzing blockchains to solve their problems or to bring efficiency into their business.

Criteria to choose a blockchain

We have understood what problem a blockchain is trying to solve and how a blockchain works. Let's understand how to identify blockchain potentials in your organization. Don't choose a blockchain for every problem. With a non-blockchain, we can still solve a business problem.

The following are the steps used to identify whether your problem needs a blockchain solution:

1. Does your business require a shared database?
2. Does your business involve multiple parties?
3. Does your system have a conflicting interest?
4. Do you want to maintain immutability for your data?

If the answer 'Yes' for all the preceding questions, then choose a blockchain. If the transactions are public, then choose the public blockchain, else a private or permissioned blockchain can serve the purpose.

Blockchain use-cases

We operate in a very complex and non-trustable environment where multiple organizations are involved in serving consumers and each organization can host its own central database. Take the case of the supply chain logistics and shipment industry. It takes three to four weeks to transfer goods overseas where multiple middlemen are involved. A lot of paperwork is required, and it is unable to trace the system when something goes wrong.

Companies like Walmart, Maersk, Samsung, FedEx, UPS, British Airways, Alibaba group, and Starbucks are exploring and researching blockchains to bring trust and efficiency into their supply chain. A blockchain is helping these organizations to trace the product from the producer to the consumer, thus reducing the process time, increase efficiency, and reduce the operation cost.

Apart from supply chain use-cases, the following are some more use-cases organizations are experimenting and developing decentralized solutions.

Figure 1.7: Blockchain use-cases

Apart from the preceding list of use-cases, we can still adopt a blockchain where we need decentralization and immutability.

Conclusion

In this chapter, we learned how a blockchain brings trust within the system through an immutable shared ledger and decentralization technology. We also learned the difference between permissionless and permissioned blockchains. With this knowledge, you will be able to identify blockchain potentials for your organization and learn where to apply blockchains and how industries will get benefited.

In the next chapter, we will explore implementing blockchain solutions with the AWS cloud blockchain services.

Points to remember

- A blockchain is a shared ledger, which records transactions in a block in an append-only manner.

- A blockchain is maintained by a peer-to-peer distributed system within the decentralized infrastructure, which is secured by the cryptographic hashing mechanism and with the support of smart contracts, it strengthens collaboration and cooperation between organizations and individuals.

- A blockchain gives benefits like transparent and true data visibility, trust, eliminate middlemen, reduced cost, interoperability, safety and auditability, faster payments with cryptocurrency, and more.

- Many organizations are adopting blockchains to solve various business problems. Example: Walmart, Maersk, Samsung, FedEx, UPS, British Airways, Alibaba group, and Starbucks.

Multiple choice questions

1. **Properties of blockchain:**
   a) Cryptographically secured
   b) Immutability
   c) Decentralized
   d) Smart Contract
   e) All the above

2. **Select a permissionless blockchain:**
   a) Hyperledger Fabric
   b) Ethereum
   c) Hyperledger Iroha
   d) Ripple

Answers

1. e
2. b

Questions

1. What is a blockchain?

2. Explain how a blockchain works.

3. Explain the difference between permissioned and permissionless blockchains.

4. List some of the use-cases of a blockchain.

Key Terms

1. **Consensus mechanism algorithms:** In the blockchain network, trust is achieved through consensus using consensus algorithms. Some of consensus algorithms are PoW, PoS, and PoA:

2. **Permissionless blockchain:** A permissionless blockchain is a decentralized network where anyone from anywhere can join and run a node, read, and write data to a blockchain. Client requests are processed by public nodes.

3. **Private and permissioned blockchains:** Private and permissioned blockchains are the same as public blockchains with one major difference that only known entities can join and transact in the network. This identity defines who can access and do what on the network. A private blockchain is used when any institution or business wants to build secured, immutable, and decentralized internal applications for auditing.

CHAPTER 2

Exploring a Blockchain on AWS

In this chapter, we will learn how AWS makes it easy to build enterprise blockchain solutions with the following services:

- AWS managed blockchain
- AWS blockchain templates
- Amazon Quantum Ledger Database
- AWS blockchain partners

Structure

In this chapter, we will discuss the following topics:

- Problems with self-hosting a blockchain network
- Understanding of an Amazon managed blockchain
- Understanding of AWS blockchain templates
- Understanding of the Amazon Quantum Ledger Database
- Advantages of using AWS blockchain services
- When to use these services?
- Who is using AWS blockchain services?

Objectives

After studying this unit, you should be able to:

- Understand an Amazon managed blockchain
- UnderstandAWS blockchain templates
- Understanding the Amazon Quantum Ledger Database
- Choose the right AWS blockchain solution for a problem

Amazon managed blockchain

Hosting a blockchain network on your own is very complex, prone to errors, and a time-consuming process. Let's explore how AWS managed blockchain makes it easy to build scalable Ethereum and Hyperledger Fabric networks.

Problems with self-hosting a blockchain network

Let's understand the steps involved in building a decentralized solution where multiple parties are involved, need to collaborate, with no central owner, and potentially low levels of trust between the parties.

The decentralized application architecture will look like the following diagram:

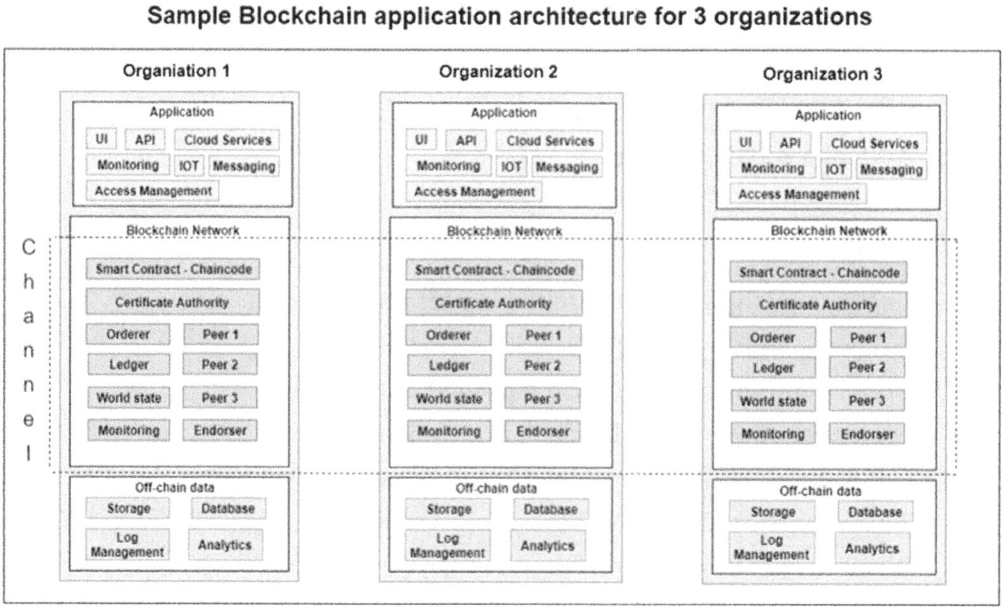

Figure 2.1: Sample blockchain application architecture

The manual steps involved to create and manage the architecture are as follows:

1. Provision and configure a permissioned blockchain network for each member.

2. Install the necessary software.

3. Configure user certificates and peer nodes.

4. Invite members and user management.

5. Configure security.

6. Enable infrastructure monitoring.

7. Enable notifications.

8. Enable network governance.

9. Enable scaling performance.

10. Configure off-chain database.

To host a blockchain network on your own involves performing a long list of the preceding manual tasks; which is very complex, prone to errors, and a time-consuming process.

What is an Amazon managed blockchain?

An Amazon managed blockchain makes it easy to build a secure permissioned blockchain network in a few clicks. It's a fully managed service that makes it easy to manage scalable blockchain networks. It supports two frameworks such as Hyperledger Fabric and Ethereum.

With an Amazon managed blockchain, you can focus only on writing business logic and application development. All the heavy lifting provisioning, deploying, and managing of these infrastructures will be taken care of by Amazon.

Advantages of an Amazon managed blockchain

The following are the advantages of using an Amazon managed blockchain for enterprises:

- **Fully managed:** With a couple of clicks, you will able to keep the network up and running with a blockchain network. An Amazon managed blockchain makes it easy to create and manage a network, invite other AWS accounts to join the network as members, and create peer nodes and membership configuration in a few minutes. Also, network participants can vote to add or remove members through the managed blockchain voting API.

- **Decentralized:** No one owns or controls the network. Once the network is created by an organization, members can join. If a member leaves the network, the network will still run as it's decentralized.

- **Reliable:** With Hyperledger Fabric for ordering service instead of Kafka, AWS uses QLDB – Quantum Ledger Database which maintains the complete history of the ledger in an immutable format.

- **Scalable:** Autoscaling can be enabled to support high transactions as the network grows. You can auto scale as many as peers as you need based on the demand. You can choose instance types based on the utilization of the CPU and memory.

- **Secure:** The network is secured with AWS **Key Management Service (KMS)** and **Virtual Private Cloud (VPC)**.

- **Easily analyze a blockchain activity:** The ledger data can be replicated to Amazon QLDB, which manages the immutable history of all data changes. QLDB allows you to query the ledger for analytics.

With the preceding features, AWS helps us to deliver blockchain solutions faster.

When to use

We can use an Amazon managed blockchain, when multiple parties are involved and work on the same goal/interest. For example, in supply chain, healthcare, financial, government, insurance, IoT, payments, media, agriculture, and more.

Who is using an Amazon managed blockchain?

As of April 2020, Verizon, GE Aviation, AT&T, Accenture, Sony Music, Philips, DTCC, GE Aviation, Workday, Liberty Mutual Insurance, Change Healthcare, and Guardian enterprises are using an Amazon managed blockchain.

AWS blockchain templates

It's a time-consuming process to provision blockchain networks. Let's explore how AWS blockchain templates make it easy to provision and operate Ethereum and Hyperledger Fabric.

What are AWS blockchain templates?

AWS has certified CloudFormation templates for Hyperledger Fabric and Ethereum blockchains. Through these templates, you will be able to easily launch secured blockchain networks in a few clicks and in a few minutes. Along with the blockchain network, AWS launches other AWS necessary resources like VPC, Subnet, **Access Control List (ACL)**, **Identity, and Access Management (IAM)**. These templates also give you the option to remove or add AWS resources.

Ethereum template

Using the Ethereum template you can:

- Create a private Ethereum network
- Join an existing private network
- Create a public Ethereum node to join the main Ethereum network

This template gives the following two options to launch the network:

- **AmazonElastic Container Service (ECS):** This creates an ECS cluster and launches docker images within VPC where you can use the network subnet and access control list.
- **EC2 instance:** This launches docker images within the EC2 instance under the same VPC.

The template also deploys EthStats and EthExplorer. EthStats, the visual interface, is used to track the network status by running the Ethereum network intelligence API in the background. EthExplorer is used to view token and transaction details.

Hyperledger fabric template

Using the Hyperledger Fabric template, you will be able to create a private and permissioned blockchain network. You can create members and peers and add new members to the network through the identity.

This template supports only containers on the EC2 instance. This template launches Hyperledger Fabric docker images within the EC2 instance. The network includes one Kafka-based order service and three organizations, each with one peer node.

The template also launches a Hyperledger Explorer Postgre SQL container which allows you to explore blocks, transactions, smart contracts, and blockchain data.

When to use

Templates are available for both public - Ethereum and permissioned network - Hyperledger Fabric and Ethereum.

We will do the hands-on of Managed blockchain and blockchain templates in the upcoming chapters after we explore Hyperledger Fabric and Ethereum.

Amazon Quantum Ledger Database

Historically, we can manage organization data in the relational database for system of records applications where traceability and auditability are very much needed, but this is not the right solution. Let's explore how Amazon's **Quantum Ledger Database(QLDB)** provides solutions for enterprises.

Why QLDB?

The problem with a traditional relational database is that it allows you to delete and overwrite the data which makes the system to lack trust and integrity. Take the example of a bank, which tracks customer balance, spending, credit, debit, loan, and so on. It is managed in a traditional relational database. Instead, we need a database that is immutable and independently verifiable.

These applications need not be decentralized, as there are no multiple parties owning the data. The bank needs a private and centralized secured immutable database, so we don't need blockchain decentralization as solving these problems with a blockchain will add more complexity and will be hard to scale. A blockchain is designed to solve a problem where multiple parties are involved with low trust. But for private organizations with a single owner who want to maintain trustable data, then decentralization is not needed. Also, the consensus mechanism in the decentralized application decreases the performance of the application.

What is QLDB?

In the preceding example, a bank should maintain the history of all the changes done to the data in a tamper-proof immutable database so that this helps them to trace the history of changes for regulation, compliance, and fraud.

Amazon QLDB is basically a database for system of records application where traceability and auditability is a must. QLDB is a fully managed centralized ledger database that provides a transparent, immutable, and cryptographically verifiable transaction log. Quantum means the change has no intermediate state.

QLDB is not decentralized, unlike Hyperledger Fabric or Ethereum where all the participants in the network will have the replicated copy of a database. Here, the ledger database is kept centralized and managed by a trusted authority or the company who owns the application.

Advantages of QLDB

The following are the advantages of adopting QLDB to build a centralized database for enterprises:

- **Cryptographically verifiable:** Data stored in QLDB are hashed and creates a chain of hashed data, this feature brings data trust.

- **Immutable and transparent:** Data stored in QLDB cannot be edited and data stored in QLDB are kept transparent to relevant parties in the system.

- **Highly scalable:** QLDB is fast and auto-scaling is available to deal with high demand.

- **Easy setup:** Just takes a few minutes to provision QLDB.

- **High performance:** QLDB is centralized in nature so there is no consensus because of which QLDB runs 2 to 3 times faster and performs with low latency.

- **Serverless:** There is no need to provision the machine; you need to manage the read or write throughput. You can concentrate only on creating an application and all the heavy lifting is managed by AWS.

- **Monitoring:** With the help of CloudWatch, we can watch key metrics such as read-events, write-events, and storage volume.

- **SQL support:** QLDB provides SQL-like API to query the ledger.

- **Document-oriented data model:** It has the flexibility to store structured, unstructured, and semi-structured data. It also supports nested documents which make querying easier.

- **ACID property:** The transaction will never be executed partially. It's always executed fully or if any steps in a transaction fails then all the previous steps in a transaction are reverted.

With the preceding features, QLDB brings trust for centralized applications.

When to use

QLDB is a right fit in a situation where organizations want to maintain a centralized database with immutability and cryptographically verifiable transaction logs. Use cases like HR and Payroll, manufacturing, insurance, retail, supply chain, and transport and logistics are a few examples where QLDB can be used.

Who is using?

As of April 2020, Accenture, Digital Asset, Realm, Splunk, Heathdirect, Osano, Smaato, Wipro, Zilliant, Driver and Vehicle Licensing Agency, and Klarna are using QLDB.

AWS blockchain partners

Currently, we do not have blockchain solutions for all major use-cases. A lot of research is happening in many organizations to build blockchain solutions, frameworks, and products to solve specific problems in multiple domains. Let's see how AWS blockchain partners help to innovate.

Why AWS blockchain partners

Since many companies are building blockchain products and frameworks, these companies require a cloud platform to host their solutions to make it available as a product for end users. These blockchain solutions/products need a platform which is cost-effective, enables faster devolvement and deployment, and takes advantage of the comprehensive suite of AWS services and third-party solutions

What are AWS blockchain partners?

An AWS partner network is a global partner program for technology and consulting businesses that leverage Amazon Web Services to build solutions and services for customers. The APN helps companies build, market, and sell their AWS offerings by providing valuable business, technical, and marketing support.

There are tens of thousands of APN partners across the globe. More than 90% of Fortune 100 companiesand more than 500 Fortune companies utilize APN partner solutions and services.

APN blockchain partners provide validated solutions for implementing blockchain technology and **distributed ledger technology (DLT)** on AWS. They specialize in leveraging a blockchain and DLT-**distributed ledger technology** to provide transparency, efficiency, and security for multi-party processes and transaction automation.

Who are the AWS blockchain partners?

As of April 2020, some of APN blockchain partners are Intel, PWC, Kaleido, R3, Tradewind, Consensys, Farmobile, Luxoft, BlockApps, and Union Bank.

Conclusion

In this chapter, we learned an overview of AWS blockchain services, how AWS makes it easy to build and manage scalable blockchain solutions with an Amazon managed blockchain and AWS blockchain templates.

We explored the Amazon QLDB to build a centralized private blockchain for organizations who want to maintain a centralized database with immutability, and cryptographically verifiable transaction logs.

In the next chapter, we will deep dive into QLDB.

Points to remember

- AWS provides following services to build enterprise blockchain solutions:
  - o AWS managed blockchain
  - o AWS blockchain template
  - o Amazon QLDB
  - o AWS blockchain partners

Multiple choice questions

1. **Select the odd one out:**
    a) AWS Managed blockchain
    b) AWS blockchain Templates
    c) Amazon Quantum Ledger Database (QLDB)
    d) AWS blockchain Partners
    e) Stellar

2. **QLDB is not decentralized.**
    a) True
    b) False

3. **AWS Managed blockchain is centralized.**
    a) True
    b) False

Answer

1. e
2. a
3. a

Questions

1. What is an AWS managed blockchain?

2. What are AWS blockchain templates?

3. What is QLDB?

4. What is AWS blockchain partners solution?

Key terms

1. **AWS blockchain partners:** The AWS partner network is a global partner program for technology and consulting businesses that leverage AWS to build solutions and services for customers.

CHAPTER 3
Exploring the Amazon Quantum Ledger Database

In this chapter, we will deep dive into Amazon QLDB and solve the real-world problems in the banking industry by building banking solutions with QLDB. We will build the record keeping system for bank auditing with Amazon QLDB which provides immutability, transparency, security, and high performance.

Structure

In this chapter, we will discuss the following topics:

- Understanding a record keeping system
- Understanding auditing in a bank
- Deep diving into QLDB
- Working of QLDB
- Building a record keeping database with QLDB for banking auditing

Objectives

After studying this unit, you should be able to:

- Understand how QLDB works
- Understand howrecord keeping works
- Build a record keeping database with QLDB for banking auditing

Pre-requisites for this chapter

The following are the pre-requisites:

- **AWS account:** If you already have an AWS account, then you can skip this step. Or else, sign up to AWS for a new account **https://console.aws.amazon.com/** .

- **SQL:** QLDB queries are like SQL queries, so SQL knowledge is required.

Record keeping

Record keeping is a process of creating, capturing, and managing the application data. Every organization manages a lot of data for their business. The data needs to be stored securely and the history of changes needs to be maintained. Also, many applications need that the data should be real-time and transparent for end-user.

Record keeping lays the foundation for a bank. Record keeping in banking is a process of recording accurate information about each transaction and events. Storing details of customer credits, debits, loans, loan transactions, asset details, international transactions, customer KYC, and other details are stored in the bank database. It is critical to store the history of events in an immutable way.

Current challenges with record-keeping

Records (data) which are being stored on the traditional databases have the following drawbacks:

- Lack of trust

- Lack of transparency

- Data tampering

- Non-traceable

With the preceding challenges, we can see that the current solutions are untrusted systems.

Auditing in a bank

Bank auditing is a mandated process by a law to ensure the books of accounts presented to the regulators and public are true and fair. It can be conducted by the charted accountants in high-level banks. Auditing undergoes the following verifications:

- Cash balance

- Tax-related

- Loan accounts

- Bank features and facilities

Tracing all the transactions/events is a costly process as banks use traditional centralized database where data can be tampered.

In the next section, we will explore how QLDB solves recordkeeping and auditing challenges in banking.

Exploring QLDB

In *Chapter 2: Exploring Blockchain on AWS*, we discussed the challenges of traceability and immutability with traditional databases. Companies spend a lot of time and money for the auditing process and to verify transactions.

With QLDB, organizations can build a tamper-proof immutable database to trace the history of changes for auditing, regulation, compliance, and fraud. QLDB is the right fit in a situation where organizations need to maintain a centralized database with immutability and cryptographically verifiable transaction logs anduse cases like HR and payroll, manufacturing, insurance, retail, supply chain, and transport, and logistics.

What is QLDB?

Amazon QLDB is a database for a system-of-records application where traceability and auditability is a must. QLDB is a fully managed, centralized ledger database that provides a transparent, immutable, and cryptographically verifiable transaction log. Amazon QLDB tracks each application data change and maintains a complete and verifiable history of changes over time.

The following are the advantages of adopting QLDB to build a centralized database for enterprises:

- **Cryptographically verifiable:** QLDB logs all the transaction details in an immutable ledger with cryptographic hashing called **Digest**. This makes the system data non-tamperable and is enabled to trace all the history of events within the organization.

- **Immutable and transparent:** QLDB is append-only, where any updates to the data will create a new entry into the database instead of updating the previous data. A journal in QLDB maintains all the changes in a chronological order with a timestamp in an immutable state. Through the journal, you can query all the history of changes made even if any data gets deleted in the ledger as the journal maintains all the history of changes.

- **Highly scalable:** QLDB is fast and auto-scaling is available on high demand.

- **Easy setup:** It just takes a few minutes to provision QLDB.

- **High Performance:** QLDB is centralized in nature so there is no consensus because of which QLDB runs 2 to 3 times faster and performs with low latency.

- **Serverless:** You don't need to provision the machine or manage read or write throughput. You need to only concentrate on creating an application and all the heavy lifting is managed by AWS.

- **Monitoring:** With the help of CloudWatch, we can watch key metrics such as read-events, write-events, and storage volume.

- **SQL support:** QLDB provides SQL-like API to query the ledger.

- **Document-oriented data model:** It has the flexibility to store structured, unstructured, and semi-structured data. It also supports nested documents which make querying easier.

- **ACID property:** A transaction is a single unit of operation. You either execute it entirely or do not execute it at all. There cannot be partial execution..

With the preceding advantages, QLDB is the solution for centralized applications.

How QLDB works?

Amazon QLDB follows the following design to store and retrieve data.

The following diagram shows how QLDB works:

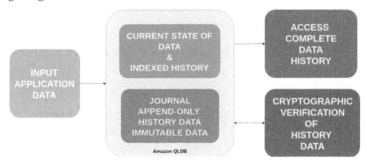

Figure 3.1: How QLDB works?

Following steps illustrates how QLDB works:

1. Application data will be loaded into the QLDB database.

2. QLDB creates the following two ledgers.

   a. One ledger stores the current state of the data.

   b. The other ledger called **Journal** stores all the historical changes as a block and chains it with the previous block as a cryptographically link.

3. We can access the complete history of data using SQL-like queries.

4. We can also cryptographically verify each change made to the data.

5. This workflow applies to all the use-cases which use QLDB.

Building a record-keeping database with QLDB for bank auditing

Let's build a simple record-keeping database for bank auditing with QLDB.

Record-keeping database architecture

In reallife, a bank database will have more tables. In this exercise we will create a simple database for a bank having only a few tables as follows:

- **Account:** This table stores all the bank account details.

- **Customer:** This table stores the customer details.

- **Banker:** This table stores bank details.

- **Tx:** This table stores every transaction of debit/credit of accounts.

- **Loan:** This table stores loan details.

- **LoanPayment:** This table stores loan payment transactions.

- **Tax:** This table stores the tax paid by the bank.

Steps in building a record-keeping database for a bank

We will perform the following steps in QLDB:

1. Create a new ledger.

2. Create tables.

3. Insert sample banking data.

4. Query data.

5. Update table data.

6. View the history of changes.

7. Verify the history data.

Step 1: Create a new ledger:

A ledger in QLDB holds tables. Data stored in the ledger are immutable and cryptographically verifiable. You can create multiple ledgers with QLDB.

We will create a ledger for bank record-keeping, and we will name the ledger as Bank-RecordKeeping.

Steps to create a ledger **are** as follows:

1. Login to the AWS console.

2. Navigate to the QLDB page **https://console.aws.amazon.com/qldb.**

3. Select **Us-East-1(N Virginia)** as the region.

4. Select **Ledgers** from the left pane and then, click on the **Create Ledger** button.

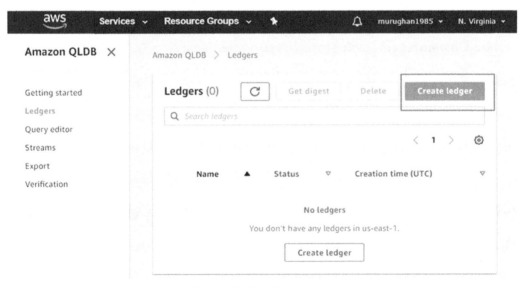

Figure 3.2: Creating a Ledger

5. Enter the ledger name as **Bank-RecordKeeping**:

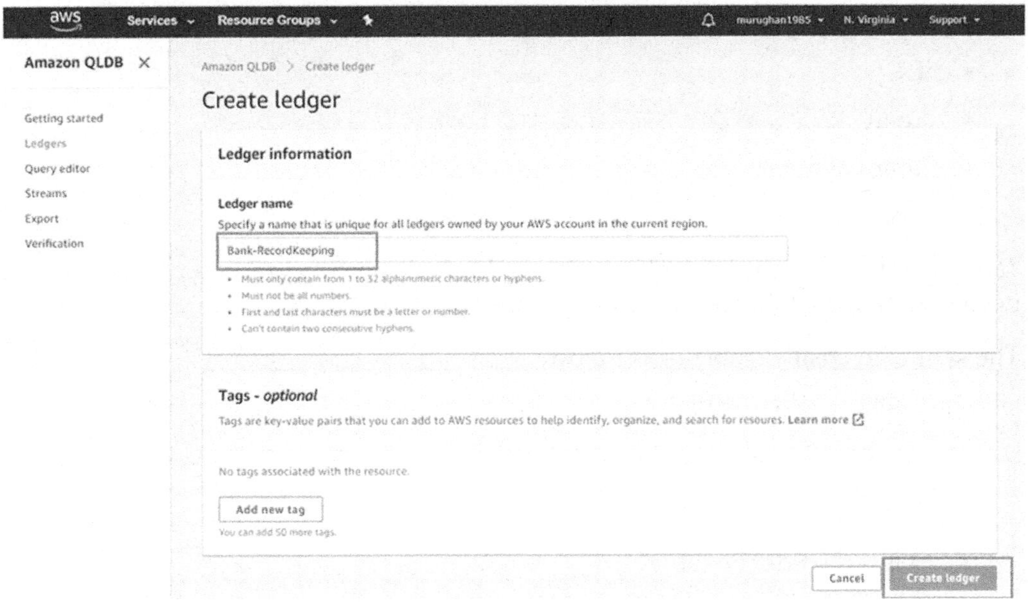

Figure 3.3: Enter ledger name

6. Click on **Create Ledger**.

7. Wait till the ledger gets created, and you will see the ledger status as **Active** as shown inthe following screenshot:

Figure 3.4: Ledger status

This step created a ledger for our bank. In the next step, we will create bank tables.

Step 2: Creating tables

A ledger can hold many tables. In this step, we will create the following seven tables which we have identified for Bank-Record keeping.

- Banker

- Customer
- Account
- Tx
- Loan
- LoanPayment
- Tax

Tables in QLDB need not have schema as QLDB supports open content, so you don't need to define the table attributes while creating a table.

The syntax to create a table is as follows:

```
CREATE TABLE <TABLE_NAME>
```

Steps to create a Banker table **are** as follows:

1. Navigate to **Query editor** from the left pane.

2. Select the **Editor** tab.

3. Enter the **CREATE TABLE Banker** statement in the editor as shown in the following screenshot:

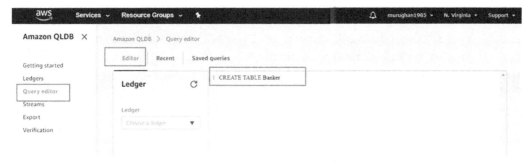

Figure 3.5: CREATE TABLE Banker

4. Choose the **Bank-RecordKeeping** ledger and click on the **Run** button:

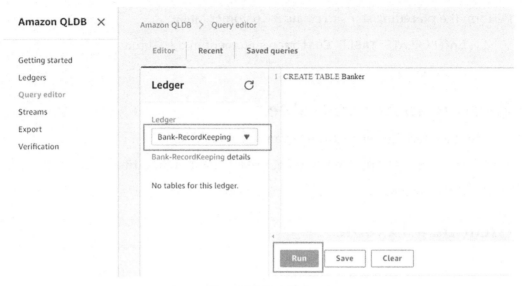

Figure 3.6: Run Code

5. Check the result status as **Success** in the output section as shown in the following screenshot:

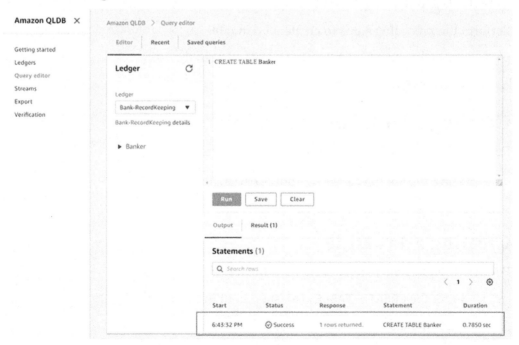

Figure 3.7: Table creation status

Creating a customer table

Perform the preceding steps to create a Customer table:

1. Enter `CREATE TABLE Customer` statement in the editor.

2. Click on **Run**.

Creating an Account table

Perform the preceding steps to create an Account table:

1. Enter the `CREATE TABLE Account` statement in the editor.

2. Click on **Run**.

Creating a Tx table

Perform the preceding steps to create a Tx table:

1. Enter the `CREATE TABLE Tx` statement in the editor.

2. Click on **Run**.

Creating a Loan table

Perform the preceding steps to create a Loan table:

1. Enter the `CREATE TABLE Loan` statement in the editor.

2. Click on **Run**.

Creating a Loan Payment table

Perform the preceding steps to create a Loan Payment table:

1. Enter the `CREATE TABLE LoanPayment` statement in the editor.

2. Click on **Run**.

Creating a Tax table

Perform the preceding steps to create a Tax table:

1. Enter the `CREATE TABLE Tax` statement in the editor.

2. Click on **Run**.

Verify if you have successfully created all the tables as below screenshot:

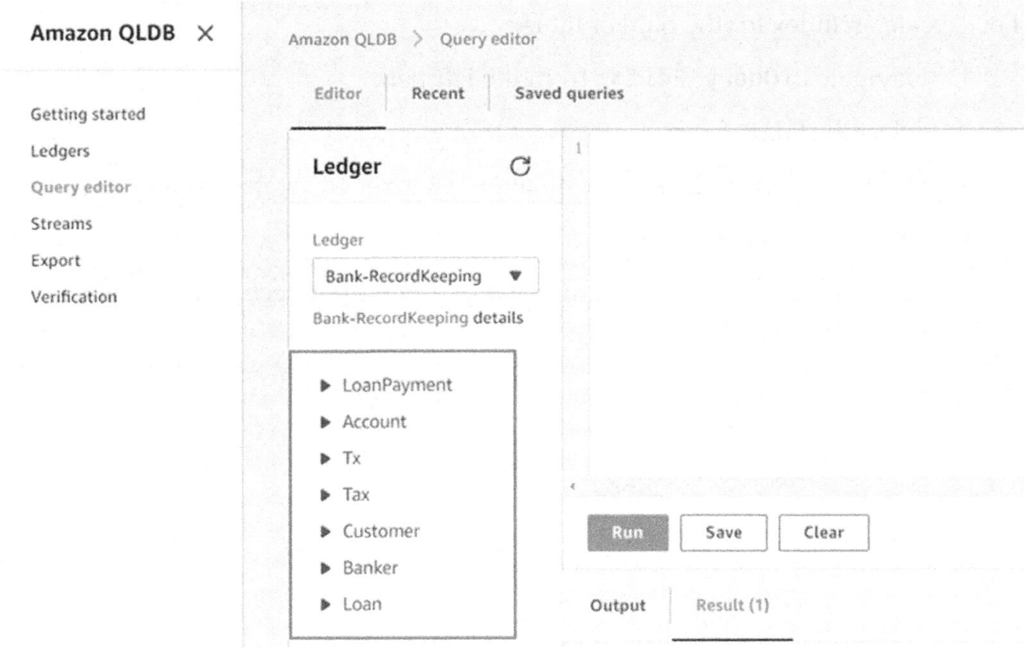

Figure 3.8: Verify all table creation

You can also view your recent queries execution status under the **Recent** tab.

We have successfully created all the required tables in this step.

Step 3: Creating Indexes

Creating indexes for each table improves query performance. Follow the following principles while creating indexes:

- Index creation should happen before inserting data into tables.
- Indexes can be created only on a single attribute.
- Composite and range indexes are not supported.
- Once you create indexes, you can't drop them.

The syntax to create indexes is as follows:

```
CREATE INDEX ON <TABLE_NAME> (id)
```

Let's create an index for each table as follows.

Let's create an index for the Banker table:

1. Navigate to **Query Editor** from the left pane.

2. Select the **Editor** tab

3. Enter the `CREATE INDEX ON Banker (BankerId)` statement in the editor.

4. Click on the **Run** button.

5. Check the result status as **Success** in the output section as shown in the following screenshot:

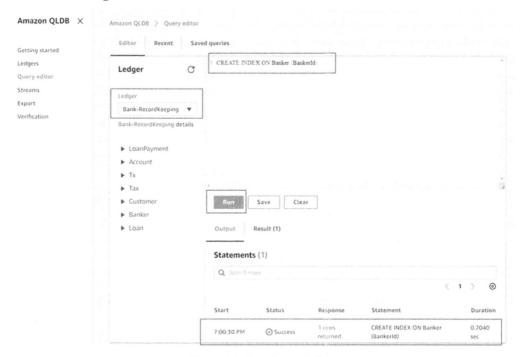

Figure 3.9: Creating an index

Creating an index for the Customer table.

Follow the preceding steps to create an index for the Customer table:

1. Enter the `CREATE INDEX ON Customer (CustomerId)` statement in the editor.

2. Click on **Run**.

Creating an index for the Account table.

Follow the preceding steps to create an index for the Account table:

1. Enter the `CREATE INDEX ON Account (AccountNumber)` statement in the editor.

2. Click on **Run**.

Creating an index for the Tx table.

Follow the preceding steps to create an index for the Tx table:

1. Enter the `CREATE INDEX ON Tx (TransactionId)` statement in the editor.

2. Click on **Run**.

Creating an index for the Loan table.

Follow the preceding steps to create an index for the Loan table:

1. Enter the `CREATE INDEX ON Loan (LoanNumber)` statement in the editor.

2. Click on **Run**.

Creating an index for the LoanPayment table.

Follow the preceding steps to create an index for the LoanPayment table:

1. Enter the `CREATE INDEX ON LoanPayment (PaymentId)` statement in the editor.

2. Click on **Run**.

Creating an index for the Tax table.

Follow the preceding steps to create an index for the Tax table:

1. Enter the `CREATE INDEX ON Tax (TaxId)` statement in the editor.

2. Click on **Run**.

Verify all the index creation by navigating to the **Recent** tab as shown in the following screenshot:

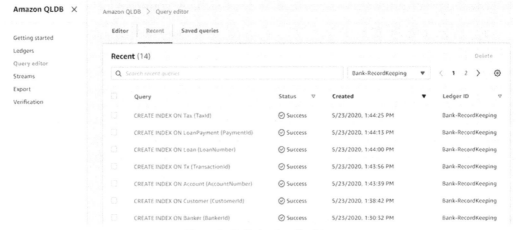

Figure 3.10: *Index for all tables*

We have created the required indexes for all the tables.

Step 4: Inserting data

While creating tables, we have not mentioned the data attributes as QLDB stores data as documents and based on the data passed, the insert statement will be added to the table. We will insert data only for a few attributes, but you can add more fields while inserting the data. The syntax to insert data is as follows:

```
INSERT INTO <TABLE_NAME>
<< {
    'KEY' : 'VALUE',
    'KEY' : 'VALUE'
    } >>
```

Let's insert sample data into each table as follows:

Inserting data into the Banker table:

1. Navigate to **Query Editor** from the left pane.

2. Select **Editor** tab.

3. Enter the following statement in the editor:

```
INSERT INTO Banker
<< {
```

```
    'BankerId' : '1',
    'Name' : 'MRGNBank',
    'Facilities' : {'SafetyLocker' : 'Yes', 'CashValut' : 'Yes',
'BurglaryAlarmSystem' : 'Yes' },
    'Address' : 'CA'
    } >>
```

4. Click on the **Run** button.

5. Check the result status as **Success** in the output section as shown in the following screenshot:

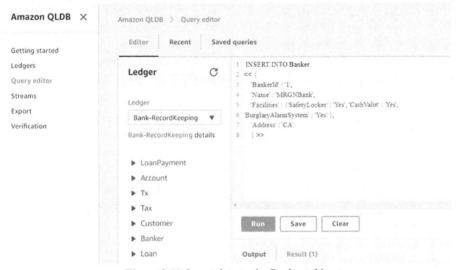

Figure 3.11: Insert data to the Banker table

Inserting data into Customer table:

Follow the preceding steps.

1. Enter the following statement in the editor

2. Run the statement

```
INSERT INTO Customer
<< {
    'CustomerId' : '1',
    'Name' : 'Murughan',
    'DOB' : '30/10/1985',
    'Address' : 'Bangalore INDIA',
    'Phone' : '1234567890'
    } >>
```

Inserting data into the Account table:

Follow the preceding steps.

1. Enter the following statement in the editor
2. Run the statement

```
INSERT INTO Account
<< {
    'AccountNumber' : '1',
    'CustomerId' : '1',
    'Type' : 'Saving',
    'Balance' : '1000'
    } >>
```

Inserting data into the Tx table:

Follow the preceding steps.

1. Enter the following statement in the editor
2. Run the statement

```
INSERT INTO Tx
<< {
    'TransactionId' : '1',
    'AccountNumber' : '1',
    'Type' : 'Debit',
    'Balance' : '100'
    } >>
```

Inserting data into the Loan table:

Follow the preceding steps.

1. Enter the following statement in the editor
2. Run the statement

```
INSERT INTO Loan
<< {
    'LoanNumber' : '1',
    'AccountNumber' : '1',
    'Type' : 'PL',
    'Amount' : '100000',
```

```
'Interest' : '12',
'Tenure' : '3'
} >>
```

Inserting data into the LoanPayment table:

Follow the preceding steps.

1. Enter the following statement in the editor
2. Run the statement

```
INSERT INTO LoanPayment
<< {
  'PaymentId' : '1',
    'LoanNumber' : '1',
    'AccountNumber' : '1',
    'AmountPaid' : '3321',
    'Month' : 'July',
    'Year' : '2019'
    } >>
```

Inserting data into the Tax table:

Follow the preceding steps.

1. Enter the following statement in the editor
2. Run the statement

```
INSERT INTO Tax
<< {
  'TaxId' : '1',
    'Type' : 'FTT',
    'AmountPaid' : '3321',
    'Month' : 'July',
    'Year' : '2019'
    } >>
```

Figure 3.12: Insert all the tables

Makes sure the table has been inserted with the sample data and then, verify from the **Recent** tab.

Step 5: Querying a table

Querying a table allows you to pull data based onfilters you pass. QLDB supports filtering data with the WHERE clause and tables can be joined while selecting data from multiple tables.

The syntax to query a table is as follows:

```
SELECT <attributes>/<*> FROM <TABLE_NAME1> and <TABLE_NAME2>
WHERE <FILTER>
```

Querying the sample data from the Customer table from the Bank-RecordKeeping ledger.

Perform the following steps to query data from a Customer table:

1. Navigate to **Query Editor** from the left pane.

2. Select the **Editor** tab

3. Enter the `Select * from Customer` statement in the editor and run the query as shown in the following screenshot:

Figure 3.13: *Read data from the Customer table*

Query data from joining two tables such as the Customer and Account table:

- To filter the data, we can use the `WHERE` clause.

- To join tables, use `FROM TABLE1 AS ALIAS, TABLE2 AS ALIAS`.

  Enter the following statement in the editor and run the query:

  ```
  SELECT c.Name, c.Address, a.AccountNumber, a.Type, a.Balance
  FROM Customer AS c, Account AS a
  WHERE c.CustomerId = '1'
  AND c.CustomerId = a.CustomerId
  ```

Figure 3.14: *Query to join tables*

We can also write complex queries like queries inside queries.

Step 6: Updating the table data

The table data can be updated with new information by mentioning the key value of a row.

The syntax to update the table is as follows:

```
UPDATE <TABLE_NAME>
SET <ATTRIBUTE> = <VALUE>
WHERE <FILTER>
```

Let's simulate multiples transactions so that the updates we make in this step can be tracked by the QLDB immutable ledger called Journal.

Add three more transactions to the Tx table. The following query inserts 3 rows into the Tx tableas follows:

1. Debit 95 dollars.

2. Debit 23 dollars.

3. Credit 600 dollars.

Run the following statement in the query editor:

```
INSERT INTO Tx
<< {
'TransactionId' : '2',
    'AccountNumber' : '1',
    'Type' : 'Debit',
    'Balance' : '95'
    },
    {
    'TransactionId' : '3',
    'AccountNumber' : '1',
    'Type' : 'Credit',
    'Balance' : '600'
    },
    {
    'TransactionId' : '4',
    'AccountNumber' : '1',
```

```
'Type' : 'Debit',
'Balance' : '23'
}>>
```

With the preceding INSERT statement, we need to update the balance of the account in the Account table.

The Current balance of the AccountNumber 1 should be 1382. Intentionally, wewill make the wrong update to the Account table. Run the following statement in the query editor:

```
UPDATE Account
SET Balance = '1280'
WHERE AccountNumber='1'
```

Let's make one more update. We will make one more mistake here. Instead of considering 600 as credit, we will consider it as debit and deduct it from the balance. The following statement will update the balance to 680 which should be 1382. Run the following statement in the query editor:

```
UPDATE Account
SET Balance = '680'
WHERE AccountNumber='1'
```

You can query the Account and Tx table to see the changes made.

Step 7: Deleting the table data

Data can be deleted from the tables, but the history table in QLDB maintains the history of all transactions.

We will delete a row from the Tx table. The following statement deletes the row in which we had earlier inserted a debit of 600. Run the following statement in the query editor:

```
DELETE
FROM Tx
WHERE TransactionId='3'
```

You can query the Tx table. You will see only three rows now. The preceding row has been deleted from the Tx table.

Step 8: Viewing the history of changes

All the changes (Insert, Delete, and Update) to the data is maintained in the QLDB history table.

Each table in QLDB maintains system-generated metadata (transactionIDs, commit time stamps, version numbers, and journal attributes) for each document in a table.

Run the following query in the editor to see the metadata:

```
SELECT * FROM _ql_committed_Account
```

Figure 3.15: View metadata

This statement returns the following metadata:

- blockAddress: This blocks the location in the journal.
  - o **strandId**: This is a unique ID of the journal partition(strand).
  - o **sequenceNo**: The index number specifies the location of the block within the strand - {strandId:"EFcC14catI5045LLneAkmU",sequenceNo:107}.
- hash: SHA-256 value of the document - {{zAUP5c8Rxtktd6vw6auCbDyIXdcGcVuNC9NSgg2wCpE=}}
- data: Data stored in a table - {AccountNumber:"1",CustomerId:"1",Type:"Saving", Balance:"680"}
- metadata: This contains metadata attributes of the document(data).
  - o **id**: This is a system generated a unique ID.
  - o **version**: For each revision, it maintains an index.
  - o **txTime**: This is document revision committed time.
  - o **txId**: This is the unique ID of the transaction that commits the document revision.

    {id:"G3OhySXfGDx2ATIfX3JxHz",version:2,txTime:2020-05-23T19: 52:20.509Z,txId:"G8ijUogV6BUCWeyFCoZsgn"}

1. **Getting the unique ID of the document:**

   Execute the following statement in **Query Editor**, which will return the unique IDa_id:

   ```
   SELECT a_id FROM Account AS a BY a_id
   WHERE a.AccountNumber = '1'
   ```

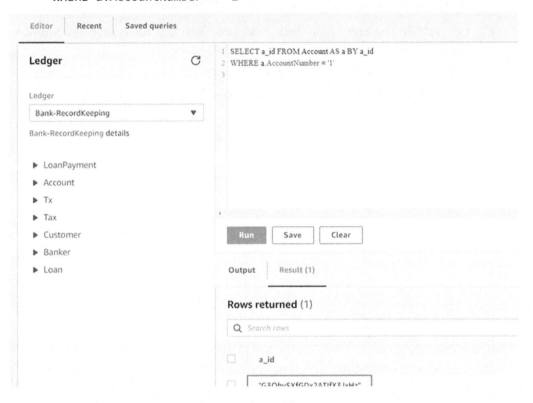

Figure 3.16: Getting unique ID of the document

2. **Searching from the history table with the precedingID:**

   QLDB provides the history function which takes input parameters as **table_name**, **start_time**, and **end_time** in ISO 8601 date and time format and in UTC.

   The syntax to get the history from the table is as follows:

   Here, enclose START-TIME and END-TIME with ` symbol (not the single quote)

   ```
   SELECT * FROM history('<TABLE_NAME>',`<START-TIME>`,`<END-TIME>`)
   AS h WHERE h.metadata.id = <a_id>
   ```

Run the following statement to get the history of the document in the Account table, replace start-time and end-time, `h.metadata.id` in the following query with your a_id value, and run the statement in the query editor:

```
SELECT * FROM history('Account', `2000T`, `2020-05-23T19:52:20.509Z`)
AS h

WHERE h.metadata.id = 'G3OhySXfGDx2ATIfX3JxHz'
```

Or exclude the start date and end date. Run the following statement by replacing `h.metadata.id` with your a_id value:

```
SELECT * FROM history(Account) AS h

WHERE h.metadata.id = 'G3OhySXfGDx2ATIfX3JxHz'
```

Figure 3.17: Searching from the history table

From the preceding output, we can see the history of changes we have made to the Account table. The result shows all the three updates made to this document. In the Account table, you will see only one row as it maintains only the current state. This way we can trace all the changes to any document in QLDB which is an immutable transaction log.

Step 9: Auditor verifying bank transactions

In this bank use-case, an auditor can verify the authenticity of the data using the QLDB Digest, which is the secured output file of your ledger's full hash chain.

With Amazon QLDB, you can efficiently verify the integrity of a document in your ledger's journal by using cryptographic hashing with SHA-256. With this, we can verify if the data is been tampered or not.

1. **Requesting a Digest:**
    a. Navigate to the **Ledgers** pane.
    b. Select your Ledger.

c. Click on the **Get digest** button as shown in the following screenshot:

Figure 3.18: Get digest

d. Save the file for later use. This file is in the Amazon Ion format and has the following details:

    I. **Digest**: This is the hash value of the Digest you requested.

    II. **Digest tip address**: This is the latest block location in Journal.

    III. **Ledger**: This is the Ledger name.

    IV. **Date**: This is the timestamp of the request.

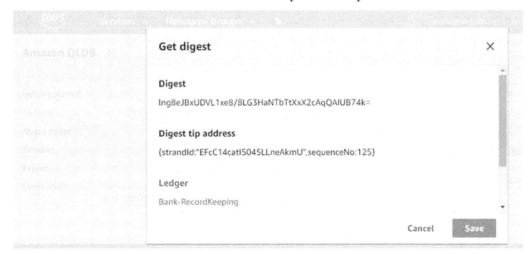

Figure 3.19: Save details

2. **Getting ID and blockAddress for the Account table document:**

We will get the details of the ID and blockAddress of the document from the Account table which we want to verify. Run the following statement to get metadata details:

```
SELECT a.metadata.id, a.blockAddress
FROM _ql_committed_Account as a
```

```
WHERE a.data.AccountNumber = '1'
```

Note down the ID and Block Address from the preceding result.

Let's verify the data. Perform the following steps:

- Navigate to the **Verification** pane.

- Select **Digest**.

- Enter **Document ID** and **Block address** as shown in the following screenshot:

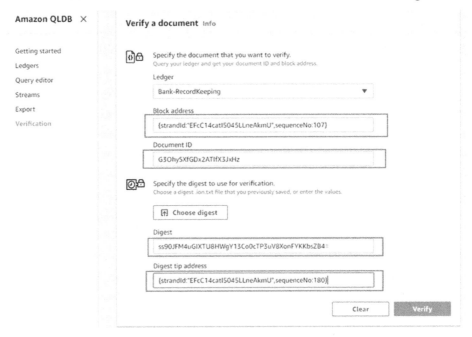

Figure 3.20: Verify data

- The verification result will look like the following screenshot:

Figure 3.21: *Verify result*

This completes our verification.

Exporting journal data

You can access the contents of the journal in your ledger for various purposes, including analytics, auditing, data retention, verification, and exporting to other systems. The following sections describe how to export journal blocks from your ledger into an Amazon Simple Storage Service (Amazon S3) bucket in your AWS account.

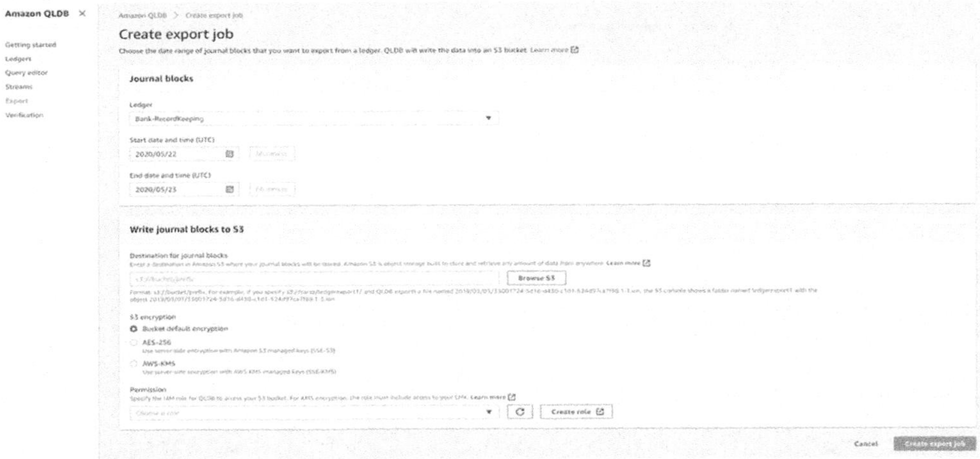

Figure 3.22: *Journal data*

Add content. A journal export job writes your data in Amazon S3 as objects in the Amazon Ion format(`.ion`).

Streaming journal data

Amazon QLDB uses an immutable transactional log, known as a journal, for data storage. The journal tracks every change made to your data and maintains a complete and verifiable history of changes over time.

You can create a stream in QLDB that captures every document revision that is committed to your journal and delivers this data to Amazon Kinesis Data Streams in near-real time. A QLDB stream is a continuous flow of data from your ledger's journal to a Kinesis data stream resource.

Figure 3.23: Streaming journal data

Add content.

You can use the Kinesis streaming platform or the Kinesis client library to consume your stream, process the data records, and analyze the data contents. A QLDB stream writes your data to Kinesis data streams in three types of records: control, block summary, and revision details.

Conclusion

Record keeping is a process of creating, capturing, and managing the application data. Record keeping requires QLDB to bring trust in the system. With QLDB, organizations can build a tamper-proof immutable database to trace the history of changes for auditing, regulation, compliance, and fraud. QLDB is a right fit in a situation where organizations want to maintain a centralized database with immutability and cryptographically verifiable transaction log.

In this chapter, we explored QLDB and designed a sample record keeping system for bank auditing with Amazon QLDB which provides immutability, transparency, security, and high performance.

In the next chapter, we will explore the Hyperledger Fabric blockchain.

Points to remember

Amazon QLDB is basically a database for a system-of-records application where traceability and auditability is a must. QLDB is a fully managed centralized ledger database that provides a transparent, immutable, and cryptographically verifiable transaction log. Amazon QLDB tracks each application data change and maintains a complete and verifiable history of changes over time.

Multiple choice questions

1. **QLDB can be used to solve many use cases like HR and Payroll, Manufacturing, Insurance, Retail, Supply Chain, and Transport, and Logistics.**

    a. True

    b. False

2. **Data stored in QLDB can be tampered.**

    a. True

    b. False

3. **How many ledgers QLDB can be created to store the transaction details.**

    a. One stores current state

    b. One stores the current state and other one maintains history

Answers

1. a

2. a

3. b

Questions

1. How does QLDB work?

2. Hands-on exercise: Add more tables to the above auditing Banking application.

3. Hands-on exercise: Build solution to HR application to store Bonus component using QLDB.

    a. Create tables, indexes to HR application.

    b. Perform transactions to HR application.

    c. Validate the transactions with QLDB.

Key Terms

1. **Record keeping:** Record keeping is a process of creating, capturing, and managing the application data. Every organization manages a lot of data for their business. It requires that data should be stored securely and maintains the history of changes.

2. **Journal:** A Journal in QLDB maintains all the changes in a chronological order with a timestamp in an immutable state. Through the Journal, you can query all the history of changes made even if the data is deleted in the ledger as the Journal maintains all the history of changes.

CHAPTER 4
Exploring Hyperledger Fabric

In this chapter, we will deep dive into the Hyperledger Fabric architecture, network, and components. Hyperledger Fabric is a blockchain framework for enterprise business applications which enable privacy and confidentiality of transactions and enables trust, transparency, and accountability in the network. Here, you will learn all the things needed to build enterprise solutions using Hyperledger Fabric.

Structure

In this chapter, we will discuss the following topics:

- Hyperledger Fabric overview
- Features of Hyperledger Fabric
- When to use Hyperledger Fabric
- Hyperledger Fabric architecture
- Hyperledger Fabric workflow
- Hyperledger Fabric models
- Hyperledger Fabric network components
- Hyperledger Fabric consensus
- Application transaction flow

Objectives

After studying this unit, you should be able to:

- Understand a permissioned blockchain
- Understand a Hyperledger Fabric blockchain
- Understand the Hyperledger Fabric architecture
- Understand the Hyperledger Fabric workflow, models, networks, and consensus
- Understand the application transaction flow

Hyperledger Fabric overview

The Hyperledger project is an open source collaborative effort hosted by the Linux foundation to advance cross-industry blockchain technologies. Hyperledger Fabric is one of the blockchain projects within the Hyperledger umbrella. It's an open source blockchain framework, distributed ledger technology which isgoverned by a diverse development community ofnearly 200 developers from 35 organizations.

Hyperledger Fabric is the blockchain framework for enterprise business applications which enables privacy and confidentiality of transactions and enables trust, transparency, and accountability in the network.

Features of Hyperledger Fabric

Hyperledger Fabric comes with many features. The following are a few important ones:

- **Permissioned blockchain:** Unlike a public blockchain where anyone can join the network without an identity, Hyperledger Fabric requires an identity and certificated authority for any user or nodes to join the network.

- **Privacy and confidentiality of transactions:** Channels allow a subset of nodes to have private communication, and the ledger data of a channel can be accessed only by the organizations thatare part of the channel. Participants can only see network features based on their roles.

- **Highly modular and configurable architecture:** It support pluggable ordering services, pluggable membership service providers, pluggable endorsement and validation policies, and pluggable consensus protocols that enable the platform to be more effective. The ledger supports multiple varieties of databases.

- **High transaction throughput performance:** Hyperledger Fabric is a highly scalable network. The transaction execution is separated from transaction ordering and commitment, while peer nodes are freed from ordering (consensus) workloads. The division of labor unburdens ordering nodes from the demands of the transaction execution and ledger maintenance.

- **Low latency of transaction confirmation:** A permissioned network is formed with only a few organizations which reduces the latency. Since there is no mining process, it makes the system fast in verifying and committing the transaction.

- **Faster and simpler data query by using CouchDB:** CouchDB executes query faster with less latency and with simpler query.

- **Smart contracts in general purpose language:** We can write smart contracts in Java, Go, or Node.js.

- **No cryptocurrency:** Cryptocurrency is not required to incent costly mining or to fuel the smart contract execution.

When to use Hyperledger Fabric

Hyperledger Fabric is the best fit where multiple parties/participants/companies are involved with low trust and work for a common goal. Hyperledger Fabric enables trust, transparency, and accountability in the network.

The following are a few usecases of Hyperledger Fabric:

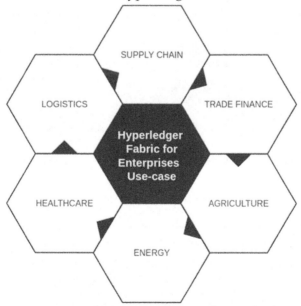

Figure 4.1: *Hyperledger Fabric use-cases*

Many organizations are experimenting/using Hyperledger Fabric for various business domains. Some of the organizations are *Maersk, Golden State Foods, McCormick and*

Co, Nestlé, Tyson Foods, Wal-Mart Stores Inc, Cambio Coffe, CLS, TradeLens, WorldWire, Unilever, Golden State Foods, and *Kroger.*

Hyperledger Fabric architecture

The following is the architecture of the Hyperledger Fabric network, which is a distributed system having multiple organizations/peers working together for a common goal. Organizations host nodes to store the transaction data into an immutable ledger to store the chaincode.

The client application executes the transaction by invoking the chaincode functions, and the client transactions are verified and endorsed by nodes and only the endorsed transaction gets stored in the ledger.

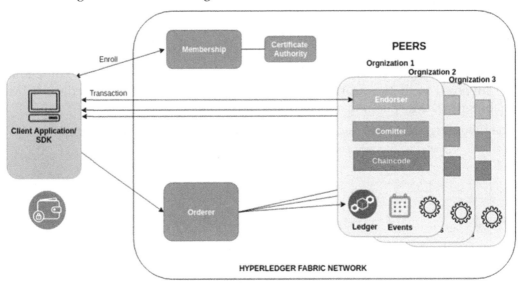

Figure 4.2: Hyperledger Fabric architecture

Hyperledger Fabric consists of the following components:

- **Transaction:** A transaction is a request from a client to execute the chaincode function.

- **Client Node:** Transactions are requested from client nodes on behalf of users, which invoke the chaincode and execute chaincode functions.

- **SDK:** Hyperledger Fabric supports Node.js and Java SDK to write smart contracts –the chaincode to interact with the Blockchain Ledger.

- **Wallet:** A wallet stores user identities which are required to interact with the network.

- **Membership:** Every actor in a blockchain network should have a digital certificate which is provided by Membership Service Provider. These certificates determine the exact permissions over resources and access to information that actors have in a blockchain network.

- **Certificated Authority:** Certificates are issued, renewed, and revoked by a Certification Authority.

- **Endorser node/peer:** Client/user requests are validated by endorsing peers to verify the certificates and simulate the chaincode but an entry to a ledger is not made.

- **Orderer node/Ordering Service:** Orderer is the communication channel for the entire network that brings data consistency across organizations. It receives endorsed transactions from the client and broadcasts it to committing peers.

- **Committer:** It validates the transaction received from ordered and makes an entry to the ledger.

- **Ledger:** The ledger records all the transactions as sequenced and immutable records. It maintains the state DB to store the current value and blockchain ledger having all the transactions.

- **Events:** Peers and chaincodes produce events on the network that applications may listen for and take actions on.

- **Channel:** Channels enable privacy within the network by creating a separate ledger between peers.

The Hyperledger Fabric architecture is modular, pluggable, flexible, and scalable.

Hyperledger Fabric workflow

Let's understand the workflow in a Fabric network when a client requests a transaction:

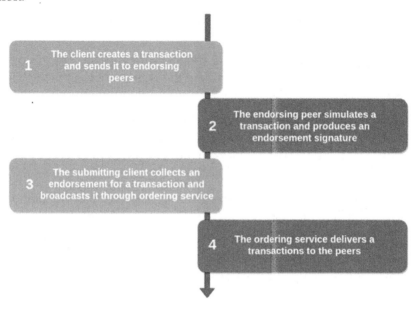

Figure 4.3: Hyperledger Fabric workflow

In the Fabric network, when the client node requests a transaction, the following steps take place:

Step1- The client creates a transaction and sends it to endorsing peers of its choice. The client submits the transaction proposal to the set of endorsing peers. The endorsing policy maintains the list of peers who act as endorsers. While submitting the transaction, we should mention the client id, chaincode id, transaction payload, time stamp, client signature, and anchor as optional.

Step2- The endorsing peer simulates a transaction and produces an endorsement signature. Once the endorser receives a transaction request, it verifies and executes the transaction in the following two stages:

- The following verifications are done by endorsing peer:
    o   Is the transaction proposal well-formed?
    o   Has the transaction not been submitted already in the past?
    o   Is the client signature valid?
    o   Is the client authorized to perform the proposed operation on the channel?

- The following are the steps in the execution stage:
  - o The endorsing peers take the transaction proposal inputs as arguments to the invoked chaincode's function.
  - o The chaincode is then simulated against the current state database to produce the transaction results, including a response value, read version dependencies, and state updates.
  - o No updates are made to the ledger at this point.

Step3: The submitting client collects an endorsement for a transaction and broadcasts it through an ordering service: Once the client receives endorsements from the selected endorser, the client transaction is accepted with the endorser's signature.

The client broadcasts the transaction proposal and response to the ordering service. The transaction will contain the read/write sets, endorsement signatures, and channel IDs.

Step4: The ordering service delivers a transaction to the peers. The ordering service creates a block with transactions and delivers it to peer nodes. Committing peers from all the organizations validate the transaction based on the endorsement policy and ensure that no change in the Ledger state and transactions in the block are tagged as being valid or invalid.

Each committing peer in an organization then appends this new block to the ledger, commits the valid transaction to the state DB, and notifies the status of the transaction to the client.

Hyperledger Fabric model

Fabric has set models like assets, ledgers, smart contracts – chaincode, channels, membership service providers, gossip protocols, and consensus. Let's understand these key design features of Hyperledger Fabric.

Assets

Assets can be tangible assets (For example: car, plane, grocery, real estate, and more) and non-tangible assets (For example: certificates, intellectual property, contracts, and more) having a monetary value.

Assets are defined as a collection of key-value pairs in binary and/or JSON format. Any time in the supply chain, when the product state changes, an entry will be made to the distributed ledger. For example, in the land registry, where the land is an asset when the next person buys the land, the ledger is updated with the new owner.

Ledger

The ledger keeps all the transactions generated by the smart contract in a sequenced, immutable format and records all changes. The ledger data is accessed through the chaincode and multiple chaincodes can access the same ledger as well. The ledger maintains data in the key-value pair format. Each peer maintains a copy of the ledger for each channel of which they are a member and there is one ledger per channel.

For flexibility, a peer can host multiple ledgers for each of the channels. Ledgers can be accessed by multiple chaincodes as well.

The ledger maintains two ledgers: one to have the current state called and the other ledger for the transaction history.

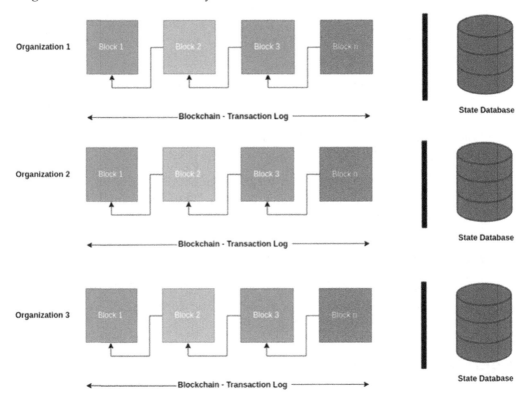

Figure 4.4: *Hyperledger Fabric model*

In the preceding diagram, we can see that Hyperledger Fabric maintains two ledgers as follows:

Ledger 1: Transaction Log:

Transaction log has following features:

- Records all transactions as a block and each block is chained with the hash of the previous block to enable immutability.

- Immutable and tamper resistance.

- Performs only Create and Read.

- Uses Level DB - Embedded with in the peer.

Ledger 2: State database:

State database has following features:

- Records the current state of asset.

- Performs Create, Read, Update, and Delete.

- New version created on update with the key-value pair.

- We can use the Couch DB to execute complex queries.

If the Couch DB is used as a state database, then we can write read-only queries using a rich query language.

Smart contract - chaincode

The smart contract implementation within Hyperledger Fabric is called a chaincode. It's basically a program which has rules and business logic, and it represents the asset or assets, transaction instructions which alter the ledger data maintained as the key-value pair.

The blockchain ledger is controlled through a smart contract. We can host more than one chaincode in any peer; a chaincode can access multiple ledgers.

Apart from the application chaincode, peers also have the system chaincode which defines operating parameters like channel rules, endorsement configuration and validation configuration for the entire channel.

Channels

Channels enable privacy within the network by creating a separate ledger between peers or among a few peers by creating a channel. Only peers belong to this channel can interact with each other. These peers collectively agree to maintain the identical ledger. Also, organizations can belong to multiple channels and maintain the separate ledger for each channel.

In the following screenshot, all the three organizations maintain a shared ledger 1, but Organization 1 and Organization 2 do private communication through a channel and maintain a different ledger 2. Organization 2 doesn't have access to Ledger 2.

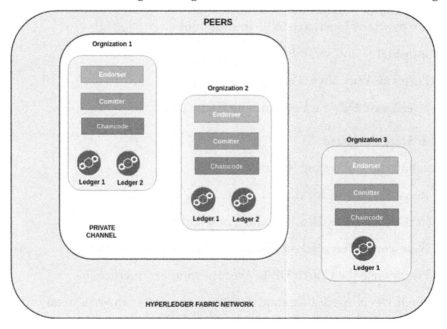

Figure 4.5: Channels

Private channels have a separate ledger which is available only to those peers who are part of that channel.

Membership service provider

Every actor (participants, peers, orderers, client applications, administrators, and more) in a blockchain network has a digital identity encapsulated in an X.509 digital certificate.

The identity determines the exact permissions over resources and access to information that actors have in a blockchain network.

For an identity to be verifiable, it must come from a trusted authority. This is achieved through a **Membership Service Provider(MSP)**.

Certificates are issued and revoked by a **Certification Authority (CA)**. MSP defines the rules that govern the valid identities for this organization. The default MSP implementation in Fabric uses X.509 certificates as identities, adopting a **Public Key Infrastructure (PKI)**. Members in an organization can create certificates for their participants and infrastructure, and the network can be governed by one or more MSPs.

Gossip protocol

A gossip protocol manages the peer discovery and channel membership by continually identifying available member peers and eventually, detecting peers that have gone offline.

Consensus

We understand that data in a blockchain is immutable and trustable. Since multiple parties are involved in the system, we need to ensure that the reliable data goes inside the blockchain where all the parties validate and agree to the process. In the blockchain network, trust is achieved through consensus.

Business agreements create a policy with an endorsement policy to verify the transaction and versioning checks are made before committing to the ledger. This also makes sure there are no double spends in the network and protect against security threats.

Consensus is achieved using the **Endorse | Order | Validate** transaction flow:

Endorse: Verify transaction and simulate the chaincode.

Order: Only endorsed transactions are ordered.

Validate: Each peer validates the transaction and commits to a ledger.

Each transaction in Hyperledger Fabric follows endorse, order and validate transaction flow.

Hyperledger Fabric network components

Let's understand the important components of the Hyperledger Fabric network.

What are organizations in the network?

Multiple organizations join and form a blockchain network; for example, in supply chain producer, supplier, factory, retailers are the organizations in the network where each one maintains the replicated copy of the ledger.

A blockchain network is not owned by anyone but it's the collective effort to keep updated with the right information. This network is created and managed by the collective effort of every organization. The network doesn't care if organizations leave in between or if the last organization leaves the network, till then the network will be running. Once the last organization exits, then the network will be deleted.

An organization can have any number of peers based on their need and performance. Each organization's application will join their own organization's peer and to the other organization peers.

Understanding of peers

Peers are basically nodes in the network. Peers store ledger data and host a chaincode. A redundant copy of the ledger and chaincode is maintained in order to avoid a single point of failure. Peers can host as many as ledgers and chaincodes based on the need.

Peers are a fundamental element of the network and the application accesses data through peers. Each peer should have a certificate to identify in the network.

Understanding of a client node

A client node interacts with peers through the SDK. The client node submits transactions to the network on behalf of a user to invoke chaincode functions. The client node submits the transaction request along with the endorsement policy to endorsers based on the configuration from the endorsement policy.

Once the client node receives the response from the endorser based on the acceptance from endorsers, the transaction will be submitted to the orderer. A client can connect to any peers in the network.

Let's understand the Hyperledger Fabric components with the help of below diagram:

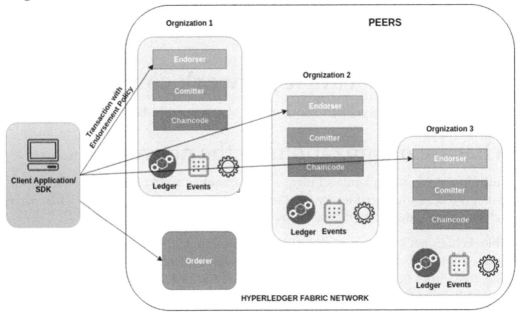

Figure 4.6: Client node

When the connected client node can access peer ledgers and chaincodes, the client node can perform the Ledger-query read or Ledger-update update operation by invoking the chaincode to execute the business logic. To generate transactions to the network, this transaction will be ordered and committed to the ledger. As the ledger-query just toread data from ledger so the response will be given immediately as it need not to go through consensus mechanism, whereas the ledger-update is an insert or update method which involves a consensus agreement and running the business login would take more time to commit to the ledger. The component Peers and Orderers ensures that the ledgers are stores up-to-date information.

Ledger-query steps are as follows:

- The client application connects to the peer.

- It creates a proposal to query the chaincode to either query or update the ledger.

- A peer invokes the chaincode to respond to a client request.

- Based on the response from the peer, the client requests transaction to the orderer node.

- An ordered node distributes transactions to all peers in the network.

- A committer validates the transaction and updates the Ledger. If the request is to read data, then just one peer can respond as they hold the requested data, so it immediately sends it back to the client.

- A committer generates an event to notify the client on his request completion.

Ledger-update steps are as follows:

- The client application connects to a peer.

- It creates a proposal to invoke the chaincode to either query or update the ledger.

- Unlike Ledger-query steps, a peer can't process the request as it's a change to the ledger. Other peers from a different organization in the network must agree to the change called **consensus**. An endorser of other organization endorsers agreement by invoking the chaincode to respond to a client request.

- Based on the response from multiple peers, the client requests the transaction to the orderer node.

- The ordered node packages the transactions into blocks and then distributes transactions to all peers in the network.

- A committer validates the transaction and updates the ledger.

- A committer generates an event asynchronously to notify the client on the progress and completion.

The client node performs the Ledger-query read or Ledger-update as mentioned in the preceding steps.

Understanding of endorsing peers

The following are the objectives of endorsing peers:

- Validates the transaction.(For example: Certificate checks)

- Simulates the chaincode - executes the chaincode but does not save the state to the ledger.

- Protects the network to stop an intentional attack and misbehaving or misconfigured nodes on the network.

- Improves scalability as only endorsers need to execute the chaincode.

The endorsement policy defines the consensus on the agreement from organizations. The endorsement policy is attached to the chaincode. A policy mentions a minimum number of approvals needed from endorsing peers or by all endorsing peers. The client transactions should meet the required policy for it to get accepted by an endorser.

Understanding of an ordering service

An ordering service is also called an orderer, and the ordering node is the communication channel for the fabric network. The blocks created by the orderer are the final blocks which will be sent to the peer nodes. The order is responsible for the consistent ledger state across the network and it ensures the order of the transactions and creates the blocks and guarantees atomic delivery.

An orderer maintains a consortium which is the list of organizations that can create channels. It can maintain multiple consortiums as well to create a multi-tenancy network. An orderer also enforces basic access control that can do anything on the network.

The ordering service implementation can be done with Solo, Raft, and Kafka. SOLO as an orderer for development or Kafka for production can be used as a messaging service.

Understanding of an Anchor peer

An Anchor peer receives the blocks and updates other peers in the organization. Gossip uses an **Anchor** peer to make sure peers in different organizations know about each other.

In the following screenshot, we can see that each organization has one Anchor peer which is communicated with an orderer.

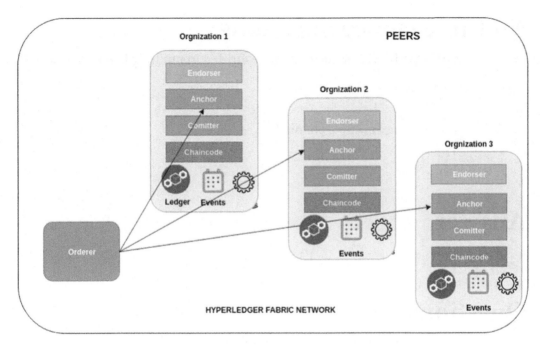

Figure 4.7: *Anchor peer*

It's mandatory to have at least one anchor peer in the organization.

Conclusion

In this chapter, we understood how Hyperledger Fabric works, the architecture of an Hyperledger Fabric network and important components and models of a fabric network. With this knowledge, we will be able to build Blockchain solutions for enterprises with Hyperledger Fabric.

In the next chapter, we will createthe Hyperledger Fabric network in AWS using an Amazon Blockchain Managed service.

Points to remember

- Hyperledger Fabric comes with many features. Here area few important features:
- Permissioned blockchain, privacy, and confidentiality of transactions, highly modular and configurable architecture, high transaction throughput performance, low latency of transaction confirmation, faster and simpler data query by using CouchDB, smart contracts in general purpose language, and no cryptocurrency.

Multiple choice questions

1. Hyperledger Fabric chaincode can be written in multiple languages.

    a) True

    b) False

2. Nodes can have multiple channels.

    a) True

    b) False

Answer

1. **a**

2. **a**

Questions

1. What are the features of Hyperledger Fabric?

2. Explain components of Hyperledger Fabric.

3. Explain the chaincode lifecycle.

4. Explain peers in Hyperledger Fabric.

5. Explain the transaction flow of Hyperledger Fabric.

Key Terms

1. **SDK:** Hyperledger Fabric supports Node.js and Java SDK to build application with nodeJS and Java language.

2. **Wallet:** A wallet stores user identities which are required to interact with the network, wallet is used to transact with Hyperledger Fabric network

CHAPTER 5

AWS Managed Blockchain to Create Fabric Network

In this chapter, we will build the Hyperledger Fabric network with Amazon Managed Blockchain. Instead of just building a Fabric network, we will solve the real-world problem in the Healthcare supply chain. We will build the healthcare supply chain system with Hyperledger Fabric and Amazon Managed blockchain services.

Structure

In this chapter, we will discuss the following topics:

- Deep dive into Amazon managed blockchain
- Understanding of the healthcare supply chain
- Current challenges in the healthcare supply chain
- Blockchain in the healthcare supply chain
- Stages in building a healthcare supply chain system with blockchain Hyperledger Fabric
- Building the Hyperledger Fabric network for the healthcare supply chain

Objectives

After studying this unit, you should be able to:

- Explore Amazon managed blockchain

- Build blockchain healthcare solutions with Amazon managed blockchain

Pre-requisites for this chapter

We will be making use of AWS resources in this chapter, so it would be great if you already have experience with AWS. Please visit https://docs.aws.amazon.com to learn more about AWS resources such as Cloud9, CloudFormation, and EC2 instance.

- **AWS account:** If you already have an AWS account, then you can skip this step. Otherwise, sign up to AWS for a new account at https://aws.amazon.com/

- **AWS CLI:** We will use the AWS CLI to provision blockchain network resources.

- **Hyperledger Fabric:** Prior knowledge of the Hyperledger Fabric architecture, fabric network models, components, and transaction flow is required.

- **Usage of Linux terminal:** We will use the Linux terminal to configure the fabric network.

- **Shell scripting:** Basic knowledge on Shell scripting is required.

- **Docker and docker-compose:** Basic understanding and working experience on docker is required as all the peers in Hyperledger Fabric run as a docker container.

Make sure to have all pre-requisites in place.

Understanding of Amazon managed blockchain

Self-hosting of the Hyperledger Fabric network for multiple organizations involves too many manual steps which are complex in nature, prone to errors, and time-consuming. We will explore how Amazon managed blockchain makes it easy.

What is Amazon managed blockchain?

Amazon managed blockchain makes it easy to build a secure permissioned blockchain network in a few clicks. It's a fully managed service that makes it easy to manage scalable blockchain networks. You can build a decentralized application using Hyperledger Fabric and the Ethereum framework with Amazon managed blockchain services.

With Amazon managed blockchain, you can focus only on writing business logic and application development. All the heavy lifting provisioning, deploying, and managing of these infrastructures will be taken care of by Amazon.

How Amazon managed blockchain works?

The following four steps are involved in building the blockchain solutions and running on AWS:

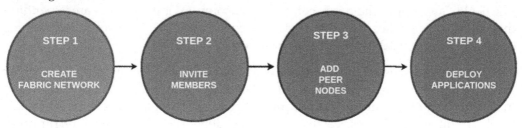

Figure 5.1: *How Amazon Managed Blockchain works?*

Step 1:

Build the blockchain network. Amazon Managed Blockchain gives two options (Hyperledger Fabric and Ethereum) to build a blockchain network.

This network can be of any size and many organizations can participate in the network. This network will be created by a member who is taking the blockchain initiative for his/her business. No one owns the network as it's a decentralized network.

Step 2:

Once the network is created, then invite other members in the business to be part of the network.

Step 3:

Once the members join the network, members will be able to create peer nodes to store the ledger, chaincode, and certificate authority.

Step 4:

Build the front-end application and deploy on AWS and start using it.

Healthcare supply chain project overview

The supply chain in healthcare industries manages pharmaceuticals, medical devices, medical supplies, patient records, and fast-moving consumer goods from supply of raw materials till disposal.

There are hundreds to thousands of parties (For example: Raw material suppliers, manufacturers, shippers, distributors, hospitals, pharmacy, and so on.) in the entire healthcare supply chain that need to collaborate and trust each other to have a better supply chain management. Healthcare supply remains fragmented and incomplete and it puts patients at risk.

Current challenges in the health care supply chain

The healthcare supply chain is becoming more complex as companies are expanding their product portfolios. There is a 200 % rise in healthcare products and customers demand more affordable and quality products.

Alverson (2003) discussed the importance of a disciplined inventory management for hospitals and suggested serious consequences of the traditional hospital purchasing, including lack of inventory control, missed contract compliance, excess inventory levels, frequent stock-outs, costly emergency deliveries, workflow interruptions, expensive rework, and increased health system labor requirements.

Here are some of the challenges the healthcare supply chain is facing:

- Quality and compliance issues are rising.
- A drug recall is increasing.
- It's very costly to trace any product in the supply chain when something goes wrong.
- Lack of trust and integrity among the parties in the supply chain.
- Each party in the supply chains work independently even though healthcare requires more collaboration.
- There is no single source of truth. Each one maintains its own source of information such as data is not transparent across the chain, end-to-end visibility of information among suppliers, manufacturers, distributors, pharmacy, hospitals, and customers is not available.
- Operating cost for the entire supply chain is very high. The cost of the supply chain in hospitals is 30 percent of the total hospital cost and healthcare spending worldwide will almost double to US$ 15 trillion.
- The industry struggles to meet on-time delivery. There are long lead times with products taking between 1,000 and 8,000 hours to pass through the whole supply chain.
- Up to 40% of healthcare provider data records are filled with errors or misleading information.
- Healthcare data breaches in organizations are estimated to cost around $380 per record in the current times.
- Drug counterfeiting which leads to losses of around $200 million.

It's very critical to improve/redesign the healthcare supply chain to help millions of people around the world for safer and affordable healthcare. It is also critical to reduce the cost of managing the supply chain for all the parties in the supply chain.

According to a study conducted by IBM, around 16% of healthcare executives are determined about their plans to implement blockchain solutions in their work this year, while around 56% are expected to adopt the blockchain by the year 2022.

Blockchain use-case in healthcare

Companies are trying to solve the healthcare issues by adopting blockchains. Here are some of the healthcare use-cases where a blockchain is the right fit:

Figure 5.2: Blockchain use-cases in healthcare

In this chapter, we will build a blockchain solution for the healthcare supply chain.

Healthcare supply chain project work flow

We will build a blockchain solution with Hyperledger fabric using AWS managed blockchain services. In the healthcare supply chain, there are many parties involved, but for this sample project, we will consider a manufacturer, distributor, hospital, and pharmacy as participants. Please take a look at the following screenshot:

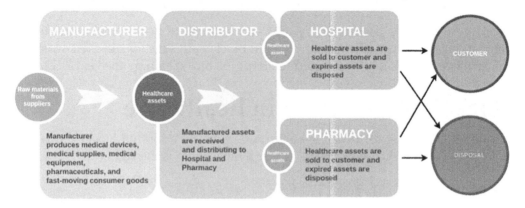

Figure 5.3: Healthcare supply chain work flow

The preceding screenshot explains the workflow of the healthcare supply chain.

Healthcare supply chain project code

The healthcare supply chain project repository is available in the following GitHub link:

Perform the following steps to download the healthcare supply channel project locally:

1. Navigate to **https://github.com/murughan1985/Healthcare-Supplychain-Blockchain.git**

2. Fork it to your GitHub account.

3. Clone it locally from your account:

   ```
   git clone https://github.com/<replace with youraccount>/Healthcare-
   Supplychain-Blockchain.git
   ```

Healthcare supply chain project architecture

We will build a layered architecture for the healthcare supply chain project. Please take a look at the following figure:

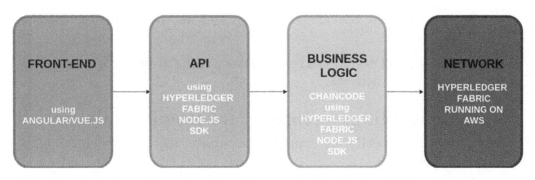

Figure 5.4: Healthcare supply chain project architecture

The layers are as follows:

- **Network:** It is the Hyperledger Fabric blockchain network as a backend which runs on AWS and is provisioned with AWS managed blockchain services.

- **Business Logic:** The chaincode that will run on the Fabric network is written with Node.js using the Hyperledger Fabric Node.js SDK. You can also write the chaincode in GoLang, Python, or Java.

- **API:** The API layer uses Node.js and express.js.

- **Front-end/UI:** This is created using Angular or Vue.js.

Note: The preceding cloned healthcare supplychain blockchain project has the following structure:

Figure 5.5: Project structure

We need to have the following order while building the complete project:

1. `healthcare-supplychain-network`: This has files to provision and configure the Fabricnetwork.

2. `healthcare-supplychain-chaincode`: This has the healthcare node.js chaincode.

3. `healthcare-supplychain-api`: The RESTful API code is written with Express.js.

4. `healthcare-blockchain-ui`: The UI application is written in Angular.

5. `healthcare-new-member:` This helps to add and configures other members to the network.

In this chapter, we will use the `healthcare-supplychain-network` directory files to provision the Fabric network.

Stages in building the healthcare supply chain project

Building a complete healthcare supply chain project requires four major stages which are as follows:

- **Stage 1:** Building a Hyperledger Fabric network for the healthcare supply chain with AWS Managed Blockchain.

- **Stage 2:** Creating a healthcare supply chain chaincode and deploying it on AWS.

- **Stage 3:** Creating an API and UI to interact with the healthcare supply chain chaincode from AWS.

- **Stage 4:** Adding Members (Distributor, Hospital, and Pharmacy) to the Fabric network on AWS.

In this chapter, we will build Stage 1: The Hyperledger Fabric network on AWS with AWS Managed Blockchain. In the next two chapters, we will work on Stage 2, Stage 3, and Stage4.

Fabric network architecture with AWS Managed Blockchain

We will create the Hyperledger Fabric network for four participants such as a Manufacturer, Distributor, Hospital, and Pharmacy using the Amazon Managed Blockchain service.

Network architecture for the healthcare supply chain project

The Fabric network for the healthcare supply chain contains four nodes such as Manufacturer, Distributor, Hospital, and Pharmacy, respectively. Each node in the network has the following components:

- Orderer node
- Certificate authority
- Peer node
- Ledger
    - o   World State Ledger

o Transaction Ledger

- Chaincode

Each member will have a Fabric client node outside the Fabric network which is connected through the VPC private link.

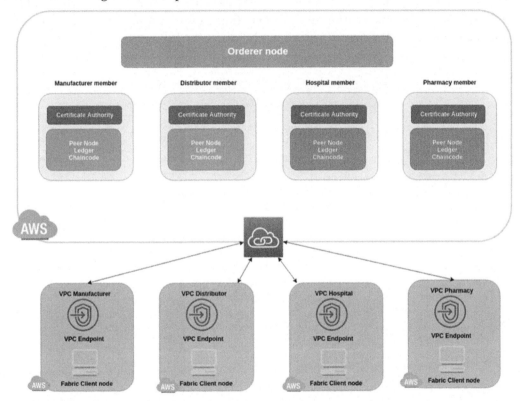

Figure 5.6: *Network architecture*

While provisioning using the AWS Managed Blockchain service, we will be provisioning only for the Manufacturer member in this chapter.

Network architecture for the Manufacturer member

The preceding architecture diagram displays all the four members, which means that each member has a different AWS account. In this chapter, we will create only one member that is the manufacturer as shown in the following figure:

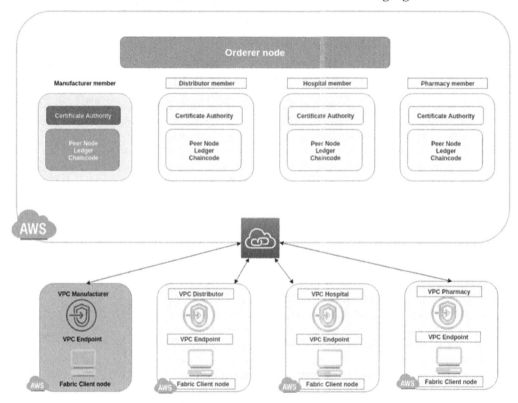

Figure 5.7: Network architecture for the Manufacturer member

The gray-colored resources will not be created in this chapter. In *chapter 6* – Add Members to the Fabric network on AWS, we will learn how to add other members to the network.

Steps in building the Hyperledger Fabric network

The following are the high-level steps to create a Fabric network:

1. Provisioning an AWS Cloud9 instance.

2. Creating a Fabric network and peer node in the AWS console with AWS Managed Blockchain.

3. Provisioning a Fabric client node.

4. Creating a Fabric channel.

5. Joining a peer node to the channel.

Step 1 – Provisioning an AWS Cloud9 instance

We can interact with the Fabric network in the following two ways:

- Create an EC2 Linux instance and create a Fabric client node.

- Create a Cloud9 instance and create a Fabric client node.

We will use the second option in this chapter to create the Fabric client node to interact with our Fabric network.

Cloud9 is a cloud-based IDE that can be accessed through a browser. It doesn't require you to install anything locally. Cloud9 provides an editor to write code with essential tools for popular languages and provides a debugger and terminal to run and debug your code. Cloud9 comes with a lot more features like code together in real-time, building a serverless application with ease, and accessing and building an application from any computer as it's a web-based tool and has terminal access to AWS.

We will use Cloud9 to provision the Hyperledger Fabric client node. In this step, we will provision a Cloud9 instance in the AWS Console. We will use the Linux terminal from Cloud9 which makes development easier as we need not worry about the OS compatibility.

Steps to provision an AWS Cloud9 instance as follows:

1. Navigate to **https://us-east-1.console.aws.amazon.com/cloud9/home/product**

2. Select the **US East(N. Virginia)** region.

3. Click on the **Create environment** button as shown in the following screenshot:

Figure 5.8: Create environment

4. Give a name for the Cloud9 instance and description.

Click on the **Next step** button as shown in the following screenshot.

Figure 5.9: Add name and description

5. Select **t2.medium** as the instance type as we need more memory to deploy our API and UI here, and then click on **Next step**.

6. Click on **Create Environment**.

7. Once the Cloud9 instance is created, clone the following `Healthcare-Supplychain-Blockchain` repo from GitHub and execute the following command in the cloud9 terminal as shown in the following screenshot:

   `cd ~`

   `git clone`

   `https://github.com/murughan1985/Healthcare-Supplychain-Blockchain.`

   `Git`

Figure 5.10: Clone sample project

8. Update your AWS CLI to the latest version. Execute the following command on the Cloud9 terminal as shown in the following screenshot:

   `sudo pip install awscli --upgrade`

```
murughan:~ $ sudo pip install awscli --upgrade
Collecting awscli
  Downloading https://files.pythonhosted.org/packages/20/fa/f4b6207d59267da0be60be3df32682d2c7479122c7cb87556bd4412675fe/awscli-1.16.198-py
2.py3-none-any.whl (1.7MB)
    100% |████████████████████████████████| 1.7MB 718kB/s
Requirement already up-to-date: colorama<=0.3.9,>=0.2.5 in /usr/local/lib/python2.7/site-packages (from awscli)
Requirement already up-to-date: rsa<=3.5.0,>=3.1.2 in /usr/local/lib/python2.7/site-packages (from awscli)
Collecting s3transfer<0.3.0,>=0.2.0 (from awscli)
  Downloading https://files.pythonhosted.org/packages/16/8a/1fc3dba0c4923c2a76e1ff0d52b305c44606da63f718d14d3231e21c51b0/s3transfer-0.2.1-p
y2.py3-none-any.whl (70kB)
    100% |████████████████████████████████| 71kB 9.0MB/s
Collecting PyYAML<=5.1,>=3.10; python_version != "2.6" (from awscli)
  Downloading https://files.pythonhosted.org/packages/9f/2c/9417b5c774792634834e730932745bc09a7d36754ca00acf1ccd1ac2594d/PyYAML-5.1.tar.gz
(274kB)
    100% |████████████████████████████████| 276kB 3.8MB/s
Collecting botocore==1.12.180 (from awscli)
  Downloading https://files.pythonhosted.org/packages/3b/27/fa7da6feb20d1dfc0ab562226061b20da2d27ea18ca32dc764fe86704a99/botocore-1.12.180-
py2.py3-none-any.whl (5.6MB)
    25% |████████                        | 1.4MB 32.2MB/s eta 0:00:01
```

Figure 5.11: Update your AWS CLI

You will see the preceding output for the successful installation of the AWS CLI.

Step 2 – Creating a Fabric network on the AWS console with AWS Managed Blockchain

In this step, we will create a Fabric network on the AWS console.

Steps to create a Fabric Network as follows:

1. Navigate to the Managed Blockchain page https://console.aws.amazon. com/managed blockchain as shown in the following screenshot:

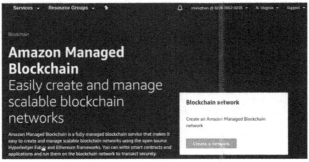

Figure 5.12: Navigate to Managed Blockchain

2. Select the Blockchain framework as **Hyperledger Fabric 1.2**. Currently, it's running on 1.2 version. Once the new version is available, you will able to use a new version.

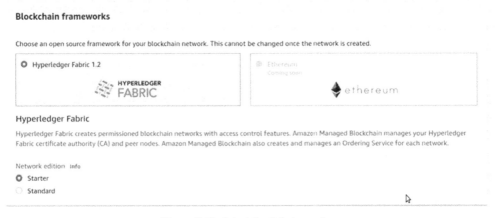

Figure 5.13: Select the Fabric version

3. Give a name for the network. We will give the name as healthcare Supplychain. *Make a note of this network name for later use.

Figure 5.14: Give the name and description

4. Enter the voting policy. The voting policy is used as a governance in the network and based on the voting from other organizations in the network, actions will be taken. Here, we will select 50% as voting which means that if there are more than 50% organization votes, we need to change them. We can also use this policy to remove the members from the network.

Figure 5.15: Configure voting

5. We will create member details in our healthcare example. We will have four members such as Manufacture, Distributor, Hospital, and Pharmacy. We will give a member name as **Manufacturer**.

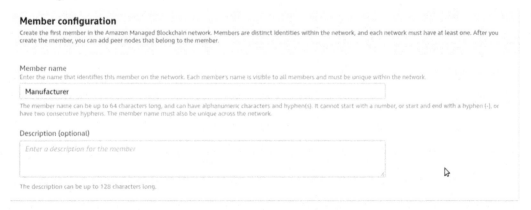

Figure 5.16: Configure members

6. Create a certificate authority for each member as Fabric requires a certificate for every identity to interact with the network. We will create CA – certificate authority, and this will create an identity for all other members in the network. Provide the **Admin username** and **Admin password**, and make a note of these credentials, as we would need them later. CA will use these credentials to create a network. **Admin123**

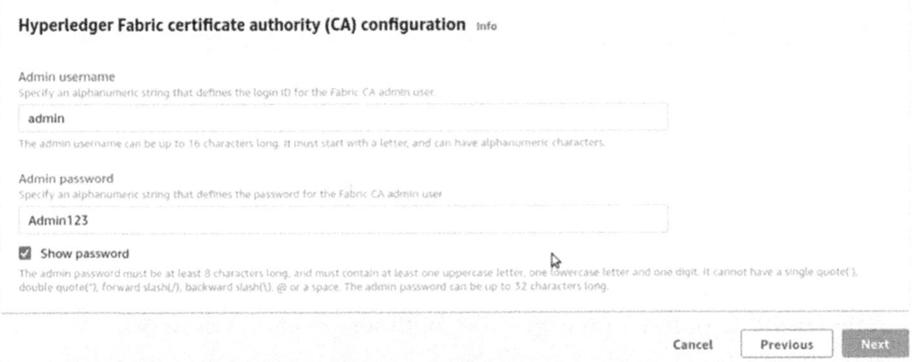

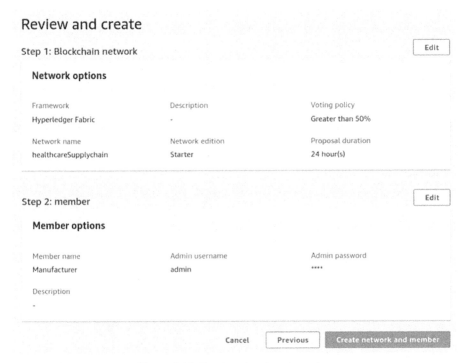

Figure 5.17: Configure CA

7. Review and create the network, and then click on **Create network and member**.

Figure 5.18: Create network and member

8. It may take around 10 minutes to create the network. Wait until the network gets created. Once it's created, note down the **Network ID** for later use. The output will look like the following screenshot:

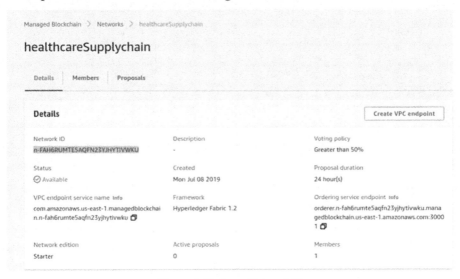

Figure 5.19: Copy Network ID

9. Select the **Members** tab, and note down the **Member ID** for later use. You should get the output as shown in the following screenshot:

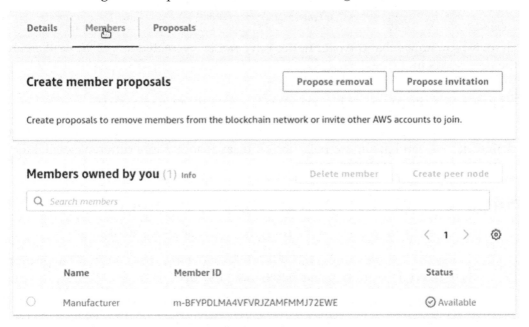

Figure 5.20: Copy Member ID

10. Click on the **Manufacturer** member to see the member and peer details:

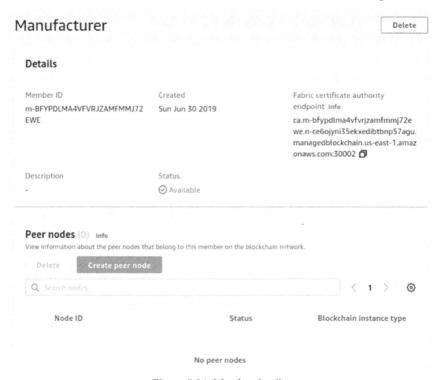

Figure 5.21: Member details

Here, we can notice that the peer nodes have not been created as yet; we will create the peer nodes in the next step.

Step 3 – Creating the manufacturer peer node

Each member will have the peer node to store host a ledger and to install the chaincode. We can have more peer nodes for availability in a different availability zone.

Steps to create the Manufacturer peer node:

1. Click on **Create peer node** from the Manufacturer details page.

2. Leave the default values, and then click on **Create peernode**. A suggestion is to select a medium instance to handle the load.

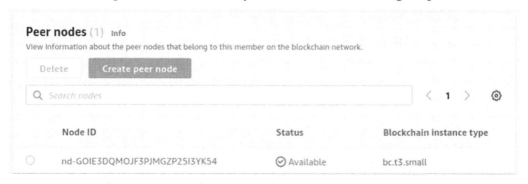

Figure 5.22: *Create peer node*

3. Once the peer node is created, you will see the following output screen:

Peer nodes (1) Info

View information about the peer nodes that belong to this member on the blockchain network.

	Delete		Create peer node	

Q Search nodes   ‹ 1 › ⚙

	Node ID	Status	Blockchain instance type
○	nd-GOIE3DQMOJF3PJMGZP25I3YK54	⊘ Available	bc.t3.small

Figure 5.23: *Check status*

So far, we have created our Fabric network and peer node. In the next section, we will create a Fabric client node.

Step 4 – Provisioning a Fabric client node using the Cloud Formation template in a Cloud9 instance

In this section, we will create a Fabric client node to interact and administer it with our Fabric network. Here, we will provision an EC2 instance with the Cloud Formation template and install Fabric CLI tools using the Cloud9 instance.

Steps to create the Manufacturer peer node:

1. In the Cloud9 Linux terminal, enter the following command with your network details as shown in the following screenshot:

```
export REGION=us-east-1
```

```
export NETWORKID=<Paste your Fabric network ID which you copied in
Step2>
```

```
export NETWORKNAME=<Paste your Fabric network name which you copied
in Step2>
```

bash - "ip-172-31 ×   Immediate   ×   ⊕

```
murughan:~ $ export REGION=us-east-1
murughan:~ $ export NETWORKID=n-CE6OJYNI35EKXEDIBTBNP57AGU
murughan:~ $ export NETWORKNAME=healthcareSupplychain
```

Figure 5.24: Set environment variables

2. Set the VPC endpoint. Execute the following command in the Cloud9 terminal, and you should get the output as shown in the following screenshot:

```
export VPCENDPOINTSERVICENAME=$(awsmanagedblockchain get-network
--region $REGION --network-id $NETWORKID --query
'Network.VpcEndpointServiceName' --output text)
echo $VPCENDPOINTSERVICENAME
```

```
murughan:~ $ export VPCENDPOINTSERVICENAME=$(aws managedblockchain get-network --region $REGION --network-id $NETWORKID --query 'Network.VpcEndpointServiceName' --output text)
murughan:~ $ echo $VPCENDPOINTSERVICENAME
com.amazonaws.us-east-1.managedblockchain.n-ce6ojyni35ekxedibtbnp57agu
murughan:~ $ 
```

Figure 5.25: Set the VPC endpoint

3. Create a CloudFormation template and execute the following command in the Cloud9 terminal which creates a key pair, VPC, subnet, security group, and an EC2 instance as our Fabric Client node:

```
cd    ~/Healthcare-Supplychain-Blockchain/healthcare-supplychain-
network

./3-vpc-client-node.sh
```

This will create a new .pem file in the format as <yournetworkname-keypair.pem>.

```
murughan:~ $ cd ~/Healthcare-Supplychain-Blockchain/healthcare-supplychain-network
murughan:~/Healthcare-Supplychain-Blockchain/healthcare-supplychain-network (master) $ ./3-vpc-client-node.sh
Creating VPC - TODO. Create the VPC, subnets, security group, EC2 client node, VPC endpoint
Create a keypair
Searching for existing keypair named healthcareSupplychain-keypair

An error occurred (InvalidKeyPair.NotFound) when calling the DescribeKeyPairs operation: The key pair 'healthcareSupplychain-keypair' does not exist
Creating a keypair named healthcareSupplychain-keypair. The .pem file will be in your /home/ec2-user directory
Create the VPC, the Fabric client node and the VPC endpoints

Waiting for changeset to be created..
Waiting for stack create/update to complete
```

Figure 5.26: Run the Cloud Formation template

4. Navigate to the CloudFormation website **https://console.aws.amazon.com/ CloudFormation/home?region=us-east-1** to see the deployment progress:

Figure 5.27: Check the deployment progress

We will wait till the Fabric client gets created for the next step.

Step 5 - ssh into the Fabric client node

When the preceding Cloud Formation stack shows the **CREATE_COMPLETE** message, we will ssh into the Fabric client node.

Steps to ssh into the Fabric client node:

1. Navigate to the **Outputs** section to see the output parameters. Copy the EC2URL field. This is your Fabric client EC2 instance URL:

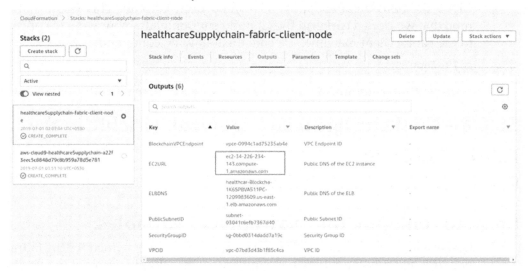

Figure 5.28: Check output parameters

2. Copy the `.pem` key pair name, which is created under the root directory in the Cloud9 instance.

```
murughan:~/Healthcare-Supplychain-Blockchain/healthcare-supplychain-network (master) $ cd ~
murughan:~ $ ls
        environment  gocode  Healthcare-Supplychain-Blockchain  healthcareSupplychain-keypair.pem  node_modules  pack
age-lock.json
```

Figure 5.29: Copy the .pem key pair name

3. ssh into the EC2 instance from the Cloud9 terminal, pass the `.pem` file, and execute the following command. You should be able to ssh successfully as shown in the following screenshot:

```
cd ~

ssh ec2-user@<paste your EC2URL> -i ~/<Fabric network name>-

keypair.pem
```

```
murughan:~ $ ssh ec2-user@ec2-34-226-234-143.compute-1.amazonaws.com -i healthcareSupplychain-keypair.pem
The authenticity of host 'ec2-34-226-234-143.compute-1.amazonaws.com (34.226.234.143)' can't be established.
ECDSA key fingerprint is SHA256:vqDAN8LLDiFNETwzJtpfCjuAQi8qySyywPY4eTXFxW4.
ECDSA key fingerprint is MD5:ee:9d:01:ce:58:4a:cb:25:5d:a9:9b:f1:93:07:f6:1f.
Are you sure you want to continue connecting (yes/no)? yes                     c
Warning: Permanently added 'ec2-34-226-234-143.compute-1.amazonaws.com,34.226.234.143' (ECDSA) to the list of known hosts.
Last login: Tue Nov 27 21:57:11 2018 from 72-21-198-66.amazon.com
     __|  __|_  )
     _|  (     /   Amazon Linux AMI
    ___|\___|___|

https://aws.amazon.com/amazon-linux-ami/2018.03-release-notes/
20 package(s) needed for security, out of 28 available
Run "sudo yum update" to apply all updates.
Starting cli ... done
[ec2-user@ip-10-0-247-155 ~]$ ▮
```

Figure 5.30: ssh into EC2

4. Clone the `HealthcareSupplychain` repo from GitHub. This is the same repo that we cloned earlierin the CLoud9 environment. Now, we will copy it to the Fabric client machine. Execute the following command:

```
git clone
```

https://github.com/murughan1985/Healthcare-Supplychain-Blockchain.git

Step 6 – Configuring an environment variable in the Fabric client node

We will capture all the Fabric network details in a file.

Steps to configure the environment variables:

1. Create a file that includes ENV export values which we defined for the fabric network. Execute the following command in the Cloud9 terminal inside the EC2 instance as shown in the following screenshot:

```
cd ~/Healthcare-Supplychain-Blockchain/healthcare-supplychain-
network
cp templates/exports-template.sh fabric-exports.sh
vi fabric-exports.sh
```

```
[ec2-user@ip-10-0-247-155 ~]$ cd ~/Healthcare-Supplychain-Blockchain/healthcare-supplychain-network
[ec2-user@ip-10-0-247-155 healthcare-supplychain-network]$ cp templates/exports-template.sh fabric-exports.sh
[ec2-user@ip-10-0-247-155 healthcare-supplychain-network]$ vi fabric-exports.sh
```

Figure 5.31: *Creating a file that includes ENV*

2. The `fabric-exports.sh` file has environment variables, which need to be updated with your Hyperledger Fabric network details. Replace the following details:

   Update these values, and then source this script:

   export REGION=us-east-1

   export NETWORKNAME=<your network name>

   export MEMBERNAME=<the member name you entered when

   creating your Fabric network>

   export NETWORKVERSION=1.2

   export ADMINUSER=<the admin user name you entered when

   creating your Fabric network>

   export ADMINPWD=<the admin user password you entered when

   creating your Fabric network>

   export NETWORKID=<your network ID, from the AWS Console>

   export MEMBERID=<your member ID, from the AWS Console>

   It should look like the below example

   export REGION=us-east-1

   export NETWORKNAME=healthcareSupplychain

   export MEMBERNAME=Manufacturer

   export NETWORKVERSION=1.2

   export ADMINUSER=admin

   export ADMINPWD=Admin123

   export NETWORKID=n-CE6OJYNI35EKXEDIBTBNP57AGU

   export MEMBERID=m-BFYPDLMA4VFVRJZAMFMMJ72EWE

3. Execute the following command to source the file as shown in the following screenshot:

   cd ~/Healthcare-Supplychain-Blockchain/healthcare-supplychain-network

source fabric-exports.sh

```
[ec2-user@ip-10-0-247-155 healthcare-supplychain-network]$ cd ~/Healthcare-Supplychain-Blockchain/healthcare-supplychain-net
work
[ec2-user@ip-10-0-247-155 healthcare-supplychain-network]$ source fabric-exports.sh
Updating AWS CLI to the latest version
Collecting awscli
```

Figure 5.32: Source fabric-export

4. When you source the file, you will be able to use these variables for later use. Scroll to the bottom to see the exported values:

```
Useful information used in Cloud9
REGION: us-east-1
NETWORKNAME: healthcareSupplychain
NETWORKVERSION: 1.2
ADMINUSER: admin
ADMINPWD: Admin123
MEMBERNAME: Manufacturer
NETWORKID: n-CE6OJYNI35EKXEDIBTBNP57AGU
MEMBERID: m-BFYPDLMA4VFVRJZAMFMMJ72EWE
ORDERINGSERVICEENDPOINT: orderer.n-ce6ojyni35ekxedibtbnp57agu.managedblockchain.us-east-1.amazonaws.com:30001
ORDERINGSERVICEENDPOINTNOPORT: orderer.n-ce6ojyni35ekxedibtbnp57agu.managedblockchain.us-east-1.amazonaws.com
VPCENDPOINTSERVICENAME: com.amazonaws.us-east-1.managedblockchain.n-ce6ojyni35ekxedibtbnp57agu
CASERVICEENDPOINT: ca.m-bfypdlma4vfvrjzamfmmj72ewe.n-ce6ojyni35ekxedibtbnp57agu.managedblockchain.us-east-1.amazonaws.com:30
002
PEERNODEID: nd-GOIE3DQMOJF3PJMGZP25I3YK54
PEERSERVICEENDPOINT: nd-goie3dqmojf3pjmgzp25i3yk54.m-bfypdlma4vfvrjzamfmmj72ewe.n-ce6ojyni35ekxedibtbnp57agu.managedblockcha
in.us-east-1.amazonaws.com:30003
PEERSERVICEENDPOINTNOPORT: nd-goie3dqmojf3pjmgzp25i3yk54.m-bfypdlma4vfvrjzamfmmj72ewe.n-ce6ojyni35ekxedibtbnp57agu.managedbl
ockchain.us-east-1.amazonaws.com
PEEREVENTENDPOINT: nd-goie3dqmojf3pjmgzp25i3yk54.m-bfypdlma4vfvrjzamfmmj72ewe.n-ce6ojyni35ekxedibtbnp57agu.managedblockchain
.us-east-1.amazonaws.com:30004
[ec2-user@ip-10-0-247-155 ~]$ []
```

Figure 5.33: Check exported values

5. Validate all the values in the peer-export file, and execute the following command:

cat ~/peer-exports.sh

6. If all the values have the correct network details, then source it by executing the following command:

source ~/peer-exports.sh

Step 7 – Enrolling an admin identity

Each member will have a certificate authority who is responsible to issue, revoke, and renew an identity for anyone/nodes to join the network.

Steps to enroll an admin identity:

1. We will download the latest version of the managed blockchain pem file, and execute the following command in Cloud9 on the Fabric client node as shown in the following screenshot:

```
aws s3 cp s3://us-east-1.managedblockchain/etc/managedblockchain-
tls-

chain.pem  /home/ec2-user/managedblockchain-tls-chain.pem
```

```
[ec2-user@ip-10-0-247-155 ~]$ aws s3 cp s3://us-east-1.managedblockchain/etc/managedblockchain-tls-chain.pem  /home/ec2-user/managedblockchain-tls-chain.pem
download: s3://us-east-1.managedblockchain/etc/managedblockchain-tls-chain.pem to ./managedblockchain-tls-chain.pem
```

Figure 5.34: *Download the latest version of the Managed Blockchain PEM file*

2. We will enroll an admin identity which we created while provisioning the Fabric network with Amazon Managed Blockchain. A certificate authority will enroll a user, and this user will be used to create the Fabric channel and to install and instantiate the Healthcare chaincode. Execute the following command as shown in the following screenshot:

```
export PATH=$PATH:/home/ec2-user/go/src/github.com/hyperledger/
fabric-

ca/bin

cd ~

fabric-ca-client enroll -u
https://$ADMINUSER:$ADMINPWD@$CASERVICEENDPOINT

--tls.certfiles /home/ec2-user/managedblockchain-tls-chain.pem -M

/home/ec2-user/admin-msp
```

```
[ec2-user@ip-10-0-247-155 ~]$ export PATH=$PATH:/home/ec2-user/go/src/github.com/hyperledger/fabric-ca/bin
[ec2-user@ip-10-0-247-155 ~]$ cd ~
[ec2-user@ip-10-0-247-155 ~]$ fabric-ca-client enroll -u https://$ADMINUSER:$ADMINPWD@$CASERVICEENDPOINT --tls.certfiles /home/ec2-user/managedblockchain-tls-chain.pem -M /home/ec2-user/admin-msp
2019/06/30 21:30:06 [INFO] Created a default configuration file at /home/ec2-user/.fabric-ca-client/fabric-ca-client-config.yaml
2019/06/30 21:30:06 [INFO] TLS Enabled
2019/06/30 21:30:06 [INFO] generating key: &{A:ecdsa S:256}
2019/06/30 21:30:06 [INFO] encoded CSR
2019/06/30 21:30:06 [INFO] Stored client certificate at /home/ec2-user/admin-msp/signcerts/cert.pem
2019/06/30 21:30:06 [INFO] Stored root CA certificate at /home/ec2-user/admin-msp/cacerts/ca-m-bfypdlna4vfvrjzanfmmj72ewe-n-ce6ojyni35ekxedibtbnp57agu-managedblockchain-us-east-1-amazonaws-com-30002.pem
```

Figure 5.35: *Enroll an admin identity*

3. Copy the certificate to the Fabric Client node and execute the following command as shown in the following screenshot:

```
mkdir -p /home/ec2-user/admin-msp/admincerts

cp ~/admin-msp/signcerts/* ~/admin-msp/admincerts/

cd    ~/Healthcare-Supplychain-Blockchain/healthcare-supplychain-
network
```

```
[ec2-user@ip-10-0-247-155 ~]$ mkdir -p /home/ec2-user/admin-msp/admincerts
[ec2-user@ip-10-0-247-155 ~]$ cp ~/admin-msp/signcerts/* ~/admin-msp/admincerts/
```

Figure 5.36: *Copy the certificate to the Fabric client node*

We created an identity for the admin user using the Fabric **Certificate Authority** (**CA**). We will now use this identity for later steps.

Step 8 - Updating the configtx channel configuration

Each channel in the Hyperledger Fabric network maintains a shared configuration of the network in a collection of configuration transactions. This configuration is called configtx. In this section, we will configure configtx for a channel.

Steps to update the configtx channel configuration:

1. Update the member ID in the channel configuration with our member details. In Step 2, we created the Fabric network and also made a note of the member ID of the Manufacturer. We will update the configtx channel with our member ID details. Execute the following command to get a member ID which we configured in *Step 6*:

   ```
   echo $MEMBERID
   ```

2. Copy `configtx.yaml` from the repo to the home directory:

   ```
   cp     ~/Healthcare-Supplychain-Blockchain/healthcare-supplychain-
   network/configtx.yaml ~
   ```

```
[ec2-user@ip-10-0-247-155 ~]$ cd ~/Healthcare-Supplychain-Blockchain/healthcare-supplychain-network
[ec2-user@ip-10-0-247-155 healthcare-supplychain-network]$ echo $MEMBERID
1-BFYPDLMA4VFVRJZAMFMMJ72EWE
[ec2-user@ip-10-0-247-155 healthcare-supplychain-network]$ cp ~/Healthcare-Supplychain-Blockchain/healthcare-supplychain-network/configtx.yaml ~
```

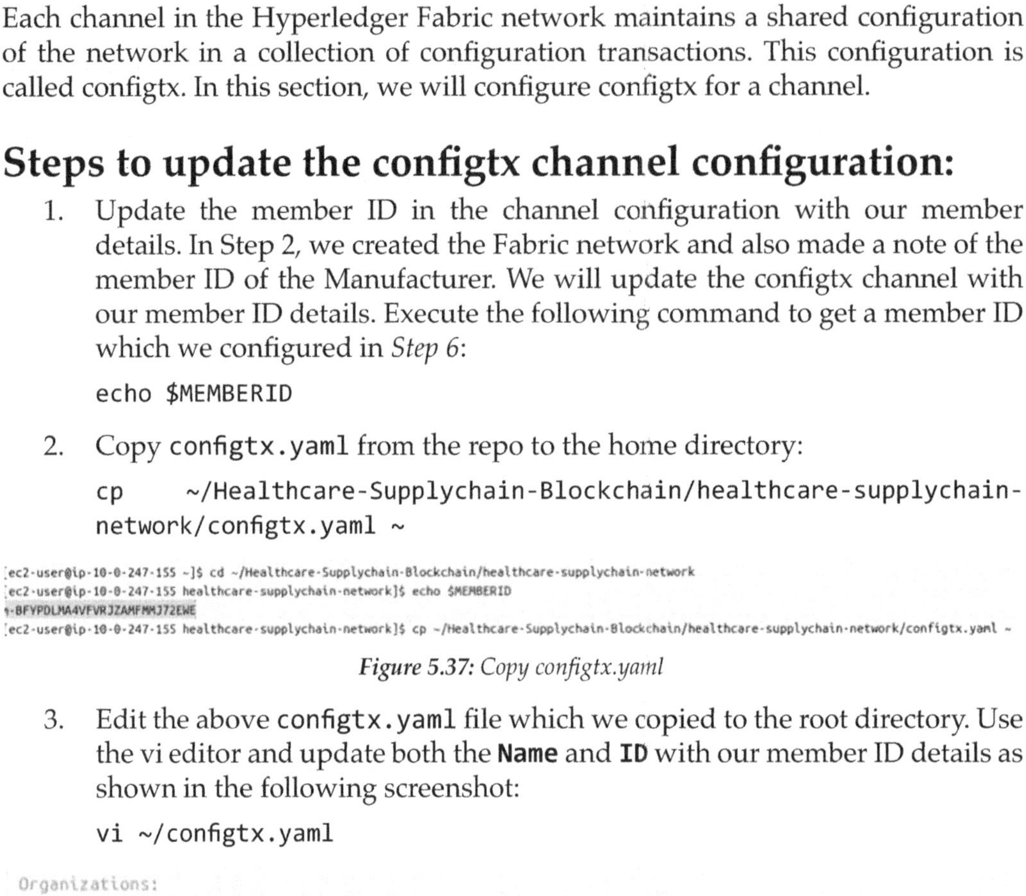

Figure 5.37: Copy configtx.yaml

3. Edit the above `configtx.yaml` file which we copied to the root directory. Use the vi editor and update both the **Name** and **ID** with our member ID details as shown in the following screenshot:

   ```
   vi ~/configtx.yaml
   ```

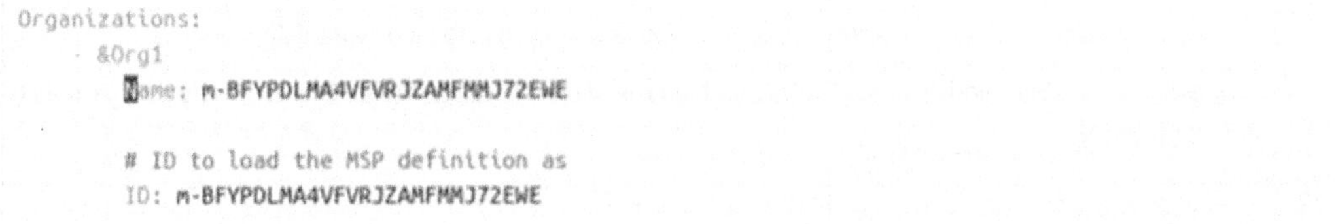

```
Organizations:
    &Org1
        Name: m-BFYPDLMA4VFVRJZAMFMMJ72EWE

        # ID to load the MSP definition as
        ID: m-BFYPDLMA4VFVRJZAMFMMJ72EWE
```

Figure 5.38: Edit the configtx.yaml file

4. Generate the configtx channel configuration by executing the following script, and you will get a similar output as shown in the following screenshot:

   ```
   docker   exec   cli   configtxgen   -outputCreateChannelTx   /opt/
   home/$CHANNEL.pb -

   profile OneOrgChannel -channelID $CHANNEL --configPath /opt/home/
   ```

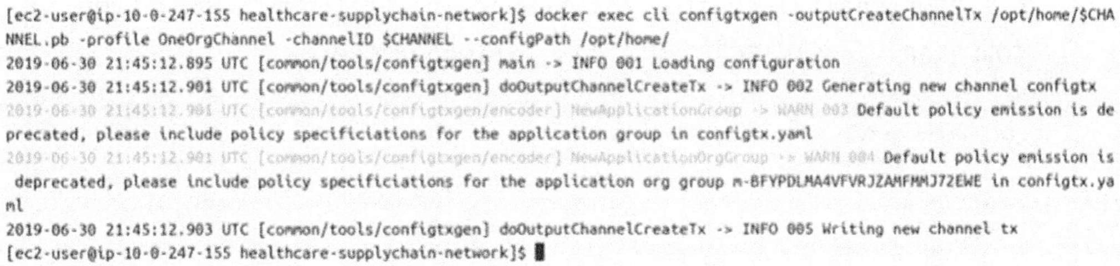

```
[ec2-user@ip-10-0-247-155 healthcare-supplychain-network]$ docker exec cli configtxgen -outputCreateChannelTx /opt/home/$CHA
NNEL.pb -profile OneOrgChannel -channelID $CHANNEL --configPath /opt/home/
2019-06-30 21:45:12.895 UTC [common/tools/configtxgen] main -> INFO 001 Loading configuration
2019-06-30 21:45:12.901 UTC [common/tools/configtxgen] doOutputChannelCreateTx -> INFO 002 Generating new channel configtx
2019-06-30 21:45:12.901 UTC [common/tools/configtxgen/encoder] NewApplicationGroup -> WARN 003 Default policy emission is de
precated, please include policy specificiations for the application group in configtx.yaml
2019-06-30 21:45:12.901 UTC [common/tools/configtxgen/encoder] NewApplicationOrgGroup -> WARN 004 Default policy emission is
 deprecated, please include policy specificiations for the application org group m-BFYPDLMA4VFVRJZAMFMMJ72EWE in configtx.ya
ml
2019-06-30 21:45:12.903 UTC [common/tools/configtxgen] doOutputChannelCreateTx -> INFO 005 Writing new channel tx
[ec2-user@ip-10-0-247-155 healthcare-supplychain-network]$ █
```

Figure 5.39: Generate the configtx

5. Verify the channel configuration and execute the following command. The output will look like the following screenshot:

    ```
    ls -lt ~/$CHANNEL.pb
    ```

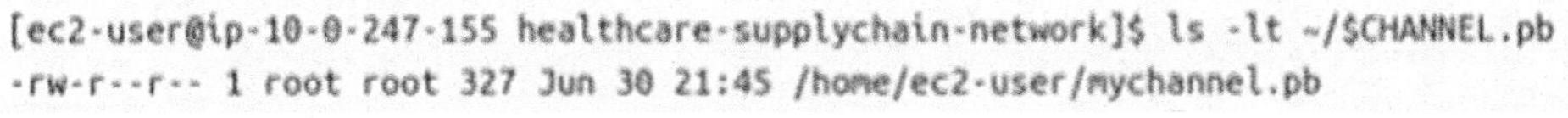

```
[ec2-user@ip-10-0-247-155 healthcare-supplychain-network]$ ls -lt ~/$CHANNEL.pb
-rw-r--r-- 1 root root 327 Jun 30 21:45 /home/ec2-user/mychannel.pb
```

Figure 5.40: Verify the channel configuration

In this step, we configured our Fabric network channel.

Step 9 - Creating a Fabric channel

Channels enable privacy within the network by creating separate ledger between peers or among a few peers by creating a channel. Only peers belonging to this channel can interact with each other. For the healthcare supply chain, we will create one channel called my channel where all the members can interact with each other.

Steps to create a Fabric channel:

1. Run the cli – command line interface container to create a channel, and execute the following command in Cloud9 on the Fabric client. You will get a similar output as shown in the following screenshot:

    ```
    docker exec -e "CORE_PEER_TLS_ENABLED=true" -e
    "CORE_PEER_TLS_ROOTCERT_FILE=/opt/home/managedblockchain-tls-
    chain.pem" -e "CORE_PEER_ADDRESS=$PEER" -e
    "CORE_PEER_LOCALMSPID=$MSP" -e "CORE_PEER_MSPCONFIGPATH=$MSP_PATH"
    ```

```
cli peer channel create -c $CHANNEL -f /opt/home/$CHANNEL.pb -o

$ORDERER --cafile $CAFILE --tls --timeout 900s
```

```
[ec2-user@ip-10-0-247-155 healthcare-supplychain-network]$ docker exec -e "CORE_PEER_TLS_ENABLED=true" -e "CORE_PEER_TLS_ROO
TCERT_FILE=/opt/home/managedblockchain-tls-chain.pem" \
>    -e "CORE_PEER_ADDRESS=$PEER" -e "CORE_PEER_LOCALMSPID=$MSP" -e "CORE_PEER_MSPCONFIGPATH=$MSP_PATH" \
>    cli peer channel create -c $CHANNEL -f /opt/home/$CHANNEL.pb -o $ORDERER --cafile $CAFILE --tls --timeout 900s
2019-06-30 21:48:22.259 UTC [channelCmd] InitCmdFactory -> INFO 001 Endorser and orderer connections initialized
2019-06-30 21:48:22.334 UTC [cli/common] readBlock -> INFO 002 Got status: &{NOT_FOUND}
2019-06-30 21:48:22.342 UTC [channelCmd] InitCmdFactory -> INFO 003 Endorser and orderer connections initialized
2019-06-30 21:48:22.544 UTC [cli/common] readBlock -> INFO 004 Got status: &{NOT_FOUND}
2019-06-30 21:48:22.551 UTC [channelCmd] InitCmdFactory -> INFO 005 Endorser and orderer connections initialized
2019-06-30 21:48:22.753 UTC [cli/common] readBlock -> INFO 006 Got status: &{NOT_FOUND}
2019-06-30 21:48:22.763 UTC [channelCmd] InitCmdFactory -> INFO 007 Endorser and orderer connections initialized
2019-06-30 21:48:22.965 UTC [cli/common] readBlock -> INFO 008 Got status: &{NOT_FOUND}
2019-06-30 21:48:22.977 UTC [channelCmd] InitCmdFactory -> INFO 009 Endorser and orderer connections initialized
2019-06-30 21:48:23.179 UTC [cli/common] readBlock -> INFO 00a Got status: &{NOT_FOUND}
2019-06-30 21:48:23.187 UTC [channelCmd] InitCmdFactory -> INFO 00b Endorser and orderer connections initialized
2019-06-30 21:48:23.389 UTC [cli/common] readBlock -> INFO 00c Got status: &{NOT_FOUND}
2019-06-30 21:48:23.396 UTC [channelCmd] InitCmdFactory -> INFO 00d Endorser and orderer connections initialized
2019-06-30 21:48:23.597 UTC [cli/common] readBlock -> INFO 00e Got status: &{NOT_FOUND}
2019-06-30 21:48:23.605 UTC [channelCmd] InitCmdFactory -> INFO 00f Endorser and orderer connections initialized
2019-06-30 21:48:23.806 UTC [cli/common] readBlock -> INFO 010 Got status: &{NOT_FOUND}
2019-06-30 21:48:23.817 UTC [channelCmd] InitCmdFactory -> INFO 011 Endorser and orderer connections initialized
2019-06-30 21:48:24.023 UTC [cli/common] readBlock -> INFO 012 Got status: &{NOT_FOUND}
2019-06-30 21:48:24.030 UTC [channelCmd] InitCmdFactory -> INFO 013 Endorser and orderer connections initialized
2019-06-30 21:48:24.232 UTC [cli/common] readBlock -> INFO 014 Got status: &{NOT_FOUND}
2019-06-30 21:48:24.240 UTC [channelCmd] InitCmdFactory -> INFO 015 Endorser and orderer connections initialized
2019-06-30 21:48:24.441 UTC [cli/common] readBlock -> INFO 016 Got status: &{NOT_FOUND}
2019-06-30 21:48:24.450 UTC [channelCmd] InitCmdFactory -> INFO 017 Endorser and orderer connections initialized
2019-06-30 21:48:24.651 UTC [cli/common] readBlock -> INFO 018 Got status: &{NOT_FOUND}
2019-06-30 21:48:24.662 UTC [channelCmd] InitCmdFactory -> INFO 019 Endorser and orderer connections initialized
2019-06-30 21:48:24.865 UTC [cli/common] readBlock -> INFO 01a Got status: &{NOT_FOUND}
2019-06-30 21:48:24.875 UTC [channelCmd] InitCmdFactory -> INFO 01b Endorser and orderer connections initialized
2019-06-30 21:48:25.077 UTC [cli/common] readBlock -> INFO 01c Got status: &{NOT_FOUND}
2019-06-30 21:48:25.085 UTC [channelCmd] InitCmdFactory -> INFO 01d Endorser and orderer connections initialized
2019-06-30 21:48:25.288 UTC [cli/common] readBlock -> INFO 01e Received block: 0
```

Figure 5.41: *Run the CLI container to create a channel*

2. The preceding command created a file called `mychannel.block` in the CLI container. Since the Fabric client is mounted with the CLI container, you can view this file from the Fabric client and execute the following command to view the channel:

```
ls -lt /home/ec2-user/fabric-samples/chaincode/hyperledger/fabric/
peer
```

```
[ec2-user@ip-10-0-247-155 healthcare-supplychain-network]$ ls -lt /home/ec2-user/fabric-samples/chaincode/hyperledger/fabric
/peer
total 16
-rw-r--r-- 1 root root 13173 Jun 30 21:48 mychannel.block
```

Figure 5.42: *View the channel*

3. At this stage, channel got created, however if the channel creation throws a time out error, then chances are that the channel got created, and you can save the genesis block with the following command. Execute the following command and the output will look like the following screenshot:

```
docker exec -e "CORE_PEER_TLS_ENABLED=true" -e

"CORE_PEER_TLS_ROOTCERT_FILE=/opt/home/managedblockchain-tls-
```

```
chain.pem" \
    -e "CORE_PEER_ADDRESS=$PEER" -e "CORE_PEER_LOCALMSPID=$MSP" -e
"CORE_PEER_MSPCONFIGPATH=$MSP_PATH" \
    cli peer channel fetch oldest /opt/home/fabric-
samples/chaincode/hyperledger/fabric/peer/$CHANNEL.block \
    -c $CHANNEL -o $ORDERER --cafile /opt/home/managedblockchain-
tls-chain.pem-tls
```

```
[ec2-user@ip-10-0-247-155 healthcare-supplychain-network]$ docker exec -e "CORE_PEER_TLS_ENABLED=true" -e "CORE_PEER_TLS_ROO
TCERT_FILE=/opt/home/managedblockchain-tls-chain.pem" \
>    -e "CORE_PEER_ADDRESS=$PEER"  -e "CORE_PEER_LOCALMSPID=$MSP" -e "CORE_PEER_MSPCONFIGPATH=$MSP_PATH" \
>    cli peer channel fetch oldest /opt/home/fabric-samples/chaincode/hyperledger/fabric/peer/$CHANNEL.block \
>    -c $CHANNEL -o $ORDERER --cafile /opt/home/managedblockchain-tls-chain.pem --tls
2019-06-30 21:51:52.315 UTC [channelCmd] InitCmdFactory -> INFO 001 Endorser and orderer connections initialized
2019-06-30 21:51:52.320 UTC [cli/common] readBlock -> INFO 002 Received block: 0
```

***Figure 5.43:** Initialize connection*

4. Validate the file mychannel.block exist and execute the following command:
   ```
   ls -lt /home/ec2-user/fabric-
   samples/chaincode/hyperledger/fabric/peer
   ```

```
[ec2-user@ip-10-0-247-155 healthcare-supplychain-network]$ ls -lt /home/ec2-user/fabric-samples/chaincode/hyperledger/fabric
/peer
total 16
-rw-r--r-- 1 root root 13173 Jun 30 21:51 mychannel.block
```

***Figure 5.44:** Validate file exist*

With this step, we created our channel called **myChannel**.

Step 10 - Joining the Manufacturer peer node to my-Channel

As we know each member of the network have peers who hold the ledger and chaincode, in this step, we will join our Manufacturer node to myChannel. Even if you are adding many peer nodes to the network, you should be able to join the channel in order to participate in the network.

Run the CLI container to create a channel, and execute the following command in Cloud9 on the Fabric client. You will get a similar output as shown in the following screenshot:

```
docker exec -e "CORE_PEER_TLS_ENABLED=true" -e

"CORE_PEER_TLS_ROOTCERT_FILE=/opt/home/managedblockchain-tls-chain.pem"
-e

"CORE_PEER_ADDRESS=$PEER" -e "CORE_PEER_LOCALMSPID=$MSP" -e
```

```
"CORE_PEER_MSPCONFIGPATH=$MSP_PATH" cli peer channel join -b $CHANNEL.
block
```

```
-o $ORDERER --cafile $CAFILE –tls
```

```
[ec2-user@ip-10-0-247-155 healthcare-supplychain-network]$ docker exec -e "CORE_PEER_TLS_ENABLED=true" -e "CORE_PEER_TLS_ROO
TCERT_FILE=/opt/home/managedblockchain-tls-chain.pem"      -e "CORE_PEER_ADDRESS=$PEER" -e "CORE_PEER_LOCALMSPID=$MSP" -e "CO
RE_PEER_MSPCONFIGPATH=$MSP_PATH"     cli peer channel join -b $CHANNEL.block  -o $ORDERER --cafile $CAFILE --tls
2019-06-30 22:13:47.078 UTC [channelCmd] InitCmdFactory -> INFO 001 Endorser and orderer connections initialized
2019-06-30 22:13:47.299 UTC [channelCmd] executeJoin -> INFO 002 Successfully submitted proposal to join channel
```

Figure 5.45: Join the channel

This completes creating the Hyperledger Fabric network with Amazon Managed Blockchain services.

Conclusion

We created a Fabric network using the AWS managed blockchain service for the Manufacturer member.

We learned how to use the AWS managed blockchain service and create the Fabric network. We can use this knowledge to build the Hyperledger Fabric network for other blockchain use-cases as well.

In the next chapter, we will write the chaincode to include business logic of the healthcare supply chain. We will also learn how to use the RESTful API to interact with the chaincode and finally, build the UI application using the Fabric-client node. js SDK.

Points to remember

- Amazon Managed Blockchain makes it easy to build a secure permissioned blockchain network in a few clicks. It's a fully managed service that makes it easy to manage scalable blockchain networks. You can build a decentralized application using Hyperledger Fabric and the Ethereum framework with Amazon Managed Blockchain services.

- AWS Managed Blockchain includes the following four steps:
  - o **Step 1:** Create a network.
  - o **Step 2:** Invite members.
  - o **Step 3:** Add peer nodes.
  - o **Step 4:** Deploy applications.

- The healthcare supply chain project has the following four participants:
  - o Manufacturer

- o   Distributor
- o   Hospital
- o   Pharmacy

Multiple choice questions

1. **Amazon Managed Blockchain makes it easy to build a secure permissioned blockchain network in a few clicks.**

    a) Yes

    b) No

2. **List the components of a node in the Fabric network.**

    a) Orderer node

    b) Certificate authority

    c) Peer node

    d) Ledger

    e) Chaincode

    f) All the above

Answer

1. a
2. f

Questions

1. What is Amazon Managed Blockchain?

2. Explain how Amazon Managed Blockchain works.

3. Create a Fabric network for the retail supply chain with Amazon Managed Blockchain.

Key terms

Amazon Managed Blockchain: Managed service to build blockchain solutions.

CHAPTER 6
Developing the Chaincode, API, and UI with the Fabric SDK on AWS

In this chapter, we will learn how to write the chaincode for the healthcare supply chain business logic, install the chaincode on the peer node, and execute chaincode functionalities. We will also learn how to create the API and UI using the Fabricnode.js SDK to interact with the chaincode deployed on AWS.

Structure

In this chapter, we will discuss the following topics:

- Understanding a chaincode
- Chaincode lifecycle
- Understanding the Fabric Node.js SDK
- Identifyingchaincode functions for the healthcare supply chain project
- Writing the healthcare chaincode with the Node.js SDK
- Installing and instantiating the healthcare chaincode on the peer
- Querying healthcare chaincode functions
- Invoking healthcare chaincode functions
- Creating the API with Express.js to interact with the chaincode
- Designing the UI with Angular to interact with the chaincode through the API

Objectives

As part of building the healthcare supply chain blockchain project, we have identified the following four stages:

Stage 1: Building the Hyperledger Fabric network for the healthcare supply chain with AWS Managed Blockchain.

Stage 2: Creating a healthcare supply chain chaincode and deploying it on AWS.

Stage 3: Creating the API and UI to interact with the healthcare supply chain chaincode from AWS.

Stage 4: Adding members (Distributor, Hospital, and Pharmacy) to the Fabric network on AWS.

In the previous chapter, we completed Stage 1. In this chapter, we will be working on Stage 2 and Stage 3.

After studying this unit, you should be able to:

- Explorea chaincode
- Write the healthcare chaincode with the Node.js SDK
- Createan API with Express.js to interact with the chaincode
- Design the UI with Angular to interact with the chaincode through the API

Pre-requisites for this chapter

We will make use of AWS resources in this chapter, so it would be great if you already have some experience with AWS. Please visit **https://docs.aws.amazon. com** to learn more about AWS resources such as Cloud9, CloudFormation, and EC2 instance.

- **AWS account:** If you already have an AWS account, then you can skip this step. Otherwise, sign up to AWS for a new account **https://aws.amazon.com/.**
- **AWS CLI:** We will usethe AWS CLI to provision the Blockchain network resources.
- **Hyperledger Fabric:** Knowledge of the Hyperledger Fabric architecture, fabric network models, components, and transaction flow is required.
- **Ubuntu and usage of Linux Terminal:** We will use the Linux terminal to configure the Fabric network.
- **Shell scripting:** Basic knowledge on Shell scripting is required.
- **JavaScript:** Programming experience in JavaScript is required as we will writethe chaincode in JavaScript.
- **Node.js:** Basic understanding and working experience with Node.js is required.

- **Express.js:** To write the RESTful API.
- **Angular:** To build the UI application.
- **Docker and docker-compose:** Basic understanding and working experience on Docker is required as all the peers in Hyperledger Fabric rung as Docker containers.
- **Visual Studio Code:** You can use VS Code as the IDE. You can still use your favorite IDE.
- **Complete Stage 1 from** *Chapter 5* **AWS Managed Blockchain to Create Fabric Network to create the Fabric network:** The Hyperledger Fabric network for the healthcare supply chain with AWS Managed Blockchain needs to be completed as we will install and interact with this network.

Make sure to have all pre-requisites in place.

Explore a chaincode

A chaincode, also called a smart contract, is a computer code having a set of agreed business rules between two parties in a business. Chaincodes are written in Node.js, Golang, or Java.

Hyperledger Fabric provides a **Software Development Kit(SDK)** for each language. We will usethe Node.js SDK in this chapter.

Understanding of a chaincode

A chaincode, also called a smart contract, is a computer code written in Node.js, Golang, or Java. It has a set of agreed business rules between two parties in a business and runs in a docker container inside the Fabric network. When a transaction is requested from an end-user, the chaincode executes business rules/functions and changes the blockchain ledger state foreach member in the network.

The chaincode hold functions to perform the read operation from the ledger or insert/update the ledger. The chaincode can invoke another chaincode in the same channel. The chaincode can be written in multiple languages, but as of now, we can write the chaincode in Go, Node.js, or Java. We will use Node.js to build our healthcare supply chain chaincode.

Chaincode use-cases

The blockchain is a revolution in the way we run a business. The chaincode allows us to automate business rules and enables trustless trust where multiple independent parties are involved. We can write a chaincode for various industries and multiple business use-cases.

Here are some of the use-cases where you can write the chaincode:

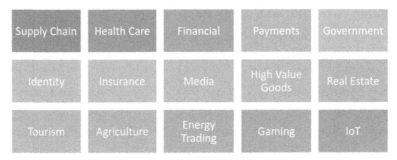

Figure 6.1: Chaincode use-cases

For example, in the case of a supply chain, all the parties/participants in the supply chain agree to common business rules. The way all the parties/participants want to transact; these rules can be coded into the system as a chaincode and executed when certain rules are met.

Understanding of the Fabric Node.js SDK

The Fabric Node.js SDK has a fabric-shim library which provides the chaincode interface for implementing the chaincode. It also provides implementation support for the chaincode written using fabric-contract-api along with fabric-chaincode-node cli to launch the chaincode.

Installing fabric-shim

The `fabric-shim` library can be installed with `npm` using the following command:
`npm install --save fabric-shim`

Once the installation is done, we will be able to use it to develop the chaincode.

Writing the chaincode

The `fabric-shim` library provides many modules to write the chaincode.

Let's understand the chaincode with the sample code

Step 1: Create a file with the chaincode name; for example: `firstChaincode.js`

Step 2: Import the `fabric-shim` library and create the chaincode class:
`const shim = require('fabric-shim');`

```
const Chaincode = class {


};
```

Step 3: The Init function is used to install and upgrade the chaincode:

```
async Init(stub) {


    // save the initial states
    await stub.putState(key, Buffer.from(aStringValue));


    return shim.success(Buffer.from('Initialized Successfully!'));
}
```

Step 4: The Invoke method is used to execute chaincode functions to change the state into the ledger:

```
async Invoke(stub) {


    // retrieve existing Chaincode states
    let oldValue = await stub.getState(key);


    // calculate new state values and saves them
    let newValue = oldValue + delta;
    await stub.putState(key, Buffer.from(newValue));


    return shim.success(Buffer.from(newValue.toString()));
}
```

Step 5: Start the chaincode and listen to an incoming request:

```
shim.start(new Chaincode());
```

This is just a sample code to get an idea of writing the chaincode. We will write more complex chaincodes in this chapter.

Understanding the chaincode lifecycle

To interact with chaincodes in Hyperledger Fabric, the chaincode follows the lifecycle of Install, Instantiate, Invoke/Query, and Upgrade.

The following is the order of the chaincode lifecycle:
  1.   Install the chaincode on a peer.

2. Instantiate the chaincode on a peer.

3. Query the peer, which returns the ledger state.

4. Invoke the chaincode to insert/update/delete the value in the state DB.

5. Upgrade the chaincode.

We will follow the same approach in the next section.

Installing the chaincode on your peer node

In this section, we will install the chaincode in our Hyperledger Fabric network created in the previous chapter.

> Note: You must complete reading *Chapter 5* AWS Managed Blockchain to Create Fabric Network to continue with the next steps.

If you have logged off from the Fabric client and logged in again, then make sure source environment variables of your Fabric network are created. The following steps will ensure that environment variables are been sourced.

The sample balance transfer chaincode is available in GitHub to transfer the balance from one account to another. Look at the chaincode by clicking on the following link:

https://github.com/hyperledger/fabric-samples/blob/release-1.4/balance-transfer/artifacts/src/github.com/example_cc/node/example_cc.js

In this chaincode, there are five functions which are as follows:

1. **Init:** This function is called while instantiating the chaincode. This function initializes the value for parameters A and B based on the values you pass.

2. **Invoke:** This function reads input values consisting of a function name and input parameter. Based on the function name, it will route the request to that function.

3. **move:** This function adds and subtracts the balance for accounts.

4. **delete:** This function will delete the values in the world state ledger but not in the transaction log as the transaction log is a blockchain ledger which is immutable.

5. **query:** This function will return the value from the world state ledger for the input parameter.

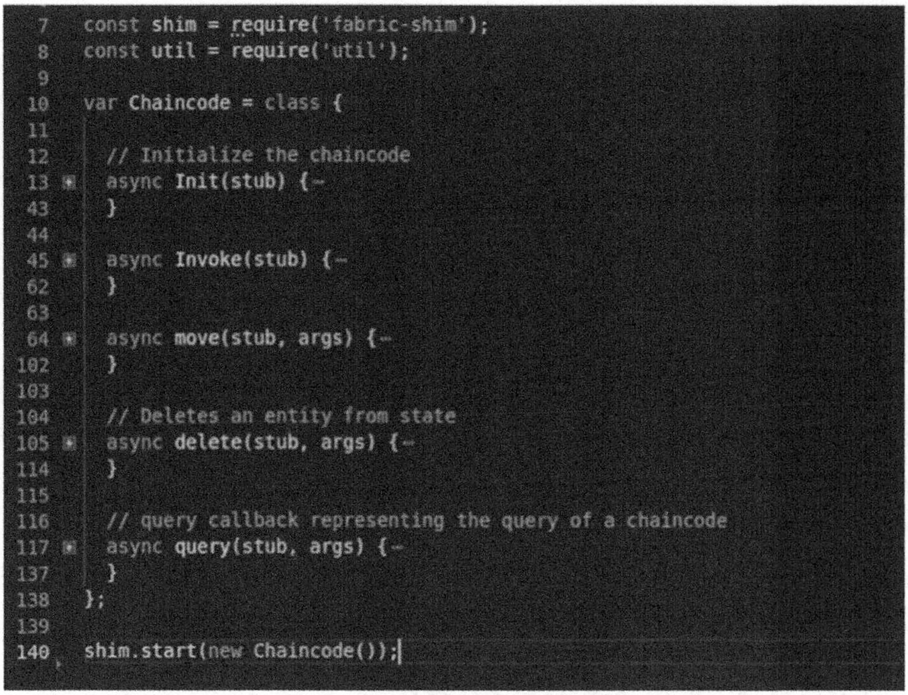

```
 7   const shim = require('fabric-shim');
 8   const util = require('util');
 9
10   var Chaincode = class {
11
12     // Initialize the chaincode
13 ▩   async Init(stub) {~
43     }
44
45 ▩   async Invoke(stub) {~
62     }
63
64 ▩   async move(stub, args) {~
102     }
103
104    // Deletes an entity from state
105 ▩   async delete(stub, args) {~
114     }
115
116    // query callback representing the query of a chaincode
117 ▩   async query(stub, args) {~
137     }
138  };
139
140  shim.start(new Chaincode());|
```

Figure 6.2: Chaincode functions

This sample balance transfer chaincode is available in the docker CLI container, so let's install the balance transfer chaincode in our newly created Hyperledger Fabric network on AWS.

Run the CLI container to install the balance transfer chaincode on the peer, and execute the following command in Cloud9 on the Fabric client. The Peer Chaincode install command is used to install the chaincode. We will pass the following arguments:

- -p specifies the path of the chaincode
- -v specifies version on the chaincode
- -n specifies the name of the chaincode

```
docker exec -e "CORE_PEER_TLS_ENABLED=true" -e
"CORE_PEER_TLS_ROOTCERT_FILE=/opt/home/managedblockchain-tls-
chain.pem" -e
"CORE_PEER_ADDRESS=$PEER" -e "CORE_PEER_LOCALMSPID=$MSP" -e
"CORE_PEER_MSPCONFIGPATH=$MSP_PATH" cli peer Chaincode install -n
balanceTransfer -v v0 -p github.com/Chaincode_example02/go
```

If you receive the status as 200, then it means that we have successfully installed the chaincode on the AWS Hyperledger Fabric network.

Instantiating the chaincode on the channel

Once the chaincode is installed, we need to instantiate the chaincode. Run the CLI container to instantiate the balance transfer chaincode, and execute the following command in Cloud9 on the Fabric client. The peer chaincode instantiate is the command which instantiates our chaincode on the peer with the value passed and passes initial values as A= 100 and B=100:

```
DOCKER EXEC -E "CORE_PEER_TLS_ENABLED=TRUE" -E
"CORE_PEER_TLS_ROOTCERT_FILE=/OPT/HOME/MANAGEDBLOCKCHAIN-TLS-CHAIN.PEM"
\ -
E "CORE_PEER_ADDRESS=$PEER" -E "CORE_PEER_LOCALMSPID=$MSP" -E
"CORE_PEER_MSPCONFIGPATH=$MSP_PATH" \ CLI PEER CHAINCODE INSTANTIATE -O
$ORDERER -C MYCHANNEL -N BALANCETRANSFER -V V0 \ -C
'{"ARGS":["INIT","A","100","B","200"]}' --CAFILE $CAFILE --TLS
```

Once you have successfully instantiated, you should see INFO 001 using default escc and INFO 002 Using default vscc message.

Querying the chaincode

Once the balance transfer chaincode is instantiated, we can query the ledger.

Run the CLI container to instantiate the balance transfer chaincode and execute the following command in Cloud9 on the Fabric client. The peer Chaincode query is the command which queries our chaincode on the peer for the value passed. We are querying the value of A and so you should get the result as 100:

```
docker exec -e "CORE_PEER_TLS_ENABLED=true" -e
"CORE_PEER_TLS_ROOTCERT_FILE=/opt/home/managedblockchain-tls-chain.pem"
\
    -e "CORE_PEER_ADDRESS=$PEER" -e "CORE_PEER_LOCALMSPID=$MSP" -e
"CORE_PEER_MSPCONFIGPATH=$MSP_PATH" \
    cli peer Chaincode query -C mychannel -n balanceTransfer -c
'{"Args":["query","a"]}'
```

The result should be equal to the value passed while instantiating the chaincode.

Invoking a transaction

Let's invoke a function to transfer a balance from account A to account B. The invoke request will change the state of a variable in the world state ledger hosted on our peer.

Run the CLI container to instantiate the balance transfer chaincode and execute the following command in Cloud9 on the Fabric client. The peer chaincode invoke is the command which invokes a function and updates the world state DB with a new value. We are transferring 10 from account A to account B, so you should get a similar output as follows:

```
docker exec -e "CORE_PEER_TLS_ENABLED=true" -e

"CORE_PEER_TLS_ROOTCERT_FILE=/opt/home/managedblockchain-tls-chain.pem"
\
    -e "CORE_PEER_ADDRESS=$PEER" -e "CORE_PEER_LOCALMSPID=$MSP" -e
"CORE_PEER_MSPCONFIGPATH=$MSP_PATH" \
    cli peer Chaincode invoke -o $ORDERER -C mychannel -n
balanceTransfer \
    -c '{"Args":["invoke","a","b","10"]}' --cafile $CAFILE –tls
```

Verify the result by querying since we have transferred 10 from account A. Now, the balance of account A should be 90. Execute the following command:

```
docker exec -e "CORE_PEER_TLS_ENABLED=true" -e

"CORE_PEER_TLS_ROOTCERT_FILE=/opt/home/managedblockchain-tls-chain.pem"
\ -

e "CORE_PEER_ADDRESS=$PEER" -e "CORE_PEER_LOCALMSPID=$MSP" -e

"CORE_PEER_MSPCONFIGPATH=$MSP_PATH" \ cli peer Chaincode query -C mychannel

-n balanceTransfer -c '{"Args":["query","a"]}'
```

Upgrading the chaincode

To upgrade the chaincode with the latest changes, we need to follow the same lifecycle: copy, install, and instantiate.

Steps to install the latest version of the balance transfer:

1. Copy the updated chaincode to the chaincode directory which is mounted for the Fabric CLI container.

2. Install the V1 version:

```
docker exec -e "CORE_PEER_TLS_ENABLED=true" -e

"CORE_PEER_TLS_ROOTCERT_FILE=/opt/home/managedblockchain-tls-

chain.pem" -e "CORE_PEER_ADDRESS=$PEER" -e

"CORE_PEER_LOCALMSPID=$MSP" -e "CORE_PEER_MSPCONFIGPATH=$MSP_
```

```
PATH"
cli peer Chaincode install -n balanceTransfer -v v1 -p
github.com/Chaincode_example02/go
```

3. Upgrade to the V1 version:

```
docker exec -e "CORE_PEER_TLS_ENABLED=true" -e
"CORE_PEER_TLS_ROOTCERT_FILE=/opt/home/managedblockchain-tls-
chain.pem" \ -e "CORE_PEER_ADDRESS=$PEER" -e
"CORE_PEER_LOCALMSPID=$MSP" -e "CORE_PEER_MSPCONFIGPATH=$MSP_PATH"
\ cli peer Chaincode upgrade -o $ORDERER -C mychannel -n
balanceTransfer -v v1 \ -c '{"Args":["init","a","100","b","200"]}'
--cafile $CAFILE –tls
```

With this sample chaincode, we learned how to write and execute the chaincode. In the next section, let us write the chaincode for our healthcare supply chain project.

Identify chaincode functions for the healthcare supply chain project

As discussed in *Chapter 5: AWS Managed Blockchain to create Fabric network,* we have identified four main members in the supply chain such as Manufacturer, Distributor, Hospital, and Pharmacy. In the real-life healthcare supply chain, there may be hundreds of members. Here, we are building a basic version, and you can extend this chaincode to work for the real-life healthcare supply chain.

Let's identify the functions required for the healthcare supply chain project:

- createManufacturer(): This function is used to create a new manufacturer.
- createAsset(): This function is used to create new healthcare assets.
- getAssetDetail(): This function is used to get asset details.
- createDistributor(): This function is used to create a new distributor.
- createHospital(): This function is used to create a new hospital.
- createPharmacy(): This function is used to create a new Pharmacy.
- transferAsset(): This function is used to transfer medical assets from one member to another.
- disposeAsset(): This function is used to dispose of a medical asset once it is expired.

I have identified minimal functions required, but you can identify more functions.

Writing the healthcare chaincode with the Node.js SDK

In the previous section, from the balance transfer chaincode example, you have understood the lifecycle of a chaincode and what constitutes a chaincode. We will do it in the same way here to write the healthcare supply chain chaincode:

This complete healthcare chaincode is available in my GitHub repo **(https:// github.com/murughan1985/Healthcare-Supplychain-Blockchain.git)** which you have cloned to the AWSEC2 Fabric client node in *Chapter 5* AWS Managed Blockchain to Create Fabric Network.

If you want to understand line by line explanation and experience writing on your own, then perform the following steps:

I have uploaded the healthcare supply chain project in my GitHub:

1. Navigate to **https://github.com/murughan1985/Healthcare-Supplychain-Blockchain.git**.

2. Fork it to your Github account.

3. Clone it locally from your account:

   ```
   git clone https://github.com/<replace with your
   account>/Healthcare-Supplychain-Blockchain.git
   ```

Steps in writing the healthcare chaincode are as follows:

Step 1: Create a healthcare chaincode file and import libraries.

Step 2: Create asset states.

Step 3: Write the Init function.

Step 4: Write the Invoke function.

Step 5: Write the function to create a Manufacturer.

Step 6: Write the function to create a Medical Asset.

Step 7: Write the function to create a Distributor.

Step 8: Write the function to create a Hospital.

Step 9: Write the function to create a Pharmacy.

Step 10: Write the function to get Asset Details.

Step 11: Write the function to transfer asset ownership.

Step 12: Write the function to dispose of an asset.

Step 13: Write the function to delete an asset.

Step 14: Add the healthcare chaincode to shim.

Step 1: Create a healthcare chaincode file and import libraries

1. From my preceding GitHub repository, you will able to see the `healthcare.js` chaincode under the `healthcare-supplychain-Chaincode\src` directory. After cloning it locally, please delete this chaincode `healthcare.js` and follow the following steps to write the healthcare chaincode on your own.

2. Create a file `healthcare.js` under the `healthcare-supplychain-Chaincode\src` directory:

3. Add the following code to import the `fabric-shim` and `util` library, and create the chaincode class as follows:

```
'use strict';

const shim = require('fabric-shim');

const util = require('util');


let Chaincode = class {
}
```

Step 2: Create asset states

1. This chaincode will track the following medical assets:
   a) Medical devices
   b) Medical supplies
   c) Medical equipment
   d) Pharmaceuticals
   e) Fast-moving consumer products
   f) Other medical devices

2. Each medical asset needs the state to define in order to know the current state of the medical asset, so we will create the following states. Add the following code inside `healthcare.js` file:

```
const stateType = {

Manufacturer: 'Manufacturered',

Distributor: 'Distributed',

Hospital: 'Delivered',
```

```
Customer: 'Sold',
Recall: 'Recalled',
Disposal: 'Disposed'
};
```

Step 3: Write the Init function

Add the Init function to initialize the chaincode with initial values, and this Init function will be used while upgrading the chaincode as well. Add the following code to `healthcare.js`:

```
async Init(stub) {
    return shim.success();
}
```

Step 4: Write the Invoke function

The Invoke function reads input values consisting of a function name and input parameters. Based on the function name, it will route the request to that function.

Read the comments for each line to get a better understanding of the code, and add the following function in`healthcare.js`:

```
async Invoke(stub) {
    //Get input parameters
let ret = stub.getFunctionAndParameters();
    //Get function name
    let method = this[ret.fcn];
    //Invoke method
    let response = await method(stub, ret.params);

    //Return the respose
    return shim.success(response);
}
```

Step 5: Write the function to create a manufacturer

For this project, we will consider thatthe manufacturer is the first person who owns the medical assets. So, as the first step in creating members, we will write a function to create a manufacturer, and the manufacturer details will be stored in the CouchDB as the world state ledger.

The createManufacturer() function does the following things:

- Reads manufacturer details as input.
- Appends the *'manufacturer'* text for the manufacturerId. For example, if you pass the manufacturer ID as 1, then it will store it as manufacturer1 in the ledger.
- Adds docType for each document in the CouchDB for better query performance.
- Checks whether the manufacturer already exists, and if so, it throws an error.
- Adds the manufacturer details to the ledger.

  Add the following function in healthcare.js:

  ```
  async createManufacturer(stub, args) {
          //Read input values
          let json = JSON.parse(args);
          let manufacturerId = 'manufacturer' +
  json['manufacturerId'];
          //Each document in CouchDB should have docType for better
  quey
  performance
          json['docType'] = 'manufacturer';


          // Check if the manufacturer already exists
          let manufacturer = await stub.getState(manufacturerId);
          if (manufacturer.toString()) {
              throw new Error('This manufacturer already exists: '
  +
  json['manufacturerId']);
          }
          //Insert into peer ledger
          await stub.putState(manufacturerId,
  Buffer.from(JSON.stringify(json)));
      }
  ```

  A sample input for this function would be as follows:

  ```
  {
  ```

```
    "manufacturerId": "1",
    "manufacturerName": "manufacturer1",
    "manufacturerLocation":"AL"
}
```

Step 6: Write a function to create a medical asset

The `createAsset()` function reads the medical asset details and stores it in the ledger. An asset can be any type of medical devices such as medical supplies, medical equipments, pharmaceuticals, fast-moving consumer products, and other medical devices.

The `createAsset()` function does the following things:

- Reads asset details as input such as `assetId`, `assetName`, `assetType`, `assetExpirtyDate`, `owner`, and `state`. You can pass more attributes as well.
- Appends the `'asset'` text for `assetId`. For example, if you pass the asset ID as 1, then it will store it as asset1 in the ledger.
- In this sample, we will assume the first owner for an asset is `Manufacturer`.
- Adds `docType` for each document in the CouchDB for better query performance.
- Check whether the asset already exists, and if so, it throws an error.
- Adds this asset detail to the ledger.

  Add the following function in `healthcare.js`:

```
async createAsset(stub, args) {
    //Read input values
    let json = JSON.parse(args);
    let assetId = 'asset' + json['assetId'];
    json['owner'] = 'manufacturer' + json['owner'];
    json['state'] = stateType.Manufacturer;
    //Each document in CouchDB should have docType for better quey
performance
    json['docType'] = 'medicaldevice';

    // Check if the assset already exists, read data from ledger
    let asset = await stub.getState(assetId);
```

```
            if (asset.toString()) {
                throw new Error('##### createAsset - This Asset already
    exists:
    ' + json['assetId']);
            }
            //Insert into peer ledger
                    await   stub.putState(assetId,  Buffer.from(JSON.
    stringify(json)));
        }
```

A sample input for this function would be as follows:

```
{
    "assetId": "1",
    "assetName": "needle",
    "assetType":"Medical Supplies",
    "assetExpirtyDate":"2019-30-12",
    "owner":"1",
    "state":"Manufacturered"
}
```

Step 7: Write a function to create a distributor

Like Step 5, we will write a function to add a distributor to the ledger.

Add the following function in `healthcare.js`:

```
    async createDistributor(stub, args) {
        //Read input values
        let json = JSON.parse(args);
        let distributorId = 'distributor' + json['distributorId'];
        json['docType'] = 'distributor';

        // Check if the distributor already exists, read data from ledger
        let distributor = await stub.getState(distributorId);
        if (distributor.toString()) {
            throw new Error('##### createDistributor - This distributor
```

```
already exists: ' + json['distributorId']);
        }
        //Insert into peer ledger
        await stub.putState(distributorId,
Buffer.from(JSON.stringify(json)));
    }
```

A sample input for this function would be as follows:

```
{
"distributorId": "1",
"distributorName": "distributor1",
"distributorLocation":"IL"
}
```

Step 8: Write a function to create a hospital

Like Step 5, we will write a function to add a hospital to the ledger.

Add the following function in `healthcare.js`:

```
    async createHospital(stub, args) {
//Read input values
        let json = JSON.parse(args);
        let hospitalId = 'hospital' + json['hospitalId'];
        json['docType'] = 'hospital';

        // Check if the hospital already exists, read data from ledger
        let hospital = await stub.getState(hospitalId);
        if (hospital.toString()) {
            throw new Error('##### createHospital - This hospital already
exists: ' + json['hospitalId']);
        }
        //Insert into peer ledger
    await stub.putState(hospitalId, Buffer.from(JSON.stringify(json)));
    }
```

A sample input for this function would be as follows:

```
{
```

```
"hospitalId": "1",
"hospitalName": "hospital1",
"hospitalLocation":"CO"
}
```

Step 9: Write a function to create a pharmacy

Like Step 5, we will write a function to add a pharmacy to the ledger.

Add the following function in `healthcare.js`:

```
    async createPharmacy(stub, args) {
        //Read input values
        let json = JSON.parse(args);
        let pharmacyId = 'pharmacy' + json['pharmacyId'];
        json['docType'] = 'pharmacy';


        // Check if the pharmacy already exists, read data from ledger
        let pharmacy = await stub.getState(pharmacyId);
        if (pharmacy.toString()) {
            throw new Error('##### createPharmacy - This pharmacy already
exists: ' + json['pharmacyId']);
        }
        //Insert into peer ledger
    await stub.putState(pharmacyId, Buffer.from(JSON.stringify(json)));
    }
```

A sample input for this function would be as follows:

```
{
"pharmacyLocation":"CA"
}
```

Step 10: Write a function to get asset details

Once the asset is created, by default the owner will be the manufacturer. `getAssetDetail ()`returns the asset details for the given `assetId`.

Add the following function in `healthcare.js`:

```
async getAssetDetail(stub, args) {
    //Read input values
    let json = JSON.parse(args);
    let assetId = 'asset' + json['assetId'];

    //read data from ledger
    let assetAsBytes = await stub.getState(assetId);
    if (!assetAsBytes || assetAsBytes.toString().length <= 0) {
        throw new Error(`${assetId} does not exist`);
    }
    return assetAsBytes;
}
```

Step 11: Write a function to transfer the asset ownership

This is the most important function in the chaincode, which helps in transferring the ownership of all the assets.

The Asset lifecycle is as follows:

1. The manufacturer owns the asset as he produces the asset.

2. Asset ownership is transferred from Manufacturer to Distributor.

3. Asset ownership is transferred from Distributor to Hospital or Pharmacy

4. Asset ownership is transferred from Hospital/Pharmacy to Customer.

5. When the medical asset expires, it will be disposed.

6. For any damage, recall the asset.

7. Delete the asset.

To create the `transferAsset()` function, add the following function in `healthcare.js`:

```
async transferAsset(stub, args) {
        //Read input value
    let json = JSON.parse(args);
        let assetId = 'asset' + json['assetId'];
```

```
        let assetAsBytes = await stub.getState(assetId);

        let asset = JSON.parse(assetAsBytes.toString());

        //update asset details

        asset.owner = json['transferTo'];

        asset.state = json['state'];

                await  stub.putState(assetId,  Buffer.from(JSON.
    stringify(asset)));

        }
```

A sample input for this function would be as follows:

```
{
"assetId": "1",
"transferTo": "pharmacy1",
"state":"Delivered"
}
```

Step 12: Write a function to dispose of an asset

If the asset expires, we should dispose of the asset, and add the following function in healthcare.js:

```
    async disposeAsset(stub, args) {
        //Read input values
        let json = JSON.parse(args);
        let assetId = json['assetId'];

        //read data from ledger
        let assetAsBytes = await stub.getState(assetId);

        if (!assetAsBytes || assetAsBytes.length === 0) {
            throw new Error(`${assetId} does not exist`);
        }
        const asset = JSON.parse(assetAsBytes.toString());
        asset.state = stateType.Disposal;
```

```
//Update peer ledger world state
await stub.putState(assetId, Buffer.from(JSON.stringify(asset)));
}
```

Step 13: Write a function to delete an asset

Assets can be deleted from the world state ledger but not from the blockchain ledger. Add the following function in `healthcare.js`:

```
async delete(stub, args) {
    let json = JSON.parse(args);
let assetId = json['assetId'];


    // Delete the key from the state in ledger
    await stub.deleteState(assetId);
}
```

Step 14: Add the healthcare chaincode to shim

To add the healthcare chaincode to the shim object, add the following statement in `healthcare.js`:

```
shim.start(new Chaincode());
```

We are now done with writing our chaincode for the healthcare supply chain project. This entire chaincode is available in my GitHub link - **https://github.com/ murughan1985/Healthcare-Supplychain-Blockchain.git** which you have already cloned into the AWC EC2instance Fabric Client node. If you have added/modified new functionalities, then update this new chaincode in the AWS EC2 instance Fabric client.

Also, the same chaincode can be extended to the real-world healthcare supply chain.

Installing and instantiating healthcare chaincode on the peer

The first step to interact with the chaincode is to install it on the peer and initialize the chaincode. After instantiating it, we will able to invoke and query the preceding healthcare chaincode functions.

Step 1 - Copy the chaincode into the CLI container

Before we copy the chaincode, let's see the CLI container's mount.

Execute the following command in Cloud9 on the Fabric client to check the mount.

```
docker inspect cli
```

You will notice that our Fabric client `./fabric-samples/Chaincode/` is mapped to the chaincode path in the peer. We will copy the chaincode into this directory.

To copy the healthcare chaincode into the peer, run the following command in the Fabric client:

```
cd ~

mkdir -p ./fabric-samples/Chaincode/healthcare

cp ./Healthcare-Supplychain-Blockchain/healthcare-supplychain-
Chaincode/src/* ./fabric-samples/Chaincode/healthcare
```

Step 2 - Install the healthcare chaincode on your peer

Once the chaincode is copied to the peer, let's install the healthcare chaincode with the CLI peer chaincode install command. In the following command, we will give the name as healthcare for our chaincode.

Run the following command in the Fabric client, and you will get a similar output as shown in the following screenshot:

```
docker exec -e "CORE_PEER_TLS_ENABLED=true" -e

"CORE_PEER_TLS_ROOTCERT_FILE=/opt/home/managedblockchain-tls-chain.pem"
-e

"CORE_PEER_LOCALMSPID=$MSP" -e "CORE_PEER_MSPCONFIGPATH=$MSP_PATH" -e

"CORE_PEER_ADDRESS=$PEER" cli peer Chaincode install -n healthcare -l
node

-v v0 -p /opt/gopath/src/github.com/healthcare
```

```
[ec2-user@ip-10-0-247-155 healthcareSupplychain]$ docker exec -e "CORE_PEER_TLS_ENABLED=true" -e "CORE_PEER_TLS_ROOTCERT_FILE=/o
pt/home/managedblockchain-tls-chain.pem"    -e "CORE_PEER_LOCALMSPID=$MSP" -e "CORE_PEER_MSPCONFIGPATH=$MSP_PATH" -e "CORE_PEER
_ADDRESS=$PEER"    cli peer chaincode install -n healthcare -l node -v v0 -p /opt/gopath/src/github.com
2019-06-30 23:04:11.318 UTC [chaincodeCmd] checkChaincodeCmdParams -> INFO 001 Using default escc
2019-06-30 23:04:11.318 UTC [chaincodeCmd] checkChaincodeCmdParams -> INFO 002 Using default vscc
2019-06-30 23:04:11.318 UTC [container] WriteFolderToTarPackage -> INFO 003 rootDirectory = /opt/gopath/src/github.com
2019-06-30 23:04:11.404 UTC [chaincodeCmd] install -> INFO 004 Installed remotely response:<status:200 payload:"OK" >
```

Step 3 - Instantiate the healthcare chaincode on the channel

This step will initialize the healthcare chaincode by executing the `Init()` function from the chaincode. By binding the healthcare chaincode to `myChannel,` which we created earlier, we can configure the endorsement policy as well in this step. For now, we will use the default membership policy.

Run the following command in the Fabric client, and you will get a similar output as shown in the following screenshot:

```
docker exec -e "CORE_PEER_TLS_ENABLED=true" -e
"CORE_PEER_TLS_ROOTCERT_FILE=/opt/home/managedblockchain-tls-chain.pem"
\
    -e "CORE_PEER_LOCALMSPID=$MSP" -e "CORE_PEER_MSPCONFIGPATH=$MSP_PATH"
-
e "CORE_PEER_ADDRESS=$PEER" \
    cli peer Chaincode instantiate -o $ORDERER -C mychannel -n healthcare
-
v v0 -c '{"Args":["init"]}' --cafile /opt/home/managedblockchain-tls-
chain.pem —tls
```

```
[ec2-user@ip-10-0-200-8 ~]$ docker exec -e "CORE_PEER_TLS_ENABLED=true" -e "CORE_PEER_TLS_ROOTCERT_FILE=/opt/home/managedblockchain-tls-chain.pem" \
>     -e "CORE_PEER_LOCALMSPID=$MSP" -e "CORE_PEER_MSPCONFIGPATH=$MSP_PATH" -e "CORE_PEER_ADDRESS=$PEER" \
>     cli peer chaincode instantiate -o $ORDERER -C mychannel -n healthcare -v v0 -c '{"Args":["init"]}' --cafile /opt/home/managedblockchain-tls-chain.pem --tls
2019-07-06 11:00:32.927 UTC [chaincodeCmd] checkChaincodeCmdParams -> INFO 001 Using default escc
2019-07-06 11:00:32.927 UTC [chaincodeCmd] checkChaincodeCmdParams -> INFO 002 Using default vscc
```

Interacting with the healthcare chaincode

The healthcare chaincode is instantiated on the peer node. It's time to execute the function we have written to create members, medical assets, and transfer assets.

Invoking healthcare chaincode functions

Let's add members such as manufacturer, distributor, hospital, and pharmacy and create an asset by invoking the respective chaincode function.
We will invoke the chaincode functions as per the following order:

1. Create a manufacturer.
2. Create an asset.
3. Create a distributor.
4. Create a hospital.
5. Create a pharmacy.

For each function, we need to pass the function name and member details as input parameters to the command peer Chaincode invoke.

Step 1: Create a manufacturer.

We will pass the function name as `createManufacturer` and manufacturer details as follows:

```
{
 "manufacturerId": "1",
 "manufacturerName": "manufacturer1",
 "manufacturerLocation":"AL"
 }
```

The following command will invoke the `createManufacturer` function and manufacturer details will be inserted inthe peer ledger.

Run the following command in the Fabric client, and you will get a similar output as shown in the following screenshot:

```
docker exec -e "CORE_PEER_TLS_ENABLED=true" -e

"CORE_PEER_TLS_ROOTCERT_FILE=/opt/home/managedblockchain-tls-chain.pem"
\

-e "CORE_PEER_ADDRESS=$PEER" -e "CORE_PEER_LOCALMSPID=$MSP" -e

"CORE_PEER_MSPCONFIGPATH=$MSP_PATH" \

cli peer Chaincode invoke -o $ORDERER -C mychannel -n healthcare \

-c '{"Args":["createManufacturer","{\"manufacturerId\": \"1\",

\"manufacturerName\": \"manufacturer1\", \"manufacturerLocation\":

\"AL\"}"]}'  -o $ORDERER --cafile /opt/home/managedblockchain-tls-chain.
pem

--tls
```

```
[ec2-user@ip-10-0-200-8 ~]$ docker exec -e "CORE_PEER_TLS_ENABLED=true" -e "CORE_PEER_TLS_ROOTCERT_FILE=/opt/home/managedblockchain-tls-chain.pem"
\
> -e "CORE_PEER_ADDRESS=$PEER" -e "CORE_PEER_LOCALMSPID=$MSP" -e "CORE_PEER_MSPCONFIGPATH=$MSP_PATH" \
> cli peer chaincode invoke -o $ORDERER -C mychannel -n healthcare \
> -c '{"Args":["createManufacturer","{\"manufacturerId\": \"1\", \"manufacturerName\": \"manufacturer1\", \"manufacturerLocation\": \"AL\"}"]}' -o
$ORDERER --cafile /opt/home/managedblockchain-tls-chain.pem --tls
2019-07-06 11:26:22.348 UTC [chaincodeCmd] chaincodeInvokeOrQuery -> INFO 001 Chaincode invoke successful. result: status:200
```

Figure 6.3: Create a manufacturer

Step 2: Create an asset

We will pass the function name as `createAsset` and asset details as follows:

```
{
 "assetId": "1",
```

```
"assetName": "needle",
"assetType":"Medical Supplies",
"assetExpirtyDate":"2019-30-12",
"owner":"1",
"state":"Manufacturered"
}
```

The following command will invoke the `createAsset` function and the asset will be inserted to the peer ledger.

Run the following command in the Fabric client, and you willget a similar output as shown in the following screenshot:

```
docker exec -e "CORE_PEER_TLS_ENABLED=true" -e
"CORE_PEER_TLS_ROOTCERT_FILE=/opt/home/managedblockchain-tls-chain.pem" \
-e "CORE_PEER_ADDRESS=$PEER" -e "CORE_PEER_LOCALMSPID=$MSP" -e
"CORE_PEER_MSPCONFIGPATH=$MSP_PATH" \
cli peer Chaincode invoke -o $ORDERER -C mychannel -n healthcare \
-c   '{"Args":["createAsset","{\"assetId\":   \"1\",   \"assetName\":
\"needle\",
\"assetType\":  \"MedicalSupplies\",  \"assetExpirtyDate\":  \"2019-12-
30\",
\"owner\": \"1\" }"]}' -o $ORDERER --cafile /opt/home/managedblockchain-
tls-chain.pem –tls
```

```
[ec2-user@ip-10-0-200-8 ~]$ docker exec -e "CORE_PEER_TLS_ENABLED=true" -e "CORE_PEER_TLS_ROOTCERT_FILE=/opt/home/managedblockchain-tls-chain.pem"
-e "CORE_PEER_ADDRESS=$PEER" -e "CORE_PEER_LOCALMSPID=$MSP" -e "CORE_PEER_MSPCONFIGPATH=$MSP_PATH" cli peer chaincode invoke -o $ORDERER -C mychann
el -n healthcare -c '{"Args":["createAsset","{\"assetId\": \"2\", \"assetName\": \"needle\",  \"assetExpirtyDate\": \"2019-07-22T11:52:20.182Z\", \
"assetOwner\": \"1\" }"]}' -o $ORDERER --cafile /opt/home/managedblockchain-tls-chain.pem --tls
2019-07-06 11:30:02.582 UTC [chaincodeCmd] chaincodeInvokeOrQuery -> INFO 001 Chaincode invoke successful. result: status:200
```

Figure 6.4: Create an asset

Step 3: Create a distributor

We will invoke a `createDistributor` function with distributor details.

Run the following command in the Fabric client, and you will get a similar output as shown in the following screenshot:

```
docker exec -e "CORE_PEER_TLS_ENABLED=true" -e
"CORE_PEER_TLS_ROOTCERT_FILE=/opt/home/managedblockchain-tls-chain.pem" \
-e "CORE_PEER_ADDRESS=$PEER" -e "CORE_PEER_LOCALMSPID=$MSP" -e
```

```
"CORE_PEER_MSPCONFIGPATH=$MSP_PATH" \
cli peer Chaincode invoke -o $ORDERER -C mychannel -n healthcare \
-c '{"Args":["createDistributor","{\"distributorId\": \"1\",
\"distributorName\":    \"distributor1\",    \"distributorLocation\":
\"IL\"}"]}'
-o $ORDERER --cafile /opt/home/managedblockchain-tls-chain.pem --tls
```

```
[ec2-user@ip-10-0-200-8 ~]$ docker exec -e "CORE_PEER_TLS_ENABLED=true" -e "CORE_PEER_TLS_ROOTCERT_FILE=/opt/home/managedblockchain-tls-chain.pem"
\
> -e "CORE_PEER_ADDRESS=$PEER" -e "CORE_PEER_LOCALMSPID=$MSP" -e "CORE_PEER_MSPCONFIGPATH=$MSP_PATH" \
> cli peer chaincode invoke -o $ORDERER -C mychannel -n healthcare \
> -c '{"Args":["createDistributor","{\"distributorId\": \"1\", \"distributorName\": \"distributor1\", \"distributorLocation\": \"IL\"}"]}' -o $ORDE
RER --cafile /opt/home/managedblockchain-tls-chain.pem --tls
2019-07-06 11:33:04.691 UTC [chaincodeCmd] chaincodeInvokeOrQuery -> INFO 001 Chaincode invoke successful. result: status:200
```

Figure 6.5: Create a distributor

Step 4: Create a hospital

We will invoke a `createHospital` function with the hospital details.

Run the following command in the Fabric client, and you will get a similar output as shown in the following screenshot:

```
docker exec -e "CORE_PEER_TLS_ENABLED=true" -e
"CORE_PEER_TLS_ROOTCERT_FILE=/opt/home/managedblockchain-tls-chain.pem"
\
-e "CORE_PEER_ADDRESS=$PEER" -e "CORE_PEER_LOCALMSPID=$MSP" -e
"CORE_PEER_MSPCONFIGPATH=$MSP_PATH" \
cli peer Chaincode invoke -o $ORDERER -C mychannel -n healthcare \
-c '{"Args":["createHospital","{\"hospitalId\": \"1\", \"hospitalName\":
\"hospital1\", \"hospitalLocation\": \"CO\"}"]}' -o $ORDERER --cafile
/opt/home/managedblockchain-tls-chain.pem --tls
```

```
[ec2-user@ip-10-0-200-8 ~]$ docker exec -e "CORE_PEER_TLS_ENABLED=true" -e "CORE_PEER_TLS_ROOTCERT_FILE=/opt/home/managedblockchain-tls-chain.pem"
\
> -e "CORE_PEER_ADDRESS=$PEER" -e "CORE_PEER_LOCALMSPID=$MSP" -e "CORE_PEER_MSPCONFIGPATH=$MSP_PATH" \
> cli peer chaincode invoke -o $ORDERER -C mychannel -n healthcare \
> -c '{"Args":["createHospital","{\"hospitalId\": \"1\", \"hospitalName\": \"hospital1\", \"hospitalLocation\": \"CO\"}"]}' -o $ORDERER --cafile /o
pt/home/managedblockchain-tls-chain.pem --tls
2019-07-06 11:34:31.256 UTC [chaincodeCmd] chaincodeInvokeOrQuery -> INFO 001 Chaincode invoke successful. result: status:200
```

Figure 6.6: Create a hospital

Step 5: Create a pharmacy

We will invoke a `createPharmacy` function with the hospital details.

Run following command in the Fabric client, and you will get a similar output as shown in the following screenshot:

```
docker exec -e "CORE_PEER_TLS_ENABLED=true" -e

"CORE_PEER_TLS_ROOTCERT_FILE=/opt/home/managedblockchain-tls-chain.pem"
\

-e "CORE_PEER_ADDRESS=$PEER" -e "CORE_PEER_LOCALMSPID=$MSP" -e

"CORE_PEER_MSPCONFIGPATH=$MSP_PATH" \

cli peer Chaincode invoke -o $ORDERER -C mychannel -n healthcare \

-c '{"Args":["createPharmacy","{\"pharmacyId\": \"1\", \"pharmacyName\":
\"pharmacy1\", \"pharmacyLocation\": \"CA\"}"]}' -o $ORDERER --cafile

/opt/home/managedblockchain-tls-chain.pem —tls
```

```
[ec2-user@ip-10-0-200-8 ~]$ docker exec -e "CORE_PEER_TLS_ENABLED=true" -e "CORE_PEER_TLS_ROOTCERT_FILE=/opt/home/managedblockchain-tls-chain.pem"
\
> -e "CORE_PEER_ADDRESS=$PEER" -e "CORE_PEER_LOCALMSPID=$MSP" -e "CORE_PEER_MSPCONFIGPATH=$MSP_PATH" \
> cli peer chaincode invoke -o $ORDERER -C mychannel -n healthcare \
> -c '{"Args":["createPharmacy","{\"pharmacyId\": \"1\", \"pharmacyName\": \"pharmacy1\", \"pharmacyLocation\": \"CA\"}"]}' -o $ORDERER --cafile /o
pt/home/managedblockchain-tls-chain.pem --tls
2019-07-06 11:36:06.048 UTC [chaincodeCmd] chaincodeInvokeOrQuery -> INFO 001 Chaincode invoke successful. result: status:200
```

Figure 6.7: *Create a pharmacy*

Make sure each invoking results in the status code 200 for successful insertion.

Querying healthcare chaincode functions

Once the balance transfer chaincode is instantiated, we can query the ledger. We have inserted all the member details and asset details into the peer node, so now let's query the ledger to get asset details.

We will query a `getAssetDetail` function and pass the input parameter `assetId` as 1.

Run the following command in the Fabric client

```
docker exec -e "CORE_PEER_TLS_ENABLED=true" -e

"CORE_PEER_TLS_ROOTCERT_FILE=/opt/home/managedblockchain-tls-chain.pem"
\

-e "CORE_PEER_ADDRESS=$PEER" -e "CORE_PEER_LOCALMSPID=$MSP" -e

"CORE_PEER_MSPCONFIGPATH=$MSP_PATH" \

cli peer Chaincode query -C mychannel -n healthcare -c

'{"Args":["getAssetDetail","{\"assetId\": \"1\"}"]}'
```

Transferring the ownership of a medical asset

Steps to transfer an asset are as follows:

Step 1 – Transfer to a distributor

Run the following command:

```
docker exec -e "CORE_PEER_TLS_ENABLED=true" -e
"CORE_PEER_TLS_ROOTCERT_FILE=/opt/home/managedblockchain-tls-chain.pem"
\
-e "CORE_PEER_ADDRESS=$PEER" -e "CORE_PEER_LOCALMSPID=$MSP" -e
"CORE_PEER_MSPCONFIGPATH=$MSP_PATH" \
cli peer Chaincode invoke -o $ORDERER -C mychannel -n healthcare \
-c '{"Args":["transferAsset","{\"assetId\": \"1\", \"transferTo\":
\"distributor1\", \"state\": \"Distributed\"}"]}' --cafile
/opt/home/managedblockchain-tls-chain.pem –tls
```

Step 2 – Transfer to a hospital

Run the following command:

```
docker exec -e "CORE_PEER_TLS_ENABLED=true" -e
"CORE_PEER_TLS_ROOTCERT_FILE=/opt/home/managedblockchain-tls-chain.pem"
\
-e "CORE_PEER_ADDRESS=$PEER" -e "CORE_PEER_LOCALMSPID=$MSP" -e
"CORE_PEER_MSPCONFIGPATH=$MSP_PATH" \
cli peer Chaincode invoke -o $ORDERER -C mychannel -n healthcare \
-c '{"Args":["transferAsset","{\"assetId\": \"1\", \"transferTo\":
\"hospital1\", \"state\": \"Delivered\"}"]}' --cafile
/opt/home/managedblockchain-tls-chain.pem –tls
```

Step 3 – Transfer to a pharmacy

Run the following command:

```
docker exec -e "CORE_PEER_TLS_ENABLED=true" -e
"CORE_PEER_TLS_ROOTCERT_FILE=/opt/home/managedblockchain-tls-chain.pem"
\
```

```
-e "CORE_PEER_ADDRESS=$PEER" -e "CORE_PEER_LOCALMSPID=$MSP" -e
"CORE_PEER_MSPCONFIGPATH=$MSP_PATH" \
cli peer Chaincode invoke -o $ORDERER -C mychannel -n healthcare \
-c '{"Args":["transferAsset","{\"assetId\": \"1\", \"transferTo\":
\"pharmacy1\", \"state\": \"Delivered\"}"]}' --cafile
/opt/home/managedblockchain-tls-chain.pem –tls
```

Step 4 – Check the current asset owner; it should be a pharmacy

Run the following command:

```
docker exec -e "CORE_PEER_TLS_ENABLED=true" -e
"CORE_PEER_TLS_ROOTCERT_FILE=/opt/home/managedblockchain-tls-chain.pem"
\
-e "CORE_PEER_ADDRESS=$PEER" -e "CORE_PEER_LOCALMSPID=$MSP" -e
"CORE_PEER_MSPCONFIGPATH=$MSP_PATH" \
cli peer Chaincode query -C mychannel -n healthcare -c
'{"Args":["getAssetDetail","{\"assetId\": \"1\"}"]}'
```

Step 5 – Transfer to a customer

Run the following command:

```
docker exec -e "CORE_PEER_TLS_ENABLED=true" -e
"CORE_PEER_TLS_ROOTCERT_FILE=/opt/home/managedblockchain-tls-chain.pem"
\
-e "CORE_PEER_ADDRESS=$PEER" -e "CORE_PEER_LOCALMSPID=$MSP" -e
"CORE_PEER_MSPCONFIGPATH=$MSP_PATH" \
cli peer Chaincode invoke -o $ORDERER -C mychannel -n healthcare \
-c '{"Args":["transferAsset","{\"assetId\": \"1\", \"transferTo\":
\"Customer\", \"state\": \"Sold\"}"]}' --cafile
/opt/home/managedblockchain-tls-chain.pem –tls
```

Step 6 – Recall the asset

Run the following command:

```
docker exec -e "CORE_PEER_TLS_ENABLED=true" -e
"CORE_PEER_TLS_ROOTCERT_FILE=/opt/home/managedblockchain-tls-chain.pem"
```

```
\
-e "CORE_PEER_ADDRESS=$PEER" -e "CORE_PEER_LOCALMSPID=$MSP" -e
"CORE_PEER_MSPCONFIGPATH=$MSP_PATH" \
cli peer Chaincode invoke -o $ORDERER -C mychannel -n healthcare \
-c '{"Args":["transferAsset","{\"assetId\": \"1\", \"transferTo\":
\"manufacturer1\", \"state\": \"Recalled\"}"]}' --cafile
/opt/home/managedblockchain-tls-chain.pem –tls
```

Step 7 – Dispose of an expired medical asset

Run the following command:

```
docker exec -e "CORE_PEER_TLS_ENABLED=true" -e
"CORE_PEER_TLS_ROOTCERT_FILE=/opt/home/managedblockchain-tls-chain.pem"
\
-e "CORE_PEER_ADDRESS=$PEER" -e "CORE_PEER_LOCALMSPID=$MSP" -e
"CORE_PEER_MSPCONFIGPATH=$MSP_PATH" \
cli peer Chaincode invoke -o $ORDERER -C mychannel -n healthcare \
-c '{"Args":["disposeAsset","{\"assetId\": \"1\"}"]}' --cafile
/opt/home/managedblockchain-tls-chain.pem –tls
```

Step 8 – Delete an asset from the world state

Run the following command:

```
docker exec -e "CORE_PEER_TLS_ENABLED=true" -e
"CORE_PEER_TLS_ROOTCERT_FILE=/opt/home/managedblockchain-tls-chain.pem"
\
-e "CORE_PEER_ADDRESS=$PEER" -e "CORE_PEER_LOCALMSPID=$MSP" -e
"CORE_PEER_MSPCONFIGPATH=$MSP_PATH" \
cli peer Chaincode invoke -o $ORDERER -C mychannel -n healthcare \
-c '{"Args":["delete","{\"assetId\": \"asset1\"}"]}' --cafile
/opt/home/managedblockchain-tls-chain.pem –tls
```

This completes writing the chaincode, and we have tested the complete lifecycle of a medical asset against the healthcare chaincode.

Creating the API to interact with the chaincode

So far, we have successfully created the Fabric network with Amazon Managed Blockchain, instantiated, and tested healthcare Chaincode functions. We are able to create members and assets. We have also tested the transfer asset functionality and it is working as expected.

In this section, we will write the RESTful API for the healthcare supply chain using the Fabric SDK and Express.js.

Understanding the fabric-client Fabric Node.js SDK

The Fabric Node.js SDK has the fabric-client library that provides APIs to interact with Fabric network peers and order services to install and instantiate the chaincode, to invoke, and query the chaincode function.

Express.js API project structure

The RESTful API is designed with the Express.js framework using fabric-client to interact with the chaincode running on the Fabric network.

Figure 6.8: *Express.js API project structure*

Look at the following files:

- `connection-profile` directory: This has the connection details of the Fabric network which is deployed on AWS.
- `config.json`: This has the configuration details about the chaincode and admin login credentials of the Fabric network.
- `connection.js`:This has code to register user and client details.
- `invoke.js`: This has reusable code to invoke chaincode functions.
- `package.json`: This has the Node.js application configuration and npm library dependencies.
- `query.js`: This has reusable code to query the ledger.
- `start.sh`: This has code to clear key stores.
- `app.js`: This is an important file that has the API code. These routes will be used to invoke chaincode functions.

app.js file has all the create, update, delete, read functions as shown in below screenshot.

Figure 6.9: Project files

Make sure you have these folder structures and files.

Running the REST API on the Fabric Client node

We will run the API on the Fabric client, which will be consumed from our UI application.

Steps to run a REST API on the Fabric Client Node:

Step1: Install Node.js .

As we are running the Node.js API, we need to install Node.js on the Fabric Client node. Run the following command:

```
curl -o-
https://raw.githubusercontent.com/creationix/nvm/v0.33.0/install.sh |
bash
```

Step 2: Install nvm.

Install the Node Version Manager, which allows us to choose the Node version. Run the following command:

```
. ~/.nvm/nvm.sh
nvm install lts/carbon
nvm use lts/carbon
```

Step 3: Install the C++ compiler.

Run the following command to install the c++ compiler:

```
sudo yum install gcc-c++ -y
```

Step 4: Install project dependencies npm.

Run the following command to install the `fabric-shim` library along with other dependent libraries:

```
cd ~/Healthcare-Supplychain-Blockchain/healthcare-supplychain-api
npm install
```

Step 5: Generate a connection profile.

This is an important step. Here, we will configure the API to interact with our Fabric network. The `gen-connection-profile.sh` file automatically creates the connection profile by using the environment variables we declared earlier:

```
cd ~/Healthcare-Supplychain-Blockchain/healthcare-supplychain-
api/connection-profile
```

```
./gen-connection-profile.sh
```

```
[ec2-user@ip-10-0-66-83 healthcare-supplychain-api]$ cd ~/Healthcare-Supplychain-Blockchain/healthcare-supplychain-api/connection-profile
[ec2-user@ip-10-0-66-83 connection-profile]$ ./gen-connection-profile.sh
/home/ec2-user/Healthcare-Supplychain-Blockchain/tmp/connection-profile:
total 8
-rw-rw-r-- 1 ec2-user ec2-user 2287 Jul  9 09:24 healthcare-connection-profile.yaml
drwxrwxr-x 2 ec2-user ec2-user 4096 Jul  9 09:24 org1

/home/ec2-user/Healthcare-Supplychain-Blockchain/tmp/connection-profile/org1:
total 4
```

Figure 6.10: *Generate a connection profile*

Look at the updated configuration with your network details in the `healthcare-connection-profile.yaml` file:

```
cd ~/Healthcare-Supplychain-Blockchain/tmp/connection-profile/

cat healthcare-connection-profile.yaml
```

```
peers:
  peer1:
    url: grpcs://nd-wvjmdyzf4zhdlljvyj4omsllfi.m-jadxrwdf5rcw3dvuct6moqiq2u.n-lwx3twmkofannedmxjjaa47gnq.managedblockchain.us-east-1.amazonaw
s.com:30003
    eventUrl: grpcs://nd-wvjmdyzf4zhdlljvyj4omsllfi.m-jadxrwdf5rcw3dvuct6moqiq2u.n-lwx3twmkofannedmxjjaa47gnq.managedblockchain.us-east-1.ama
zonaws.com:30004
    grpcOptions:
      ssl-target-name-override: nd-wvjmdyzf4zhdlljvyj4omsllfi.m-jadxrwdf5rcw3dvuct6moqiq2u.n-lwx3twmkofannedmxjjaa47gnq.managedblockchain.us-
east-1.amazonaws.com
    tlsCACerts:
      path: /home/ec2-user/managedblockchain-tls-chain.pem

certificateAuthorities:
  ca-org1:
    url: https://ca.m-jadxrwdf5rcw3dvuct6moqiq2u.n-lwx3twmkofannedmxjjaa47gnq.managedblockchain.us-east-1.amazonaws.com:30002
    httpOptions:
      verify: false
    tlsCACerts:
      path: /home/ec2-user/managedblockchain-tls-chain.pem
    registrar:
      - enrollId: admin
        enrollSecret: Admin123
```

Figure 6.11: *Connection profile*

Step 6: Configure admin credentials.

Update admin credentials you have used in the previous chapter while creating the Fabric network using Amazon Managed Blockchain on the AWS console:

```
cd ~/Healthcare-Supplychain-Blockchain/healthcare-supplychain-api

vi config.json
```

Developing the Chaincode, API, and UI with the Fabric SDK on AWS ■ 137

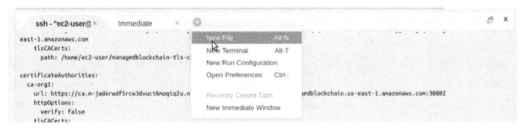

```
ssh - "ec2-user@ ×        Immediate        ×   +

  "host":"localhost",
  "port":"3000",
  "channelName":"mychannel",
  "chaincodeName":"healthcare",
  "eventWaitTime":"30000",
  "peers":[
      "peer1"
  ],
  "admins":[
      {
          "username":"admin",
          "secret":"Admin123"
      }
  ]
```

Figure 6.12: Configure admin credentials

Step 7: Run the API.

After verifying all the network configuration, it's time to run the API:

```
cd ~/Healthcare-Supplychain-Blockchain/healthcare-supplychain-api

nvm use lts/carbon

node app.js &
```

```
[ec2-user@ip-10-0-66-83 healthcare-supplychain-api]$ cd ~/Healthcare-Supplychain-Blockchain/healthcare-supplychain-api
[ec2-user@ip-10-0-66-83 healthcare-supplychain-api]$ nvm use lts/carbon
Now using node v8.16.0 (npm v6.4.1)
[ec2-user@ip-10-0-66-83 healthcare-supplychain-api]$ node app.js &
[1] 5061
[ec2-user@ip-10-0-66-83 healthcare-supplychain-api]$ [2019-07-09T09:25:21.883] [INFO] HealthcareAPI - ****************** SERVER STARTED *****
******************
[2019-07-09T09:25:21.885] [INFO] HealthcareAPI - ************** Listening on: http://localhost:3000 ******************
[2019-07-09T09:25:22.953] [INFO] HealthcareAPI - ##### New request for URL /health
```

Figure 6.13: Running the API

The API is now running on `localhost:3000` in the Fabric Client node.

Testing the healthcare API

This step will be done in a new terminal in Cloud9.

```
ssh - "ec2-user@ ×     Immediate     ×   +                                              ⊡  ✕
east-1.amazonaws.com
   tlsCACerts:
      path: /home/ec2-user/managedblockchain-tls-c       New File          Alt-N
                                                          New Terminal      Alt-T
certificateAuthorities:                                   New Run Configuration
   ca-org1:
      url: https://ca.m-jødxrwdf5rcw3dvuct6moqiq2u.n      Open Preferences   Ctrl-.          jedblockchain.us-east-1.amazonaws.com:30002
      httpOptions:
         verify: false                                   Recently Closed Tabs
      tlsCACerts:                                         New Immediate Window
```

Figure 6.14: Open new terminal

Steps to test the healthcare API:

Step 1: ssh to your Fabric Client.

Navigate to the Cloud Formation output section to see the output parameters. Copy the EC2 URL field. This is your Fabric Client EC2 instance URL:

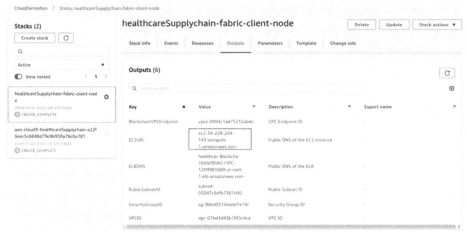

Figure 6.15: ssh to your Fabric Client

Copy the `.pem` key pair name, which is created under the root directory in the Cloud9 instance:

Figure 6.16: Copy the .pem key pair name

ssh into the EC2 instance from the Cloud9 terminal, pass the `.pem` file, and execute the following command. You will be able to `ssh` successfully as shown in the following screenshot:

```
cd ~

ssh ec2-user@<paste yyour EC2URL> -i ~/<Fabric network name>-
keypair.pem
```

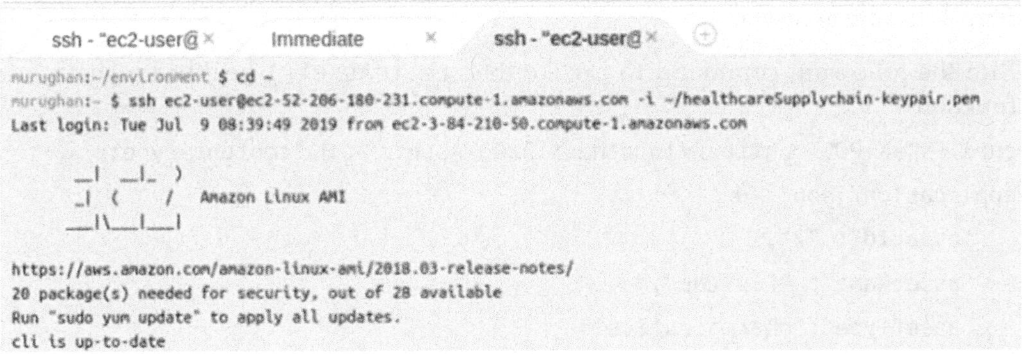

Figure 6.17: ssh into the EC2 instance

Step 2: Register user.

We need to create an identity before interacting with the Fabric network. We will register a new user called `user1` and run the following command in the Fabric Client. This invokes the API method to register `user1`:

```
curl -s -X POST http://localhost:3000/users -H "content-type:
application/x-www-form-urlencoded" -d 'username=user1&orgName=Org1'
```

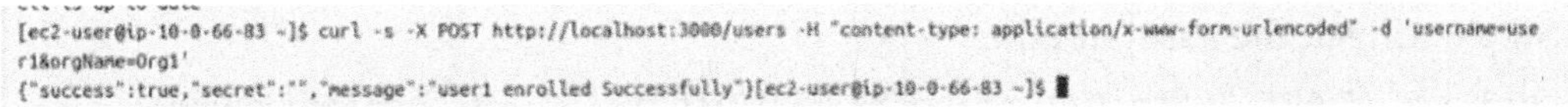

Figure 6.18: Registering a user

Step 3: Create a Manufacturer.

Run the following command to invoke the `createManufacturer()` healthcare chaincode function to add new a manufacturer using the API **http://localhost:3000/manufacturer** method, and run the following code:

```
curl -s -X POST "http://localhost:3000/manufacturer" -H "content-type:
application/json" -d '{
    "manufacturerId": "2",
    "manufacturerName": "manufacturer1",
    "manufacturerLocation":"AL"
}'
```

Figure 6.19: Creating a Manufacturer

Step 4: Create an asset.

Run the following command to invoke the `createAsset()` healthcare chaincode function:

```
curl -s -X POST "http://localhost:3000/Assets" -H "content-type:
application/json" -d '{
    "assetId": "2",
    "assetName": "Lipitor",
    "assetType":"pharmaceuticals",
    "assetExpirtyDate":"2019-12-30",
    "owner":"2",
    "state":"Manufacturered"
}'
```

Step 5: Create a Distributor, Hospital, and Pharmacy to pass the right data.

Repeat the previous steps to create a Distributor, Hospital, and Pharmacy to pass the right data.

Step 6: Check the asset details:

```
curl -s -X GET "http://localhost:3000/assets/2" -H "content-type:
application/json"
```

{"transactionId":"686e3be13c9cfc4d518358293b469fed028e019deae0c2fea84ae176e8947c4f"}[ec2-user@ip-10-0-66-83 ~]$ curl -s -X GET "http://localh
ost:3000/assets/2" -H "content-type: application/json"
[{"assetId":"2","assetName":"Lipitor","assetType":"pharmaceuticals","assetExpirtyDate":"2019-12-30","owner":"manufacturer2","state":"Manufact

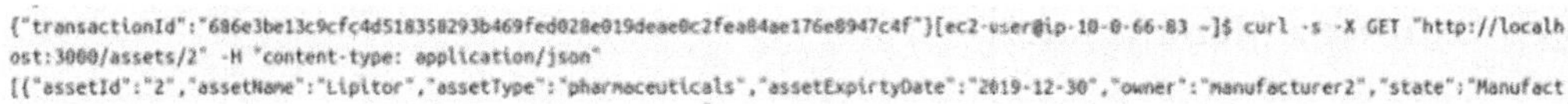

Figure 6.20: Check the asset details

Step 7: Transfer the asset:

```
curl -s -X POST "http://localhost:3000/transfer" -H "content-type:
application/json" -d '{
    "assetId": "1",
    "transferTo": "distributor2",
    "state": "Distributed"
}'
```

Step 8: Dispose of an asset:

```
curl -s -X POST "http://localhost:3000/disposal" -H "content-type:
application/json" -d '{
    "assetId": "2"
}'
```

Step 9: Recall the asset:

```
curl -s -X POST "http://localhost:3000/transfer" -H "content-type:
application/json" -d '{
 "assetId": "5",
 "transferTo": "manufacturer2",
 "state": "Recalled"
}'
```

This completes creating the API using `fabric-shim` library. We have successfully run the application and tested all the chaincode functions using the API method.

Designing the UI application for the healthcare supply chain project

We will create a simple UI with Angular which interacts with the AWS Managed Blockchain network through the API.

Execute the steps in the Cloud9 new terminal:

Figure 6.21: *Create a new terminal*

Steps to design the UI application:

Step 1: ssh to your Fabric Client node:

```
cd ~
ssh ec2-user@<paste yyour EC2URL> -i ~/<Fabric network name>-
keypair.pem
```

Step 2: Install the node:

```
curl -o-
https://raw.githubusercontent.com/creationix/nvm/v0.33.0/install.sh    |
bash
```

Step 3: Installnvm:

```
. ~/.nvm/nvm.sh
nvm install lts/carbon
nvm use lts/carbon
```

Step 4: Install Angular UI dependencies:

```
cd ~/Healthcare-Supplychain-Blockchain/healthcare-blockchain-ui
npm install
```

Step 5: Configure to node.js API to ELB:

```
vi src/environments/environment.ts
```

Replace `api_url` and `socket_url` from your CloudFormation stack output:

```
export const environment = {
  production: false,
  host: '',
  port: '',
  dbhost: '',
  dbport: '',
  api_url: 'http://ngo10-elb-2090058053.us-east-1.elb.amazonaws.com/',
  test: 'test',
  socket_url: 'ws://ngo10-elb-2090058053.us-east-1.elb.amazonaws.com'
};
```

Figure 6.22: Configure to node.js API to ELB

```
api_url: '</>',
  socket_url: '<>'
```

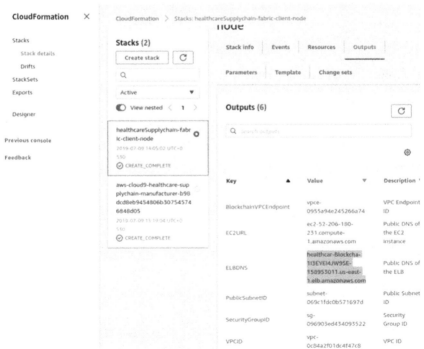

Figure 6.23: Replace api_url and socket_url

Make sure at the end of the link / is added to `api_url` as shown in the following screenshot:

```
export const environment = {
  production: false,
  host: '',
  port: '',
  dbhost: '',
  dbport: '',
  api_url: 'http://healthcar-Blockcha-1I3EYEI4JW9SE-158953011.us-east-1.elb.amazonaws.com/',
  test: 'test',
  socket_url: 'ws://healthcar-Blockcha-1I3EYEI4JW9SE-158953011.us-east-1.elb.amazonaws.com
};
```

Figure 6.24: Add to api_url

Step 6: Start the UI application and interact with your chaincode:

`cd ~/Healthcare-Supplychain-Blockchain/healthcare-blockchain-ui nvm use`

`lts/carbon npm start &`

The application is now running on port 8080. This completes running the UI application to interact with our healthcare chaincode running on the Amazon Managed Blockchain Fabric node.

Conclusion

We discussed how to write the chaincode in Node.js using the Fabric Node SDK for the healthcare supply chain project, how to design the API using a node.js express. js framework and UI to interact with the chaincode running on the Fabric node on AWS.

In the next chapter, we will learn how to invite other members such as a Distributor, Hospital, and Pharmacy to join our Fabric network.

Points to Remember

- A chaincode, also called a smart contract, is a computer code written in Node.js, Golang, or Java.

- The Fabric Node.js SDK has the `fabric-shim` library that provides the chaincode interface for implementing the chaincode.

- The chaincode follows the lifecycle as follows:

    Install | Instantiate | Invoke/Query | Upgrade

Multiple choice questions

1. **Chaincode are written only with Node.js.**

   a) Yes

   b) No

2. **UI can be designed in varieties of languages/frameworks.**

   a) Yes

   b) No

Answers

1. **b**
2. **a**

Questions

1. What is a chaincode?
2. Write a sample chaincode for a retail supply chain.
3. Design the UI and API for a retail supply chain.

Key terms

1. Chaincode lifecycle:

   a) Install the chaincode on a peer.

   b) Instantiate the chaincode on a peer.

   c) Query the peer, which returns the ledger state.

   d) Invoke the chaincode to insert/update/delete the value in the state DB.

   e) Upgrade the chaincode.

2. **Fabric Node.js SDK**: The Fabric Node.js SDK has the `fabric-shim` library that provides the chaincode interface for implementing the chaincode. It also provides implementation support for chaincodes written using `fabric-contract-api` along with the `fabric-Chaincode-nodeCLI` to launch the chaincode.

3. **Express.js:** The RESTful API is designed with the Express.js framework using `fabric-client` to interact with the chaincode running on the Fabric network.

CHAPTER 7

Adding Members to the Fabric Network on AWS

In this chapter, we will add members (distributor, hospital, and pharmacy) to the Fabric network on AWS.

Structure

In this chapter, we will discuss the following topics:

- Inviting a member to join the Fabric network
- Configuring a Fabric network to add a new member
- Creating a peer node for a new member
- Creating a Fabric client node for a new member
- Installing and instantiating chaincode
- Running the chaincode

Objectives

As a part of building the healthcare supply chain blockchain project, we have identified four stages as follows:

Stage 1: Building a Hyperledger Fabric network for healthcare supply chain with AWS-managed blockchain.

Stage 2: Creating a healthcare supply chain chaincode and deploying it on AWS.

Stage 3: Creating API and UI to interact with the healthcare supply chain chaincode from AWS.

Stage 4: Adding members (distributor, hospital, and pharmacy) to the Fabric network on AWS.

In the previous two chapters, we have completed stages 1 to 3. In this chapter, we will work on stage 4.

After studying this unit, you should be able to:

- Add a distributor member to the Fabric network
- Learn to add more members to the network

Pre-requisites for this chapter

We will make use of more AWS resources in this chapter, so it would be great if you already have experience with AWS. Otherwise, visit **https://docs.aws.amazon.com** to learn about these AWS resources Cloud9, CloudFormation, and EC2 instance.

- **AWS account for manufacturer:** If you already have an AWS account then you can skip this step. Otherwise, sign-up to AWS for a new account by visiting https://aws.amazon.com/.

- **AWS account for distributor:** Create a new AWS account for the distributor, if you already have an AWS account, then you can skip this step. Otherwise, sign-up to AWS for a new account at https://aws.amazon.com/.

- **AWS CLI:** We will use AWS CLI to provision blockchain network resources.

- Hyperledger Fabric: Understand Hyperledger Fabric architecture, fabric network models, components, and transaction flow.

- **Ubuntu and usage of Linux terminal:** We will use the Linux terminal to configure the Fabric network.

- **Shell scripting:** Basic knowledge of shell scripting.

- Stage 1 from *Chapter 5* AWS Managed Blockchain to Create Fabric Network Hyperledger Fabric network for healthcare supply chain with AWS-managed blockchain should be completed.

- Stage 2 from *Chapter 6* Developing the Chaincode, API, and UI with the Fabric SDK on AWS: Healthcare chaincode installed, and API is tested to interact with this network.

- **Docker and docker-compose:** Basic understanding and working experience on Docker as all the peers in Hyperledger Fabric run as a Docker container.

- Visual Studio Code: VS Code as IDE, you can still use your favorite IDE.

Fabric network architecture for manufacturer and distributor

In the previous chapter, we created the Fabric network with one member, that is, the manufacturer. In the real-world, each member in the network is an independent organization. So, each member will need to create a different peer node to join the network.

We will create one more member that is a distributor in this chapter. You can use the same steps to add other members to join the Fabric network.

Our healthcare supply chain project has four members, which means each member has a different AWS account. In this chapter, we will add a distributor to the Fabric network as shown in the following screenshot:

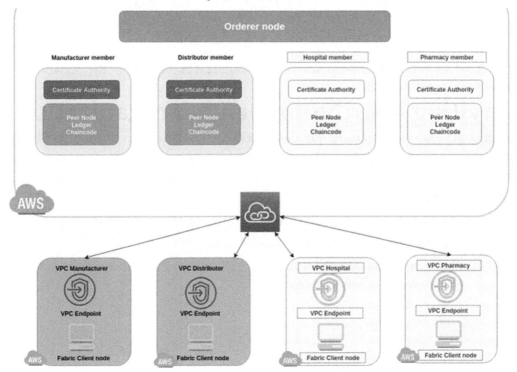

***Figure 7.1:** The architecture of Fabric network*

Please note, the gray-colored resources will not be created in this chapter. We will create a peer and a client node for the hospital in the next section.

Steps for members to join and participate in the Fabric network

The following are the high-level steps to participate in the network:

1. The first member of the network invites a new member.

2. The new member accepts the request and joins the Fabric network.

3. The new member creates a Peer node.

4. The new member creates a Fabric Client node.

5. The new member installs and instantiates chaincode.

6. The first and new member becomes an endorsing peer to approve the transactions.

7. The new member invokes chaincode functions.

8. This new member can also invite the next member to join the network.

Inviting distributor member organization

In this step, the manufacturer member will invite the distributor to join the network.

Steps to invite the member are as follows:

1. Log in to the AWS console with a manufacturer account (the AWS account used in the previous two chapters).

2. Navigate to **https://console.aws.amazon.com/managedblockchain.**

3. Select **healthcareSupplychain** network from the list.

4. Navigate to the **Members** tab and click on the **Propose invitation** button as shown in the following screenshot:

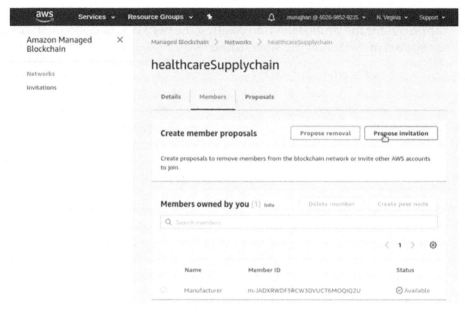

Figure 7.2: *Propose invitation*

5. Select the manufacturer id as the manufacturer is sending the invitation, enter the AWS account ID of the distributor, and click on **Create**.

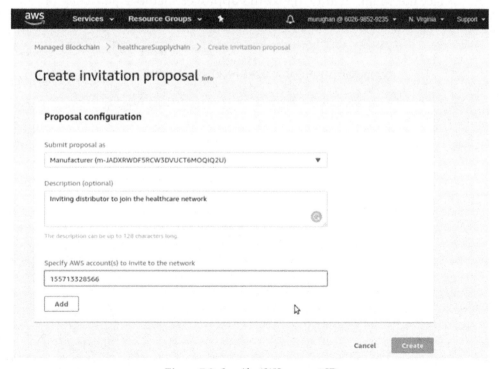

Figure 7.3: *Specify AWS account ID*

6. Once the invitation is created, this should be approved as we have set 50% approval for the proposal while creating the network, click on the **Proposal ID** as shown in the following screenshot:

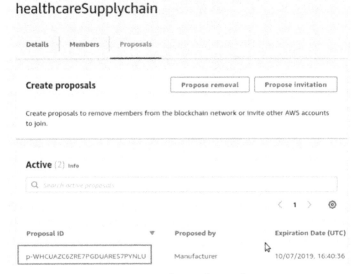

Figure 7.4: Proposal created

7. Select the Manufacturer ID as the approver member and click on the **Yes** button to approve the invite request to the distributor.

Figure 7.5: Approve Proposal

8. This will send an invitation link to the distributor.

Distributor member joining the Fabric network

For the members to join the Fabric network, they should get an invitation from the existing member from the network. Once the invitation is received, a new member will be able to join and participate in the network.

In this section, we will create the following resources:

1. Create a Cloud9 instance.
2. Accept the proposal to join the network.
3. Create and configure the Peer node.
4. Create and configure the Fabric Client node.

Step 1 – Provisioning an AWS Cloud9 instance for the distributor

Cloud9 is a cloud-based IDE that can be accessed through a browser and doesn't require to be installed locally. Cloud9 provides an editor to write the code with essential tools for popular languages, provides a debugger and terminal to run and debug your code. We will create a Cloud9 instance to provision network resources.

Steps to provision an AWS Cloud9 instance

1. Navigate to **https://us-east-1.console.aws.amazon.com/cloud9/home/ product.**
2. Select `US East(N. Virginia)` region.
3. Click on the **Create Environment** button.
4. Give a name and description for the Clound9 instance. Click on **Next step**.
5. Select **t2.medium** as an instance type as we need more memory to deploy our API and UI here. Then, click on **Next step**.
6. Click on **Create Environment.**
7. Once the Cloud9 instance is created, clone the following `Healthcare-Supplychain-Blockchain` repository from GitHub and execute the following command in the Cloud9 terminal.

    ```
    cd ~

    git clone
    ```
    https://github.com/murughan1985/Healthcare-Supplychain-Blockchain.git

8. Update your AWS CLI to the latest version. Execute the following command on the Cloud9 terminal:

```
sudo pip install awscli –upgrade
```

```
ec2-user:~ $ git clone https://github.com/murughan1985/Healthcare-Supplychain-Blockchain.git
Cloning into 'Healthcare-Supplychain-Blockchain'...
remote: Enumerating objects: 9937, done.
remote: Counting objects: 100% (9937/9937), done.
remote: Compressing objects: 100% (7443/7443), done.
remote: Total 9937 (delta 1870), reused 9911 (delta 1845), pack-reused 0
Receiving objects: 100% (9937/9937), 28.64 MiB | 32.92 MiB/s, done.
Resolving deltas: 100% (1870/1870), done.
ec2-user:~ $ sudo pip install awscli --upgrade
```

Figure 7.6: Update AWS CLI

Step 2 – Creating a distributor member in AWS Managed Blockchain

For the member distributor to join the network, log in to the AWS console with the distributor's credentials.

Steps to create distributor member

1. Navigate to **https://console.aws.amazon.com/managedblockchain.**

2. Click on the **Invitations** pane on the left.

3. Choose the **Fabric network** from the invitation list.

4. Click on **View details** to see the network details of the healthcare supply chain Fabric network

5. Click on **Accept Invitation** to join the network.

Figure 7.7: Accept invitation

6. Enter the member name as **Distributor**.

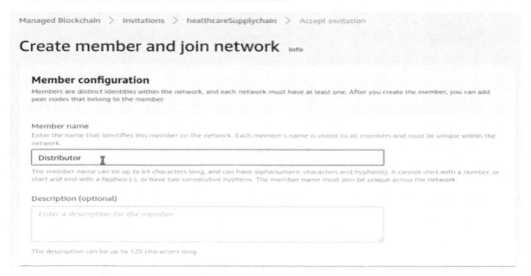

Figure 7.8: Enter member name

7. Enter `Admin username` and password, click on `Create member and join network`.

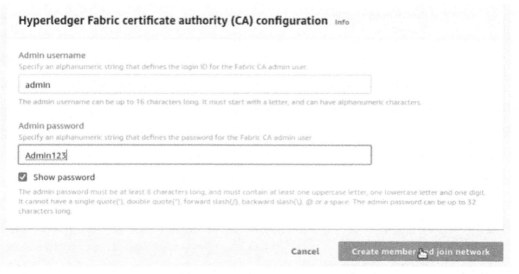

Figure 7.9: Enter admin username and password

8. Make a note of these credentials for later use.

9. Check the member creation status as available.

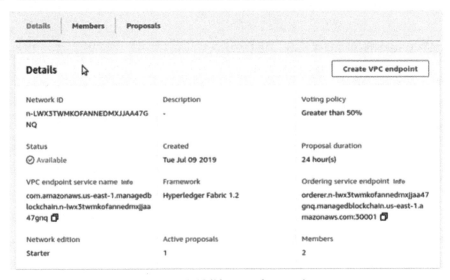

Figure 7.10: *Validate member creation*

10. Click on the **Members** tab, you can notice that we now have two members, **Manufacturer** and **Distributor**.

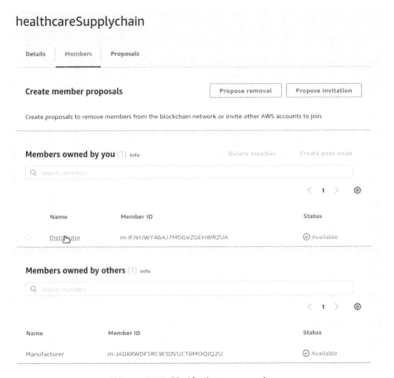

Figure 7.11: *Verify the two members*

Step 3 – Creating a distributor peer node

Let's create a peer node for distributor participants.

Steps to create a manufacturer peer node

1. Click on the newly created distributed member id from Managed Blockchain Services page and click on **Create peer node** from the **Distributor** details page.

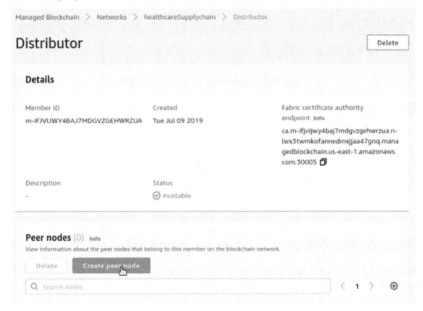

Figure 7.12: Create peer node

2. Leave the default values and click on **Create peer node.** A suggestion is to select a medium instance to handle the load.

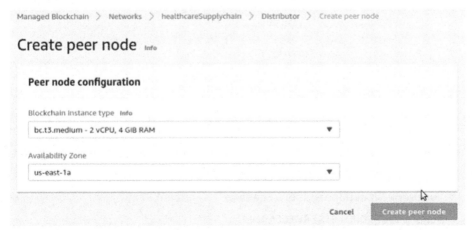

Figure 7.13: Select a medium instance

3. Once the peer node is created, you should see the following output screen:

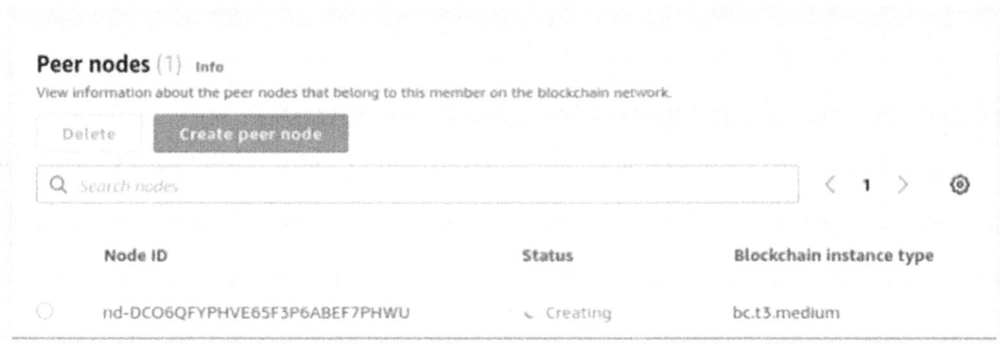

Peer nodes (1) Info

View information about the peer nodes that belong to this member on the blockchain network.

Delete	Create peer node

Q Search nodes   ‹ 1 › ⚙

Node ID	Status	Blockchain instance type
○ nd-DCO6QFYPHVE65F3P6ABEF7PHWU	Creating	bc.t3.medium

Figure 7.14: Confirm peer node creation

4. Wait for some time till the peer creation status shows as **Available**.

Step 4 – Provisioning Fabric Client node using CloudFormation template in Cloud9 instance

Let's provision Fabric Client node.

Steps to create Manufacturer peer node

1. In the Cloud9 Linux terminal, enter the following command to set the environment variables of your network as shown in the following screenshot:

```
export REGION=us-east-1
export NETWORKID=<Paste your Fabric network ID>
export NETWORKNAME=<Paste your Fabric network name which you
copied>
```

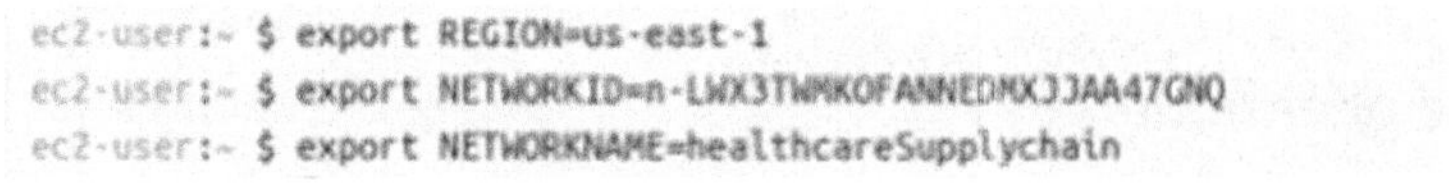

```
ec2-user:~ $ export REGION=us-east-1
ec2-user:~ $ export NETWORKID=n-LWX3TWMKOFANNEDMXJJAA47GNQ
ec2-user:~ $ export NETWORKNAME=healthcareSupplychain
```

Figure 7.15: Set environment variable

2. Set the VPC endpoint. Execute the following command in the Cloud9 terminal, and you should get the output as shown in the following screenshot:

```
export VPCENDPOINTSERVICENAME=$(aws managedblockchain get-network
--region $REGION --network-id $NETWORKID --query
'Network.VpcEndpointServiceName' --output text)
echo $VPCENDPOINTSERVICENAME
```

3. Create a CloudFormation template and execute the following command in the Cloud9 terminal which creates a key pair, VPC, subnet, security group, and EC2 instance as our Fabric Client node.

    ```
    cd ~/Healthcare-Supplychain-Blockchain/healthcare-supplychain-
    network
    ```

    ```
    ./3-vpc-client-node.sh
    ```

    This will create a new `.pem` file in the format as `<yournetworkname-keypair.pem>`, ignore the error message.

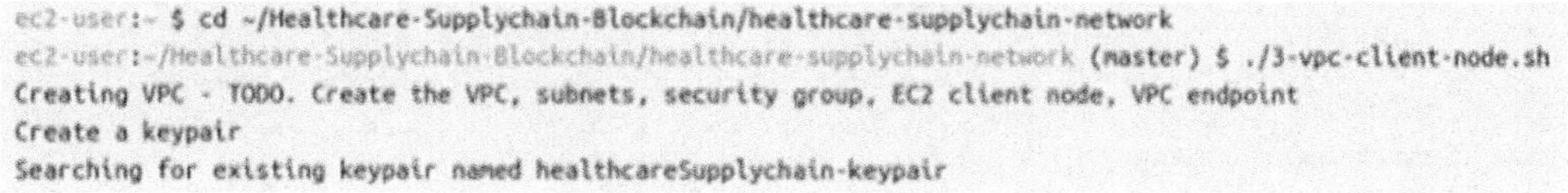

    ```
    ec2-user:~ $ cd ~/Healthcare-Supplychain-Blockchain/healthcare-supplychain-network
    ec2-user:~/Healthcare-Supplychain-Blockchain/healthcare-supplychain-network (master) $ ./3-vpc-client-node.sh
    Creating VPC - TODO. Create the VPC, subnets, security group, EC2 client node, VPC endpoint
    Create a keypair
    Searching for existing keypair named healthcareSupplychain-keypair
    ```

    Figure 7.16: *create a new .pem file*

4. Navigate to CloudFormation **https://console.aws.amazon.com/ CloudFormation/home?region=us-east-1** to see the deployment progress.

    We will wait till the Fabric Client gets created for the next step.

Step 5 – ssh into the Fabric Client node

Once the preceding CloudFormation stack shows the **CREATE_COMPLETE** message, we will ssh into the Fabric Client node.

Navigate to the **Outputs** section to see the output parameters. Copy the **EC2URL** field, this is your Fabric Client EC2 instance URL.

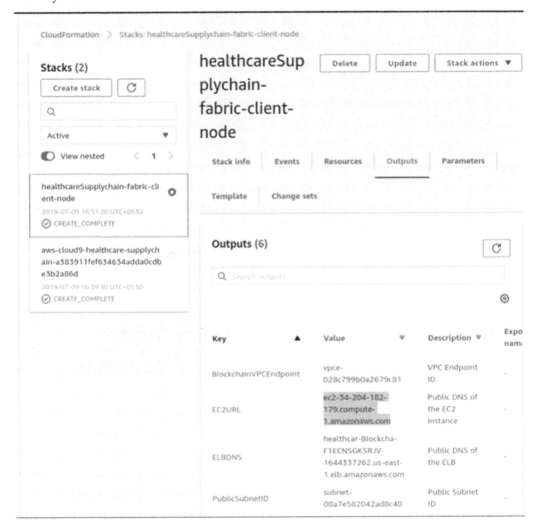

Figure 7.17: Copy the EC2URL

Copy the `.pem` key pair name, which is created under the root directory in the Cloud9 instance. ssh into the EC2 instance from the Cloud9 terminal and pass the `.pem` file. Execute the following command and you should be able to `ssh` successfully as shown in the following screenshot:

```
cd ~

ssh ec2-user@<paste your EC2URL> -i ~/<Fabric network name>-

keypair.pem
```

Clone the HealthcareSupplychain repository from GitHub, it's the same repo that we had cloned before onto the Cloud9 environment. Now let us copy it to the Fabric Client machine.

Execute the following command:

```
git clone
https://github.com/murughan1985/Healthcare-Supplychain-Blockchain.git
```

Step 6 – Configuring the environment variable in the Fabric Client node

We will capture all the Fabric network details in a file.

Steps to configure the environment variables

1. Create a file that includes ENV export values which we have defined for the Fabric network. Execute the following command in the Cloud9 terminal inside the EC2 instance as shown in the following screenshot:

    ```
    cd    ~/Healthcare-Supplychain-Blockchain/healthcare-supplychain-
          network

    cp templates/exports-template.sh fabric-exports.sh

    vi fabric-exports.sh
    ```

2. The fabric-exports.sh file has environment variables that need to be updated with your Hyperledger Fabric network details. Update these values, then source this script:

    ```
    export REGION=us-east-1

    export NETWORKNAME=<your network name>

    export MEMBERNAME=<the member name you entered when

    creating your Fabric network>

    export NETWORKVERSION=1.2

    export ADMINUSER=<the admin user name you entered when

    creating your Fabric network>

    export ADMINPWD=<the admin user name you entered when

    creating your Fabric network>

    export NETWORKID=<your network ID, from the AWS Console>

    export MEMBERID=<your Distributor member ID, from the AWS

    Console>
    ```

It will look as shown in the following screenshot:

```
# Update these values, then 'source' this script
export REGION=us-east-1
export NETWORKNAME=healthcareSupplychain
export MEMBERNAME=Manufacturer
export NETWORKVERSION=1.2
export ADMINUSER=admin
export ADMINPWD=Admin123
export NETWORKID=n-6KFLB4HGOFFZ3ELHSNJMASOUYI
export MEMBERID=m-IFJVIJWY4BAJ7MDGVZGEHWRZUA
```

Figure 7.18: Update environment variables

Execute the following command to source the file:

```
cd     ~/Healthcare-Supplychain-Blockchain/healthcare-supplychain-
network
```

```
source fabric-exports.sh
```

3. When you source the file, you will be able to use these variables for later. Scroll to the bottom to see the exported values.

4. Validate all the values in the peer-export file, and execute the following command:

```
cat ~/peer-exports.sh
```

5. If all the values are having your right network details, then source it by executing the following command:

```
source ~/peer-exports.sh
```

Step 7 – Enrolling admin identity

Each member will have Certificate Authority who is responsible to issue, revoke, and renew identity for anyone/nodes to join the network.

Steps to enroll admin identity

1. We will be downloading the latest version of Managed Blockchain PEM file. Execute the following command in Cloud9 on Fabric Client node:

```
aws s3 cp s3://us-east-1.managedblockchain/etc/managedblockchain-
tls-
```

```
chain.pem  /home/ec2-user/managedblockchain-tls-chain.pem
```

2. We will be enrolling an admin identity which we have created while provisioning Fabric network with Amazon Managed Blockchain. The Certificate Authority will enroll this user and this user will be used to create

a Fabric channel, install, and instantiate Healthcare chaincode. Execute following command:

```
export PATH=$PATH:/home/ec2-user/go/src/github.com/hyperledger/
fabric-

ca/bin

cd ~

fabric-ca-client enroll -u
https://$ADMINUSER:$ADMINPWD@$CASERVICEENDPOINT

--tls.certfiles /home/ec2-user/managedblockchain-tls-chain.pem -M

/home/ec2-user/admin-msp
```

3. Copy the certificate to the Fabric Client node and execute the following command:

```
mkdir -p /home/ec2-user/admin-msp/admincerts

cp ~/admin-msp/signcerts/* ~/admin-msp/admincerts/
```

The code will look as follows:

```
[ec2-user@ip-10-0-225-13 ~]$ cd ~
[ec2-user@ip-10-0-225-13 ~]$ fabric-ca-client enroll -u https://$ADMINUSER:$ADMINPWD@$CASERVICEENDPOINT --tls.certfiles /home/ec2-user/managedblockchain-tls-ch
ain.pem -M /home/ec2-user/admin-msp
2019/07/09 11:37:23 [INFO] TLS Enabled
2019/07/09 11:37:23 [INFO] generating key: &{A:ecdsa S:256}
2019/07/09 11:37:23 [INFO] encoded CSR
2019/07/09 11:37:23 [INFO] Stored client certificate at /home/ec2-user/admin-msp/signcerts/cert.pem
2019/07/09 11:37:23 [INFO] Stored root CA certificate at /home/ec2-user/admin-msp/cacerts/ca-m-ifjvijwy4baj7mdgvzgehwrzua-n-lwx3twnkofannednxjjaa47gnq-managedb
lockchain-us-east-1-amazonaws-com-30005.pem
[ec2-user@ip-10-0-225-13 ~]$ mkdir -p /home/ec2-user/admin-msp/admincerts
[ec2-user@ip-10-0-225-13 ~]$ cp ~/admin-msp/signcerts/* ~/admin-msp/admincerts/
```

Figure 7.19: Enrolling an admin identity

We have created an identity for admin user using FabricCA (Certificate Authority), we will use this identity for later steps.

Step 8 – Share distributor public key with the manufacturer

The distributor member should share the admin certificate and root CA certificate with the manufacturer and these certificates will be shared via S3.

Update the `region` and `memberID` of distributor in the following command:

```
cd ~/Healthcare-Supplychain-Blockchain

vi healthcare-new-member/s3-handler.sh
```

The code will be as follows:

```
set +e

region=us-east-1
memberID=<your member ID, from the AWS Console>
```

Figure 7.20: Update the region and member Id

Update the distributor member Id which you have noted while creating the distributor member using Managed Blockchain. Run the following command to copy public keys to s3:

```
cd ~/Healthcare-Supplychain-Blockchain
```

```
./healthcare-new-member/s3-handler.sh createS3BucketForNewMember
```

```
./healthcare-new-member/s3-handler.sh copyCertsToS3
```

The output will be as follows:

```
[ec2-user@ip-10-0-225-13 Healthcare-Supplychain-Blockchain]$ cd ~/Healthcare-Supplychain-Blockchain
[ec2-user@ip-10-0-225-13 Healthcare-Supplychain-Blockchain]$ ./healthcare-new-member/s3-handler.sh createS3BucketForNewMember
creating s3 bucket for new member : m-ifjvijwy4baj7mdgvzgehwrzua-newmember
{
    "Location": "/m-ifjvijwy4baj7mdgvzgehwrzua-newmember"
}
Creating the S3 bucket complete
[ec2-user@ip-10-0-225-13 Healthcare-Supplychain-Blockchain]$ ./healthcare-new-member/s3-handler.sh copyCertsToS3
Copying the certs for the new org to S3
{
    "ETag": "\"34697efcf0a7589365ef2336fa2cbd07\""
}
{
    "ETag": "\"8c8f42c2c9cdb0f89f8d7f51ffddc7f8\""
}
Copying the certs for the new org to S3 complete
```

Figure 7.21: Copying public keys to s3

Configuring the network to add a new distributor member

For this section, we will log in to the manufacturer's AWS account. As the manufacturer is the first member of the network, the manufacturer should configure the network to include the distributor member details.

Step 1 – Creating an MSP folder for the distributor

Update the member ID of the distributor and run the following command:

```
cd ~/Healthcare-Supplychain-Blockchain
vi healthcare-new-member/s3-handler.sh
```

```
region=us-east-1
memberID=m-IFJVIJWY48AJ7MDGVZGEH&RZUA
```

Figure 7.22: Update the member ID of Distributor

Update the member Id and save the changes. Run the following command to copy the distributor's public keys from S3 to the MSP directory:

```
cd ~/Healthcare-Supplychain-Blockchain
```

```
./healthcare-new-member/s3-handler.sh copyCertsFromS3
```

The output will be as follows:

```
[ec2-user@ip-10-0-66-83 Healthcare-Supplychain-Blockchain]$ cd ~/Healthcare-Supplychain-Blockchain
[ec2-user@ip-10-0-66-83 Healthcare-Supplychain-Blockchain]$ ./healthcare-new-member/s3-handler.sh copyCertsFromS3
Copying the certs from S3
{
    "AcceptRanges": "bytes",
    "ContentType": "binary/octet-stream",
    "LastModified": "Tue, 09 Jul 2019 11:39:47 GMT",
    "ContentLength": 1115,
    "ETag": "\"34697efcf0a7589365ef2336fa2cbd07\"",
    "Metadata": {}
}
{
    "AcceptRanges": "bytes",
    "ContentType": "binary/octet-stream",
    "LastModified": "Tue, 09 Jul 2019 11:39:48 GMT",
    "ContentLength": 993,
    "ETag": "\"8c8f42c2c9cdb0f89f8d7f51ffddc7f8\"",
    "Metadata": {}
}
/home/ec2-user/m-ifjvijwy4baj7mdgvzgehwrzua-msp/:
total 8
drwxrwxr-x 2 ec2-user ec2-user 4096 Jul  9 11:43 admincerts
drwxrwxr-x 2 ec2-user ec2-user 4096 Jul  9 11:43 cacerts

/home/ec2-user/m-ifjvijwy4baj7mdgvzgehwrzua-msp/admincerts:
total 4
-rw-rw-r-- 1 ec2-user ec2-user 1115 Jul  9 11:43 cert.pem

/home/ec2-user/m-ifjvijwy4baj7mdgvzgehwrzua-msp/cacerts:
total 4
-rw-rw-r-- 1 ec2-user ec2-user 993 Jul  9 11:43 cacert.pem
Copying the certs from S3 complete
```

Figure 7.23: Copying the distributor's public keys

Verify msp (membership service provider) and you should have a directory name that ends with -msp once you run the following command:

```
ls -l ~
```

The output is as follows:

```
[ec2-user@ip-10-0-66-83 Healthcare-Supplychain-Blockchain]$ ls -l -
total 129428
drwx------  7 ec2-user ec2-user      4096 Jul  9 08:49 admin-msp
-rw-rw-r--  1 ec2-user ec2-user      2359 Jul  9 08:50 configtx.yaml
-rw-rw-r--  1 ec2-user ec2-user       612 Nov 27  2018 docker-compose-cli.yaml
drwxrwxr-x 12 ec2-user ec2-user      4096 Nov 27  2018 fabric-samples
drwxrwxr-x  5 ec2-user ec2-user      4096 Nov 27  2018 go
-rw-rw-r--  1 ec2-user ec2-user 132489256 Jun  7  2018 go1.10.3.linux-amd64.tar.gz
drwxrwxr-x  9 ec2-user ec2-user      4096 Jul  9 09:24 Healthcare-Supplychain-Blockchain
-rw-rw-r--  1 ec2-user ec2-user      3290 Apr 30 17:27 managedblockchain-tls-chain.pem
drwxrwxr-x  4 ec2-user ec2-user      4096 Jul  9 11:43 m-ifjvijwy4baj7mdgvzgehwrzua-msp
-rw-r--r--  1 root     root          327 Jul  9 08:50 mychannel.pb
-rw-rw-r--  1 ec2-user ec2-user       512 Jul  9 08:46 peer-exports.sh
```

Figure 7.24: Verify msp (membership service provider)

Step 2 – Updating the configtx channel configuration to include the distributor member

Earlier we created only one organization, since now we are adding the second organization that is distributor, the organization's details need to be updated in the configtx.yaml file.

vi ~/configtx.yaml

You need to update two sections here:

1. Add Org2 section after Org1 section.

   &Org2

     Name: <Distributor member ID>

     ID: <Distributor member ID>

     MSPDir: /opt/home/m-ifjvijwy4baj7mdgvzgehwrzua-msp

     AnchorPeers:

     - Host:

     Port:

   The code will now look as shown in the following screenshot:

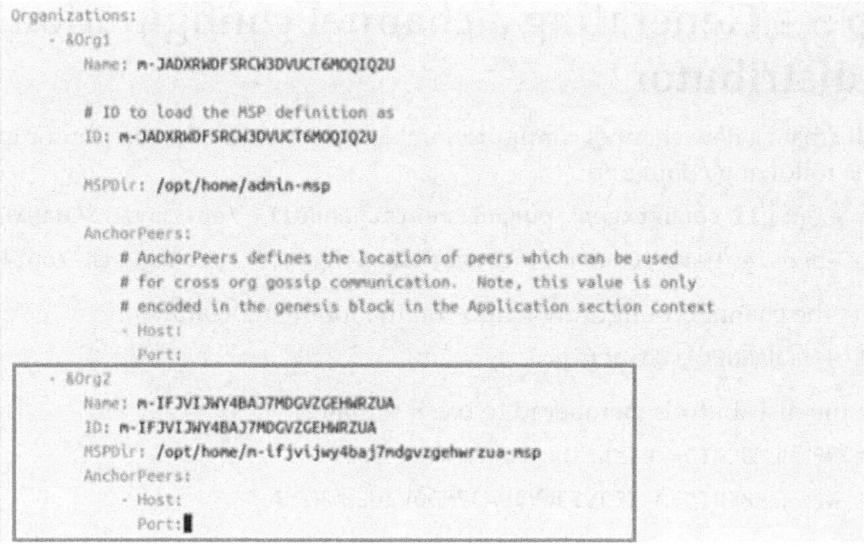

Figure 7.25: Add Org2 section

2. At the bottom of the file, add the following content:

```
TwoOrgChannel:
  Consortium: AWSSystemConsortium
  Application:
  <<: *ApplicationDefaults
  Organizations:
  - *Org1
  - *Org2
```

The code will look as shown in the following screenshot:

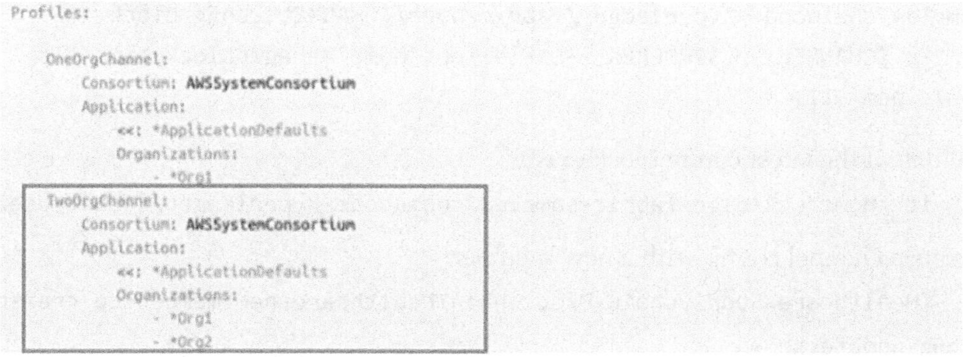

Figure 7.26: Update channel

Generate a new **configtx.yaml** channel creation.

Step 3 – Generating a channel configuration for the distributor

We will create a new channel configuration block to include the distributor member. Run the following command:

```
docker exec cli configtxgen -outputCreateChannelTx /opt/home/$CHANNEL-two-org.pb -profile TwoOrgChannel -channelID $CHANNEL --configPath /opt/home/
```

Validate the channel configuration and run the following command:

```
ls -lt ~/$CHANNEL-two-org.pb
```

Export the distributor's member id to use it for later:

```
export NEWMEMBERID=<Distributor Member ID>
export NEWMEMBERID=m-IFJVIJWY4BAJ7MDGVZGEHWRZUA
```

Generate a new member configuration and run the following command:

```
docker exec cli /bin/bash -c "configtxgen -printOrg $NEWMEMBERID --configPath /opt/home/ > /tmp/$NEWMEMBERID.json"
```

Validate the new member generation:

```
$ docker exec cli ls -lt /tmp/$NEWMEMBERID.json
```

Get the latest configuration block using cli peer channel fetch command:

```
docker exec -e "CORE_PEER_TLS_ENABLED=true" -e
"CORE_PEER_TLS_ROOTCERT_FILE=/opt/home/managedblockchain-tls-chain.pem"  \
    -e "CORE_PEER_ADDRESS=$PEER" -e "CORE_PEER_LOCALMSPID=$MSP" -e
"CORE_PEER_MSPCONFIGPATH=$MSP_PATH" \
    cli peer channel fetch config /opt/home/fabric-
samples/chaincode/hyperledger/fabric/peer/$CHANNEL.config.block \
    -c $CHANNEL -o $ORDERER --cafile /opt/home/managedblockchain-tls-
chain.pem –tls
```

Validate if the latest config block exist:

```
ls -lt /home/ec2-user/fabric-samples/chaincode/hyperledger/fabric/peer
```

Create a channel config with a new member:

```
cd ~/Healthcare-Supplychain-Blockchain/healthcare-new-member cp create-
config-update.sh ~
```

Replace the member Id which is the distributor member id:

```
docker exec -e "CHANNEL=mychannel" -e "MEMBERID=<replace with
```

```
distributor's
member id>" -e "BLOCKDIR=/opt/home/fabric-
samples/chaincode/hyperledger/fabric/peer" cli /opt/home/create-config-
update.sh
```

Validate the channel config block:

```
ls -lt /home/ec2-user/fabric-samples/chaincode/hyperledger/fabric/peer
```

Step 4 – Endorsing peer signing new channel configuration

Any changes to the network should get endorsed by network members, in this step the manufacturer will endorse the preceding configurations. Run the following command:

```
export  BLOCKDIR=/opt/home/fabric-samples/chaincode/hyperledger/fabric/
peer
docker exec -e "CORE_PEER_TLS_ENABLED=true" -e
"CORE_PEER_TLS_ROOTCERT_FILE=/opt/home/managedblockchain-tls-chain.pem"
\
    -e "CORE_PEER_ADDRESS=$PEER" -e "CORE_PEER_LOCALMSPID=$MSP" -e
"CORE_PEER_MSPCONFIGPATH=$MSP_PATH" \
    cli bash -c "peer channel signconfigtx -f
${BLOCKDIR}/${NEWMEMBERID}_config_update_as_envelope.pb"
```

File size is bigger as we have included the digital signature of the manufacturer.

```
ls -lt /home/ec2-user/fabric-samples/chaincode/hyperledger/fabric/peer
```

Step 5 – Update the channel with the new configuration

The manufacturer updates the channel using peer channel update command, run the following command. This will make changes to the channel to include the new member, that is, the distributor.

```
docker exec -e "CORE_PEER_TLS_ENABLED=true" -e
"CORE_PEER_TLS_ROOTCERT_FILE=/opt/home/managedblockchain-tls-chain.pem"
\
    -e "CORE_PEER_ADDRESS=$PEER" -e "CORE_PEER_LOCALMSPID=$MSP" -e
"CORE_PEER_MSPCONFIGPATH=$MSP_PATH" \
```

```
cli bash -c "peer channel update -f
${BLOCKDIR}/${NEWMEMBERID}_config_update_as_envelope.pb -c $CHANNEL -o
$ORDERER --cafile /opt/home/managedblockchain-tls-chain.pem --tls"
```

Step 6 – Sharing genesis block with the distributor

The mychannel.block file is created if the previous steps consisted of an endpoint of ordering service. The distributor should be able to connect to ordering service through this endpoint. We will copy this file to S3 so that the distributor can copy mychannel.block, run the following command:

```
cd ~/Healthcare-Supplychain-Blockchain
./healthcare-new-member/s3-handler.sh createS3BucketForCreator
./healthcare-new-member/s3-handler.sh copyChannelGenesisToS3
```

Step 7 – Copying genesis block to the distributor

For this step, we will log in to the distributor's AWS account.

Copy mychannel.block from the manufacture's S3 bucket.

```
cd ~/Healthcare-Supplychain-Blockchain
./healthcare-new-member/s3-handler.sh copyChannelGenesisFromS3
ls -l /home/ec2-user/fabric-
samples/chaincode/hyperledger/fabric/peer/mychannel.block
```

Instantiating and running healthcare chaincode on the distributor

For this section, we will log in to the distributor AWS account. So far, we have configured the channel to include the distributor, let's start the distributor peer node and interact with the healthcare chaincode.

Step 1 – Starting peer node on the distributor

Join the peer node to the channel and run the following command:

```
docker exec -e "CORE_PEER_TLS_ENABLED=true" -e
"CORE_PEER_TLS_ROOTCERT_FILE=/opt/home/managedblockchain-tls-chain.pem"
\
```

```
    -e "CORE_PEER_ADDRESS=$PEER" -e "CORE_PEER_LOCALMSPID=$MSP" -e
"CORE_PEER_MSPCONFIGPATH=$MSP_PATH" \
    cli peer channel join -b $CHANNEL.block -o $ORDERER --cafile $CAFILE
--
tls
```

Step 2 – Copying chaincode

Copy the healthcare chaincode to the container's mount directory and run the following command:

```
cd ~

mkdir -p ./fabric-samples/chaincode/healthcare

cp ./Healthcare-Supplychain-Blockchain/healthcare-supplychain-
chaincode/src/* ./fabric-samples/chaincode/healthcare
```

Step 3 – Installing chaincode

Install the healthcare chaincode on the distributor and run the following command:

```
docker exec -e "CORE_PEER_TLS_ENABLED=true" -e
"CORE_PEER_TLS_ROOTCERT_FILE=/opt/home/managedblockchain-tls-chain.pem"
-e
"CORE_PEER_LOCALMSPID=$MSP" -e "CORE_PEER_MSPCONFIGPATH=$MSP_PATH" -e
"CORE_PEER_ADDRESS=$PEER" cli peer chaincode install -n healthcare -l
node
-v v0 -p /opt/gopath/src/github.com/healthcare
```

Step 4 – Instantiating chaincode

To instantiate healthcare chaincode on the distributor, run the following command:

```
docker exec -e "CORE_PEER_TLS_ENABLED=true" -e
"CORE_PEER_TLS_ROOTCERT_FILE=/opt/home/managedblockchain-tls-chain.pem"
\
    -e "CORE_PEER_LOCALMSPID=$MSP" -e "CORE_PEER_MSPCONFIGPATH=$MSP_PATH"
-
e "CORE_PEER_ADDRESS=$PEER" \
    cli peer chaincode instantiate -o $ORDERER -C mychannel -n healthcare
-v v0 -c '{"Args":["init"]}' --cafile /opt/home/managedblockchain-tls-
chain.pem -tls
```

Step 5 – Invoking chaincode functions

Let's create a sample medical asset, which invokes the `createAsset()` chaincode function, run the following command:

```
docker exec -e "CORE_PEER_TLS_ENABLED=true" -e
"CORE_PEER_TLS_ROOTCERT_FILE=/opt/home/managedblockchain-tls-chain.pem" \
-e "CORE_PEER_ADDRESS=$PEER" -e "CORE_PEER_LOCALMSPID=$MSP" -e
"CORE_PEER_MSPCONFIGPATH=$MSP_PATH" \
cli peer chaincode invoke -o $ORDERER -C mychannel -n healthcare \
-c '{"Args":["createAsset","{\"assetId\": \"10\", \"assetName\":
\"needle\", \"assetType\": \"MedicalSupplies\", \"assetExpirtyDate\":
\"2019-12-30\", \"owner\": \"10\" }"]}' -o $ORDERER --cafile
/opt/home/managedblockchain-tls-chain.pem –tls
```

This step will not get executed as this transaction requires the manufacturer to endorse this change.

Step 6 – Get channel information

Run the following command to see the invoke details:

```
docker exec -e "CORE_PEER_TLS_ENABLED=true" -e
"CORE_PEER_TLS_ROOTCERT_FILE=/opt/home/managedblockchain-tls-chain.pem"
\
    -e "CORE_PEER_ADDRESS=$PEER" -e "CORE_PEER_LOCALMSPID=$MSP" -e
"CORE_PEER_MSPCONFIGPATH=$MSP_PATH"  \
    cli peer channel getinfo -o $ORDERER -c $CHANNEL --cafile $CAFILE –tls
```

Note down the peer address of the manufacturer peer and the distributor peer to use in the next command.

Step 7 – Invoke chaincode with the preceding peer address details

Run the following command to invoke chaincode:

```
docker exec -e "CORE_PEER_TLS_ENABLED=true" -e
"CORE_PEER_TLS_ROOTCERT_FILE=/opt/home/managedblockchain-tls-chain.pem"
\
   -e "CORE_PEER_ADDRESS=$PEER" -e "CORE_PEER_LOCALMSPID=$MSP" -e
```

```
"CORE_PEER_MSPCONFIGPATH=$MSP_PATH"          \

  cli peer chaincode invoke -o $ORDERER -C $CHANNEL -n healthcare      -c
'{"Args":["createAsset","{\"assetId\": \"10\", \"assetName\": \"needle\",
\"assetType\":   \"MedicalSupplies\",   \"assetExpirtyDate\":   \"2019-12-
30\",
\"owner\": \"10\" }"]}' \

  --cafile $CAFILE --tls --peerAddresses <peerAddress of A> \

  --peerAddresses <peerAddress of B> \

  --tlsRootCertFiles  /opt/home/managedblockchain-tls-chain.pem --
tlsRootCertFiles /opt/home/managedblockchain-tls-chain.pem
```

Before we run this, we need to update the endorsement policy.

Endorsing distributor transaction from the manufacturer

For this section, we will log in to the manufacturer AWS account.

Step 1 – Manufacturer updating endorsement policy

Run the following command to update the endorsement policy:

```
export CHAINCODEVERSION=v2
docker exec -e "CORE_PEER_TLS_ENABLED=true" -e
"CORE_PEER_TLS_ROOTCERT_FILE=/opt/home/managedblockchain-tls-chain.pem"
\
    -e "CORE_PEER_ADDRESS=$PEER" -e "CORE_PEER_LOCALMSPID=$MSP" -e
"CORE_PEER_MSPCONFIGPATH=$MSP_PATH" \
    cli peer chaincode install -n $CHAINCODENAME -v $CHAINCODEVERSION -p
$CHAINCODEDIR
```

Step 2 – Update endorsement policy

Run the following command to update the endorsement policy:

```
    docker exec -e "CORE_PEER_TLS_ENABLED=true" -e
"CORE_PEER_TLS_ROOTCERT_FILE=/opt/home/managedblockchain-tls-chain.pem"
\
```

```
        -e "CORE_PEER_ADDRESS=$PEER" -e "CORE_PEER_LOCALMSPID=$MSP" -e
"CORE_PEER_MSPCONFIGPATH=$MSP_PATH" \
        cli peer chaincode upgrade -o $ORDERER -C $CHANNEL -n
$CHAINCODENAME -v $CHAINCODEVERSION \
      -c '{"Args":["init","a","100","b","200"]}' --cafile $CAFILE --tls \
      -P "OR('<Account A member ID>.member','<Account B member
ID>.member')"
```

Step 3 – Distributor updates chaincode

Run the following command to update the chaincode:

```
export CHAINCODEVERSION=v2
docker exec -e "CORE_PEER_TLS_ENABLED=true" -e
"CORE_PEER_TLS_ROOTCERT_FILE=/opt/home/managedblockchain-tls-chain.pem"
\
    -e "CORE_PEER_ADDRESS=$PEER" -e "CORE_PEER_LOCALMSPID=$MSP" -e
"CORE_PEER_MSPCONFIGPATH=$MSP_PATH" \
    cli peer chaincode install -n $CHAINCODENAME -v $CHAINCODEVERSION -p
$CHAINCODEDIR
```

Step 4 – Verify from distributor account

Run the following command to verify from the distributor account:

```
docker exec -e "CORE_PEER_TLS_ENABLED=true" -e
"CORE_PEER_TLS_ROOTCERT_FILE=/opt/home/managedblockchain-tls-chain.pem"
\
    -e "CORE_PEER_ADDRESS=$PEER" -e "CORE_PEER_LOCALMSPID=$MSP" -e
"CORE_PEER_MSPCONFIGPATH=$MSP_PATH" \
cli peer chaincode invoke -o $ORDERER -C $CHANNEL -n $CHAINCODENAME \
    -c '{"Args":["invoke","a","b","10"]}' --cafile $CAFILE –tls
```

Step 5 – Querying chaincode functions

Run the following command to query the chaincode functions:

```
docker exec -e "CORE_PEER_TLS_ENABLED=true" -e
"CORE_PEER_TLS_ROOTCERT_FILE=/opt/home/managedblockchain-tls-chain.pem"
\
```

```
-e "CORE_PEER_ADDRESS=$PEER" -e "CORE_PEER_LOCALMSPID=$MSP" -e
"CORE_PEER_MSPCONFIGPATH=$MSP_PATH" \
cli peer chaincode query -C mychannel -n healthcare -c
'{"Args":["getAssetDetail","{\"assetId\": \"10\"}"]}'
```

This completes adding distributor organization to the network.

Adding hospital and pharmacy organization

Follow the preceding steps to add a hospital and pharmacy member to the network. If we need privacy and confidentiality within the network, then we can create a separate channel between the organizations. For example, in healthcare supply chain the distributor might sell for a different prices in a pharmacy and in a hospital. This detail should be kept private between the distributor and the hospital. For this, follow the same preceding steps from the beginning.

Conclusion

We have built our complete network to include the distributor and hospital members as organizations within the Fabric network. In a real-life use case, there will be more organizations, and we need to use the same steps to include new members in the network. We have also created a peer node, Fabric Client node for the distributor and hospital.

You have learned to invite other members to the Fabric network, you have learned to build end-to-end Blockchain solution with AWS Managed Blockchain.

In the next chapter, we will explore Ethereum.

Points to remember

- We have added all the participants to the network, we can invite any number of participants to the network.

Multiple-choice questions

1. Chaincode is written only with Node.js:
   a) Yes
   b) No

2. UI can be designed in varieties of languages/frameworks.

   a) Yes

   b) No

Answer

1. b

2. a

Questions

1. What are the steps to invite members to the network?

2. Invite participants to the retail supply chain.

Key terms

1. **Following are the high-level steps to participate in the network:**

   a) The first member of the network invites a new member.

   b) The new member accepts the request and joins the Fabric network.

   c) The new member creates a peer node.

   d) The new member creates the Fabric Client node.

   e) The new member installs and instantiates chaincode.

   f) The first and the new member become an endorsing peer to approve the transactions.

   g) The new member invokes chaincode functions.

   h) This new member can also invite the next member to join the network.

CHAPTER 8

Deep Dive into Ethereum Blockchain

Ethereum is called a *World Computer*, which is an open source general-purpose public blockchain framework to build decentralized applications. Ethereum is a platform for anyone to program decentralized applications for multiple use cases where you want to eliminate middlemen from the system and conduct direct business between peers. For example, redesigning of Uber in Ethereum will remove the intermediates, the consumer and driver can do business directly, which reduces the cost for the consumer, and the driver gets paid more.

Structure

In this chapter, we will discuss the following topics:

- Ethereum platform
- Ethereum Virtual Machine
- Ethereum accounts
- Ether denominations
- Gas and Ether
- Transactions in the Ethereum blockchain
- Ethereum network
- Ethereum test network

- Ethereum main network

Objectives

After studying this unit, you should be able to:

- Get in-depth knowledge about Ethereum blockchain
- Understand how Ethereum works
- Understand Ethereum concepts

Ethereum platform

After the launch of Bitcoin, people started to understand the power of blockchain and wanted to explore beyond fund transfer. However, Bitcoin is not designed to be a general-purpose blockchain, that's when the birth of Ethereum took place by *Vitalik Buterin* in December 2013. Primarily intended as a means to execute smart contracts in a decentralized fashion, and can be used to build applications for many industries.

Ethereum peer-to-peer network

Applications built on Ethereum follows the following architecture:

- Ethereum blockchain peer-to-peer network acts as a database.
- The application's business logic is written as a smart contract with solidity language and runs on the Ethereum network.
- The frontend application called as *DApps* (**Decentralized Applications**) uses web3.js library to interact with smart contracts.

Ethereum blockchain is a distributed peer-to-peer network:

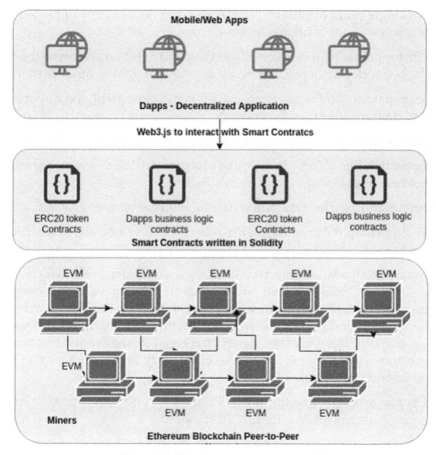

Figure 8.1: Ethereum peer-to-peer network

Transactions are processed by the public nodes which form the blockchain network. These nodes are not controlled by any central authority rather it's a public peer-to-peer network where anyone can join and participate in the mining. Each node records transactions within blocks that are immutable.

Data stored in these blocks are verified with signature and proof-of-work consensus. Each block is linked with the previous block hash and forms a blockchain.

Features of Ethereum blockchain

The following are some of the features of the Ethereum blockchain:

- **Global singleton**: Ethereum network has multiple nodes, each node stores the replicated copy of the same ledger.

- **Multi-user:** Ethereum can hold as many accounts as possible.

- **No single point of failure:** Since each node stores a copy of the ledger, there is always a node available to serve.

- **Unstoppable:** As it is decentralized in nature and no one owns the network, the network cannot be stopped by any government or other authority.

- **Transparent:** All the transactions are kept transparent and anyone can join and do transactions in the network.

- **Atomicity:** Either the complete operation runs or nothing happens.

- **Immortal:** The object can never be externally deleted, it can only voluntarily commit suicide.

- **Immutability:** The data stored in Ethereum are tamper-resistant.

- **Turing-complete language:** This allows the development of smart contracts for blockchain and decentralized applications.

- **Smart contracts:** A smart contract is a computer code which has a set of business rules between two parties in a business. Smart contracts are deployed into the Ethereum blockchain and run on the Ethereum blockchain as a self-operating computer program that automatically executes while specific conditions are met or executed based on the event. Once the contract executes a particular action, it makes an entry into the blockchain ledger as an immutable record.

- **Cryptocurrency token:** With Ethereum you can create your own cryptocurrency token with ERC20 standard.

With Ethereum, a developer need not worry about how to create his own peer-to-peer network and does not depend on any centralized infrastructure. Ethereum provides a general-purpose language called *solidity,* in which developers code for a broad variety of requirements and deploy on the Ethereum peer-to-peer network. Ethereum also allows us to create private blockchain networks.

Ethereum virtual machine

Ethereum Virtual Machine (EVM) is the heart of an Ethereum network that executes smart contracts and processes complex requests. These smart contract programs are written in solidity. All the nodes in the Ethereum networks run EVM and execute smart contracts. Each EVM in the network produces an identical state change for every transaction.

Since the nodes are decentralized and thousands of nodes process the request, there is no downtime for the Ethereum network. As all the nodes process/validate the request, it takes around 10 minutes to create a new block. 10 minutes seems to be very high compared to the current applications that respond in milliseconds. However, the problem Ethereum solves is big, so 10 mins is not too bad and the Ethereum team is researching to improve this.

EVM executes smart contract code as a trustless system and global singleton. The EVM is a stack-based VM with an ephemeral memory byte-array and persistent key-value storage. The smart contract is compiled to bytecode and then EVM runs this bytecode.

You can read in more detail through Ethereum white paper release by *Vitalik Buterin* in the year 2013 **(https://github.com/ethereum/wiki/wiki/White-Paper)** and the Ethereum Yellow Paper that has the complete Ethereum network details **(https://github.com/ethereum/yellowpaper)**.

Ethereum accounts

In Ethereum, users and smart contracts should have an account. An account in the Ethereum network is the unique identity provided to the users and contracts to participate in the network, each user and contract is identified with the account address which is 160-bit code.

There are two types of accounts in Ethereum:

1. Externally owned account (accounts)
2. Contract account (contracts)

Externally-owned account (accounts)

Every participant in the Ethereum network including humans, mining nodes, and automated agents is identified through an account address which is a unique identifier.

An example of an externally owned account:

Address: 0x742d35Cc6634C0532925a3b844Bc454e4438f44e

You can view the top Ethereum accounts at **https://etherscan.io.**

In the following screenshot, we can see the top 5 Ethereum accounts:

Figure 8.2: Externally owned account (accounts)

Accounts have the following characteristics:

- The account maintains the state in the ledger
- The ledger maintains the balance of the account
- All the account balances are maintained in the Ethereum network
- Every account has a private and public key
- Accounts can send Ether to another account
- Accounts initiate the transaction in the blockchain network
- You must have an account to interact with the Ethereum network.

Contract account (contracts)

Each smart contract deployed onto the Ethereum network has an address which is called a contract account (contracts). Decentralized applications will interact with smart contracts through the contract account.

Have a look at an example of contract address:
0xdac17f958d2ee523a2206206994597c13d831ec7

You can view the top ERC20 cryptocurrency token smart contact accounts at **https:// etherscan.io.**

In the following screenshot, we can see the Tether ERC20 cryptocurrency token smart contact account:

Figure 8.3: *Contract account (contracts)*

Contracts have the following characteristics:

- Contracts maintain both balances as well as storage
- Contracts hold the code which will be executed by the EVM
- Contracts don't have a private key
- Contracts can also send and receive Ether

Each smart contract has a unique address.

Ether denominations

Ether is the cryptocurrency used in Ethereum and the symbol is ETH, every transaction within Ethereum involves cost (Ether) to be paid. If the call to the blockchain network is just to read the data then it's free of cost, but every state change to the blockchain will incur a cost, this will be paid to the node that processes the request in the blockchain.

Ether has multiple denominations, each denomination has a name, the smallest denomination is Wei which is 18 decimals, that is, 1 Ether = 1,000,000,000,000,000,000 Wei.

Unit	Wei Value	Wei
wei	1 wei	1
Kwei (babbage)	1e3 wei	1,000
Mwei (lovelace)	1e6 wei	1,000,000
Gwei (shannon)	1e9 wei	1,000,000,000
microether (szabo)	1e12 wei	1,000,000,000,000
milliether (finney)	1e15 wei	1,000,000,000,000,000
ether	1e18 wei	1,000,000,000,000,000,000

Figure 8.4: Ether denominations

Let's do a small exercise to find out the denomination for two Ether. *EtherConverter* is a great tool to convert the different Ethereum units. Navigate to **https://etherconverter. online/** and enter 2 in the Ether textbox.

In the following screenshot, we can see all the denominations for the 2 Ether along with the equivalent value in USD and EUR.

Figure 8.5: Ether Converter

This is a very handy tool to find denominations.

Gas and transactions

Since transactions are processed by public nodes in an Ethereum network and nodes store smart contracts, these nodes should get paid from the user who initiates the transaction.

Every transaction in the Ethereum network requires Ether to be paid for miners.

What is Gas in Ethereum?

Gas is the unit of measurement for every transaction in the Ethereum network:

- Gas is required to be paid for each activity performed on the Ethereum blockchain.
- A transaction fee is charged as some amount of Ether and is taken from the account balance of the transaction originator.
- A fee is paid for transactions to be included by miners.
- The more the fee, the higher the chances for the transactions to be picked up by the miners for inclusion in the block.
- Providing too little gas will result in a failed transaction.

Terms within Gas

- **Gas cost:** This is a constant computation cost.
- **Gas price:** This is the price of the gas in Ether or other cryptocurrencies.
- **Gas limit:** Maximum amount of gas that can be used per block.
- **Gas fee:** Amount of gas needed to execute a transaction.

What are transactions in Ethereum?

The term *transaction* is used in Ethereum to refer to the signed data package that contains a message to be sent from an externally owned account to another account on the blockchain. Ethereum blocks contain both a transaction list and the most recent *state* of the ledger of these transactions. Any state change in the blockchain is called a transaction.

Examples of a transaction

- Transferring Ether or ERC20 tokens.
- Deploying solidity smart contract.

- Executing smart contract functions that change the state of the blockchain.

The transaction contains the following details:

- **Recipient:** The recipient's address.
- **Sender:** A signature to identify the sender.
- **Value:** Amount of Wei to transfer from sender to receiver.
- **Start gas:** Units of gas this transaction can consume.
- **Gasprice:** Total amount of Wei the sender is willing to pay to the node that processes this request.

Calculating transaction cost

Before we initiate any transaction, it's better to calculate the transaction cost for a successful transaction.

To estimate the transaction cost, we can use the following formula:

*Total cost = gasUsed * gasPrice*

The following opcode gas cost table is from Ethereum Yellow Paper, through this, you can derive the gas needed for any operation.

For example, to multiply a number it takes 5 gas, which we can see in the following table the Mnemonic MUL required Gas of 5.

Value	Mnemonic	Gas Used	Subset	Removed from stack	Added to stack	Notes	Formula
0x00	STOP	0	zero	0	0	Halts execution.	
0x01	ADD	3	verylow	2	1	Addition operation	
0x02	MUL	5	low	2	1	Multiplication operation.	
0x03	SUB	3	verylow	2	1	Subtraction operation.	
0x04	DIV	5	low	2	1	Integer division operation.	
0x05	SDIV	5	low	2	1	Signed integer division operation (truncated).	
0x06	MOD	5	low	2	1	Modulo remainder operation	
0x07	SMOD	5	low	2	1	Signed modulo remainder operation.	
0x08	ADDMOD	8	mid	3	1	Modulo addition operation.	
0x09	MULMOD	8	mid	3	1	Modulo multiplication operation.	
0x0a	EXP	FORMULA		2	1	Exponential operation.	(exp == 0) ? 10 : (10 + 10 * (1 + log256(exp)))
0x0b	SIGNEXTEND	5	low	2	1	Extend length of two's complement signed integer.	
0x10	LT	3	verylow	2	1	Less-than comparison.	
0x11	GT	3	verylow	2	1	Greater-than comparison.	
0x12	SLT	3	verylow	2	1	Signed less-than comparison.	
0x13	SGT	3	verylow	2	1	Signed greater-than comparison.	
0x14	EQ	3	verylow	2	1	Equality comparison.	
0x15	ISZERO	3	verylow	1	1	Simple not operator.	

Figure 8.6: Calculating transaction cost

The complete list of opcode gas costs is available here **https://github.com/ djrtwo/evm-opcode-gas-costs/blob/master/opcode-gas-costs_EIP-150_revision-1e18248_2017-04-12.csv.**

While you send a transaction to the network, it's very important to provide enough gas to complete your request. The transactions will be canceled halfway for requests with insufficient gas, so it's very critical to understand how much to provide. *Ethgasstation* is a great tool to calculate the gas required for a successful transaction. Navigate to **https://ethgasstation.info/index.php.**

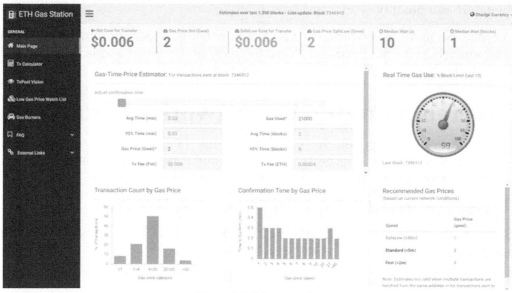

Figure 8.7: Eth gas station

To calculate Gas, click on the Tx Calculator tab and enter a value in Gas Used field.

Figure 8.8: Transaction view

This shows us the prediction for sender request with Gas 30000, 98% percentage of success rate, 24 seconds to confirm and transaction fee in Ether is 0.0003 and Fiat USD $0.0402.

Ethereum public network

Ethereum blockchain is a distributed peer-to-peer network, requests are processed by the public nodes which form the blockchain network. Each node records transaction within blocks which are in immutable, data stored in these blocks are verified with signature and proof-of-work consensus.

Anyone can join the network, each node in the network is a machine running an Ethereum client (Geth). Each node has a full copy of the ledger and is synchronized with the latest data. Any node can process the sender request.

Ethereum production network - MainNet

The production version of the public Ethereum blockchain network is called Ethereum MainNet that runs on TCP port 30303 and runs a protocol called DEVp2p.

Understanding of Ethereum client

Smart contracts are converted into the EVM bytecode via an EVM compiler and uploaded onto the Blockchain using an Ethereum client.

The Ethereum client is software that allows a user to do the following:

- Approve transactions/blocks
- Create/manage accounts on Ethereum
- Send/receive transactions to/from your Ethereum accounts
- Deploy smart contracts onto blockchain
- Mining Ether on the Ethereum blockchain

List of Ethereum clients

The following are some Ethereum clients designed with multiple languages:

- Go-ethereum (Geth) - Go language
- Parity - Rust language
- Cpp-Ethereum - C++ language
- Pyethapp - Python language
- Ethereum(J) - Java language

Installing Geth

Install go-ethereum with the following command on Linux to connect to main Net:

```
sudo apt-get install software-properties-common
```

```
sudo add-apt-repository -y ppa:ethereum/ethereum
```

```
sudo apt-get update
```

```
sudo apt-get install Ethereum
```

After successful installation, execute geth command.

To install Geth on any other OS, please refer to Ethereum documentation available at **https://github.com/ethereum/go-ethereum/wiki/Building-Ethereum.**

Exploring Ethereum blockchain with Etherscan

Etherscan is a block explorer and analytics platform for all the transactions within Ethereum main network.

Let's look at the Ethereum MainNet by navigating to **https://etherscan.io/.**

On the home page, you are provided with Ether price, latest blocks, latest transactions, and search by (account address, contract address, transaction hash, block no, token, and ens).

Figure 8.9: Exploring Ethereum on Etherscan

Let's explore the search functionality by entering 0xEA674fdDe714fd979de3EdF0F56AA9716B898ec8 sample account address in search box.

Figure 8.10: Search functionality

The search result for this account address lists the details as shown in the following screenshot:

- Overview of this account
- Amount of Ether this account holds
- Different cryptocurrency ERC20 tokens
- Number of blocks mined
- Latest 25 transactions (you can click on each of this transaction to see more transaction details)
- ERC20 token transaction
- Mined blocks
- Mined uncles
- Comments

Figure 8.11: Explore account details

Navigate to the Blockchain tab and select View Txns to explore transaction details as shown in *Figure 8.12*. In the result screen, we can see the recent transaction details:

- Transaction hash
- Block number
- Time
- From account
- To account
- Ether transferred value
- Transaction fee

Figure 8.12: View transaction

Let's explore the blocks. Navigate to the **Blockchain** tab and select the **View Blocks** option, this result shows the recent block details as shown in *Figure 8.13*:

- Block number
- Age
- Number of transactions in a block
- Miner detail
- Gas used
- Gas limit
- Avg gas price

- Reward

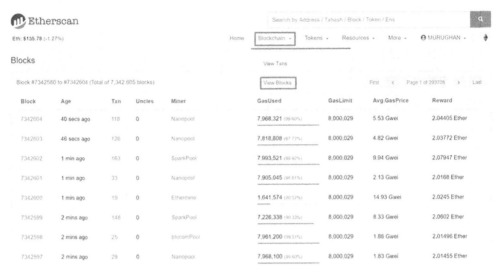

Figure 8.13: View blocks

Click on any of the block numbers from the preceding result to see more block detail as shown in the following screenshot:

Figure 8.14: View block details

Etherscan gives some more options to explore ERC-20 tokens, view pending transactions, forked blocks, uncles, top accounts, ERC-721 tokens, verified tokens, and more options to explore public blockchain.

Exploring Ethereum blockchain with Ethstats

Another useful blockchain explorer to check the health of the Ethereum network is EthStats.

Navigate to **https://ethstats.net/** to see the current state of the Ethereum network.

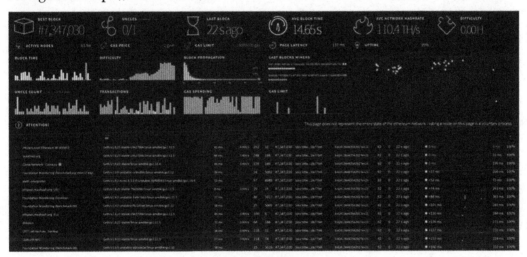

Figure 8.15: Ethstats

This beautiful dashboard shows the Ethereum network details like latest block, uncle block, last block, average block time, active nodes, gas price, gas limit, and more metrics.

Ethereum test networks - TestNet

Every transaction in Ethereum involves cost where the blockchain state change is involved, so it's not a good idea to use MainNet while in the development stage. Instead, we can use TestNet which is similar to MainNet and is used to test the DApps and smart contracts in the development and testing phases where the real Ether is not used.

There are multiple TestNet available, mainly:

- Ropsten
- Kovan

- Rinkeby

Take a look at the Ropsten test network at **https://ropsten.etherscan.io/.**

These test networks (Ropsten, Kovan, and Rinkeby) have the same functionality as that of Etherscan but as a test environment.

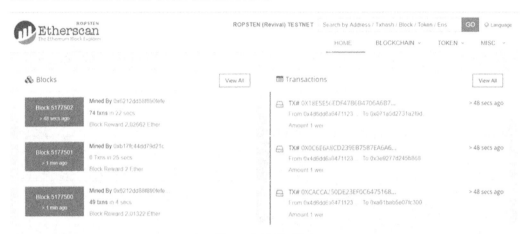

Figure 8.16: TestNet

Ropsten test network has all the functionality as Etherscan to test smart contracts and tokens.

Ethereum private and permissioned network

With Ethereum we can create private and permissioned blockchain as well where only known people have joined. As the members of the network are known, mining is not required.

Private network

A private blockchain is used when any institution or business wants to build secure, immutable, and centralized internal applications for auditing. For example, banks could use a private network to store all the customer transaction details for auditing and tracking purposes.

Permissioned network

Permissioned blockchain is the same as public blockchain with one major difference that only known entities can join and transact in the network. This identity defines who can access and do what on the network. Permissioned blockchain is used when multiple parties are involved and are working on the same goal/interest. For example, in the supply chain, health care, agriculture, and more.

We shall explore more on this in the upcoming chapters.

Exercise - Transferring Ether between accounts

In this exercise, we will create a wallet with two accounts, and transfer the fund from one account to another in Ethereum peer-to-peer distributed network.

Steps to transfer fund between two accounts:

1. Add a *MetaMask* wallet in the Chrome browser.
2. Create an Ethereum account in MetaMask.
3. Get a fake Ether to one account.
4. Create a recipient account.
5. Initiate the transaction by mentioning gas and recipient address.
6. Check the transaction status in Etherscan.
7. Check the recipient balance.

Step 1 – Add MetaMask wallet in Chrome browser

A wallet is a software that manages Ethereum accounts. Wallets are used to send transactions to the Ethereum network and to track the account balance. A wallet doesn't hold cryptocurrency, it just holds the keys, and the user signs the transaction with a private key.

MetaMask is a wallet, bridge to the Ethereum network for both the main and test network which is installed as a browser extension. We use the Chrome browser for this exercise:

1. Search for *MetaMask* extensions in the Chrome browser, and add them to Chrome:

Figure 8.17: MetaMask extensions in the Chrome browser

2. After successful installation of MetaMask, it will appear in the Chrome browser toolbox.

Step 2 – Create an Ethereum account in MetaMask

In this step, we will create an Ethereum account:

1. Select the **MetaMask** toolbar from the Chrome browser and get started.

Welcome to MetaMask

Connecting you to Ethereum and the Decentralized Web.
We're happy to see you.

GET STARTED

Figure 8.18: Click on GET STARTED

2. If you already have an Ethereum account, then select **IMPORT WALLET** or click on **CREATE A WALLET,** and agree to conditions mentioned in Metamask.

New to MetaMask?

No, I already have a seed phrase

Import your existing wallet using a 12 word seed phrase

Yes, let's get set up!

This will create a new wallet and seed phrase

IMPORT WALLET

CREATE A WALLET

Figure 8.19: Create a wallet

3. Create the password for your wallet.

Figure 8.20: Provide a password

4. Now, make a note of the secret backup phrase that will be displayed, copy the seed key. It is very important to save the seed key; with this key, you will be able to recover the wallet or use a different system to log in.

Figure 8.21: Seed key

5. Select the phrase in the same order in which you noted it in the previous step.

Figure 8.22: Enter seed key

6. Click on **Confirm** to create the account in a wallet. You will be redirected to the MetaMask home page. Ethereum account has been created with zero Ether.

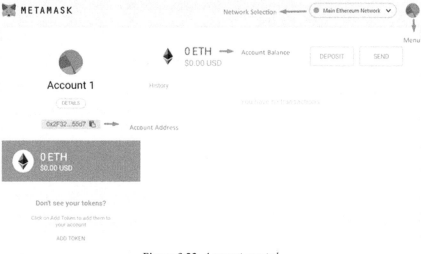

Figure 8.23: Account created

This Account 1 will be used to interact with both the test and main network.

Step 3 – Get fake Ether to one account

Let's add some Ether to **Account 1:**

1. Let's get some free fake Ether to transact with the Ethereum test network. Select Ropsten as the network from the top corner and then click on the **DEPOSIT** button which will navigate to the faucet.

Figure 8.24: Get free fake Ether

2. Request for 1 Ether from the faucet.

Figure 8.25: Request for Ether

3. Now check your account balance for **Rosten Test Network,** the current balance should be 1 Ether.

Step 4 – Create a recipient account

Let's create another Ethereum account for the recipient:

1. Click on the **Menu** and choose the **Create Account** option and name the account as Account 2.

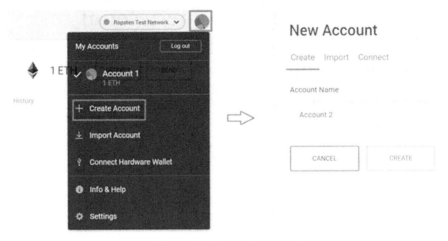

Figure 8.26: Create Account 2

2. Here, you can even give a different name for the account instead of Account 2.

Step 5 – Initiate the transaction by mentioning the Gas and recipient address

Let's transfer some Ether to **Account 1**:

1. Select **Account 1** to transfer fund:

Figure 8.27: Transfer to Account 1

2. Click on the **SEND** button.

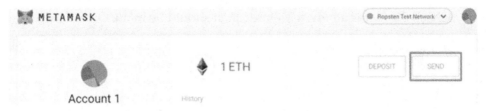

Figure 8.28: Send Ether

3. Select recipient **Account 2,** enter the amount of Ether you want to send, and click on **Next.** Validate all the details, and confirm the transaction. Your request is now sent to the peer-to-peer test network. Your request will be processed by any public node and a block will be created by any public node in the Ropsten test network.

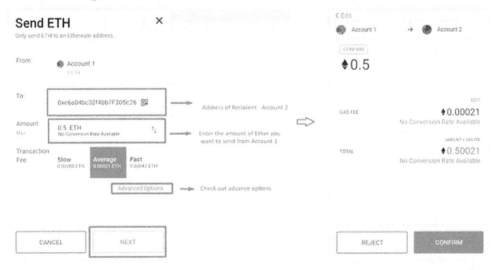

Figure 8.29: Validate

4. Check the status in MetaMask, note that the status is still **PENDING**, this is because it takes time to mine your request.

Figure 8.30: Check the status

5. Check the status again in MetaMask, it should be in a **CONFIRMED** state.

Figure 8.31: Check status to confirmed state

You can see the transaction details by clicking on the **CONFIRMED** link in the preceding screenshot.

Step 6 – Check the transaction status in Etherscan

Let's view transaction detail in Etherscan:

1. Click on Etherescan explorer option.

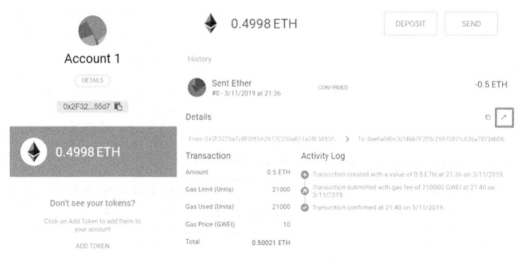

Figure 8.32: Etherescan explorer

2. Check all the details of your transaction in Etherescan Ropsten TestNet.

3. Here we can see all the gas used for the transaction and other details of the transaction.

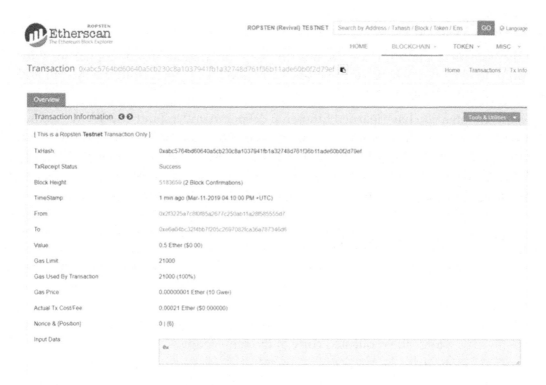

Figure 8.33: Gas used for the transaction

Step 7 – Check Account 2 balance

Let's check the balance of Account 2:

1. If the transaction is successful, then Account 2 should have 0.5 Ether.

Figure 8.34: Check the balance

2. This completes the steps to transfer funds between accounts. You can try the same steps to transfer real Ether by selecting the main network in MetaMask.

Conclusion

Ethereum is a platform for anyone to program decentralized applications for multiple use cases where you want to eliminate middlemen from the system and conduct direct business between peers.

In this chapter, you have learned Ethereum deeper to understand how EVM executes smart contracts and processes user requests. You have also understood the difference between accounts and contacts, gas and Ether denominations. You have learned to use Etherscan and the usage of MetaMask wallet.

In the next chapter, we will create an Ethereum network in AWS.

Points to remember

- Ethereum is called a World Computer, which is an open source general-purpose public blockchain framework to build decentralized applications.
- Ethereum has the following features:
    - o *Global singleton:* Ethereum network has multiple nodes, each node stores the replicated copy of the same ledger.
    - o *Multi-user:* Ethereum can hold as many accounts as possible.
    - o *No single point of failure*: Since each node stores the copy of the ledger, there is always a node available to serve.
    - o *Unstoppable:* As it is decentralized in nature and no one owns the network, the network cannot be stopped by any government or other authority.
    - o *Transparent:* All the transactions are kept transparent, and anyone can join and transact in the network.
    - o *Atomicity:* Either complete operation runs or nothing happens.
    - o *Immortal:* The object can never be externally deleted, it can only voluntarily commit suicide.
    - o *Immutability:* Data stored in Ethereum are tamper-resistant.
    - o *Turing-complete language:* This allows the development of smart contracts for blockchain and decentralized applications.
    - o *Smart contracts:* A smart contract is a computer code having a set of business rules between two parties in a business. Smart contracts are deployed into the Ethereum blockchain and run on the Ethereum blockchain as a self-operating computer program that automatically executes while specific conditions are met or executed based on the event. Once the contract executes a particular action, it makes an entry into the blockchain ledger as an immutable record.

o *Cryptocurrency token:* With Ethereum you can create your own cryptocurrency token with ERC20 standard.

Multiple-choice questions

1. **Chaincode is written only with Node.js:**

    a. Yes

    b. No

2. **UI can be designed in a variety of languages/frameworks.**

    a. Yes

    b. No

Answer

1. b

2. a

Questions

1. What is Ethereum blockchain?

2. How does Ethereum blockchain work?

Key terms

1. **Ethereum:** Ethereum blockchain is a distributed peer-to-peer network. Transactions are processed by the public nodes which form the blockchain network.

2. **EVM:** It is the heart of the Ethereum network that executes smart contracts and processes complex requests.

3. **Ethereum accounts:** In Ethereum, users and smart contracts should have an account. An account in the Ethereum network is the unique identity provided to the user and contracts to participate in the network. Each user and contract is identified with the account address which is a 160-bit code. There are two types of accounts in Ethereum:

    a. Externally-owned account (accounts)

    b. Contract account (contracts)

4. **Wei**: Ethereum is the smallest denomination.

5. **Gas**: Gas is the unit of measurement for every transaction in the Ethereum network.

6. **Transactions**: The term *"transaction"* is used in Ethereum to refer to the signed data package that contains a message to be sent from an externally-owned account to another account on blockchain.

7. **Etherscan**: Blockchain explorers

8. **Ethstats**: Check whether the health of the Ethereum network is EthStats.

9. **Ethereum TestNet**: This is used to test the DApps and smart contracts in the development and testing phases where real Ether is not used. There are multiple TestNets available, mainly: Ropsten, Kovan, and Rinkeby.

10. **MetaMask**: Ethereum wallet.

CHAPTER 9

AWS Blockchain Template to Create Private Ethereum

In the previous chapter, we have understood how Ethereum and AWS blockchain services works. In this chapter, we will deep dive into **AWS Blockchain Template** by building an Ethereum private network on AWS.

Structure

In this chapter, we will discuss the following topics:

- AWS blockchain templates for Ethereum
- Deployment options - ECS and Docker-local
- Create a VPC and Subnets
- Create security groups
- Create an IAM role
- Create a Bastion host
- Provision private Ethereum network
- Connect to the EthStats and the EthExplorer
- Connect to Ethereum network through MetaMask wallet

Note: This chapter involves creating many AWS resources and involves a lot of configurations so, please make sure to verify each step.

Pre-requisites for this chapter

We will be primarily using AWS resources in this chapter, so it would be great if you already have some experience with AWS. Otherwise, Visit **https://docs.aws. amazon.com** to learn AWS resources IAM user, IAM role, key pair, VPC, subnet, security groups, EC2 instance, **Elastic Container Service (ECS)**, **Elastic Container Registry(ECR)**, Bastion host, and Load balancer.

- AWS account: If you already have an AWS account then you can skip this step. Otherwise, sign up on AWS for a new account: **https://aws.amazon. com/**

- Creating an IAM user: It's not advisable to use an AWS root account for day to day activity, instead, we should create anew identity and provide only necessary access through IAM. Please follow this link to create a new IAM user **https://docs.aws.amazon.com/IAM/latest/UserGuide/getting-started_ create-admin-group.html**

- Creating a key pair: Public-key cryptography is used to secure the blockchain network in AWS. You require a key pair to login into the blockchain network created through AWS. We will use this key pair to SSH to the blockchain network. Create a key pair in the same region where you will be launching the Ethereum node.

We will be using US East 2 (Ohio) region, to provision all the AWS resources in this chapter.

Steps to create a key pair

1. Go to AWS EC2 console **https://console.aws.amazon.com/ec2/**.
2. Select the **US East 2 (Ohio)** region.
   a) As of now, AWS blockchain templates are available in US East 1 (NVirginia), US East 2 (Ohio), and US West 2 (Oregon) regions only.
   b) We will be using US East 2 (Ohio) region here to provision all the AWS resources.
3. Navigate to the Key Pairs section, click on the **Create Key Pair** button to give a name, and create a new key pair.
4. `.pem` file will be downloaded automatically to your computer. Keep the `.pem` file safe.
5. This key pair will be used in future steps.

AWS Blockchain templates for Ethereum

We have understood the difficulty and complexity involved in self-hosting a blockchain network, and how AWS blockchain services make it easier to build blockchain solutions. We can now focus on writing business logic, and AWS takes care of creating and managing infrastructure.

AWS blockchain templates provide a fast and easy way to create and deploy blockchain networks on AWS for Ethereum and Hyperledger Fabric. You can create both private and public Ethereum networks with AWS.

AWS provides a certified CloudFormation template to create a blockchain network. AWS CloudFormation allows us to model our complete infrastructure in a text file to provision the resources in an automated way. This file acts as a single source of truth and helps us to treat the infrastructure as code.

Following screenshot shows the components of a blockchain network created using AWS Blockchain Templates:

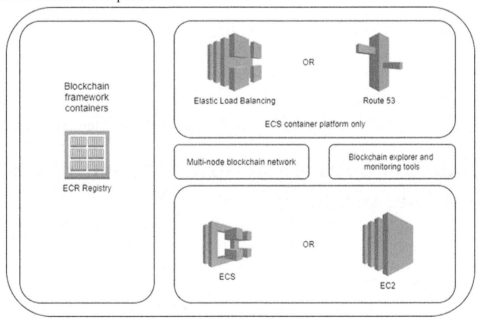

Figure 9.1:*AWS Blockchain Templates*

AWS provides two deployment options to run a blockchain network:

- **ECS: Elastic Container Service (ECS)** is a highly scalable and high-performance docker container orchestration service, which runs and scales Ethereum containers.

- **Docker-local:** Docker running on EC2 instance.

Benefits of AWS blockchain templates

Following are the benefits of using AWS blockchain templates:

- Faster and error-free deployment.
- Option to choose between Ethereum and Hyperledger Fabric template.
- Provides monitoring tools like the *EthStats* and the *EthExplorer*.
- Pay only for the resources you use.

AWS blockchain templates provide a fast and easy way to create blockchain networks.

AWS Ethereum template network architecture

In this section, we will explore the AWS Ethereum CloudFormation template architecture, components, and AWS resources from our Ethereum blockchain network.

As of now, AWS has Ethereum template only in following three regions:

- US East 1 - N Virginia
- US East 2 - Ohio
- US West 2 - Oregon

We will be using the US East 2 (Ohio) region here, to provision all the AWS resources.

Ethereum network architecture with ECS container platform

We will be using ECS Cloud Formation template to create Ethereum private network. This template creates a network which consists of the following resources:

- AWS Virtual Private Cloud to provide network access to all AWS resources in this architecture.
- Two public subnet in different availability zone and one private subnet.
- **Elastic Container Registry(ECR)** to maintain all the Ethereum docker images.
- Elastic Container Service creates three EC2 instances (two EC2 instances for the client, and one EC2 instance for miner) and provisions multiple Ethereum docker containers.
- Elastic Load Balancer manages the traffic to nodes.
- External connections are handled through one Bastion host which redirects requests to Load Balancer and to the Ethereum nodes.

- Security groups for Load Balancer and EC2 instance.
- IAM role for EC2 instance and Load Balancer.
- EthStats to monitor the health of blockchain network.
- EthExplorer to explore the blocks in the network.

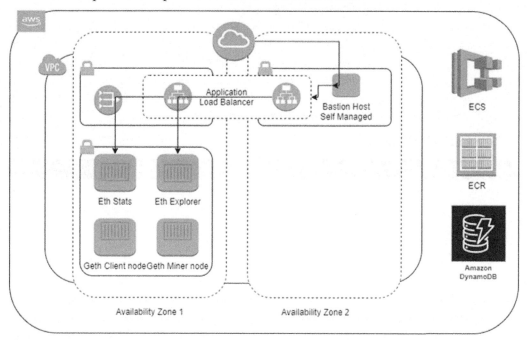

Figure 9.2:Ethereum network architecture with ECS container platform

Let's create the Ethereum network, by provisioning the above resources step by step.

Create a VPC and subnets

We will create a virtual network with VPC and provision all the Ethereum resources into this virtual network. We will also create two private subnets and one public subnet.

Create Elastic IP address

Here, we will create a static Elastic IP address which is a public IPV4 address, that enables communication with the internet.

Steps to create an Elastic IP address are as follows:

1. Open **https://console.aws.amazon.com/vpc/**.
2. Use the same region as Ohio (us-east-2).

3. Select Elastic IPs option.
4. Click on **Allocate new address**.

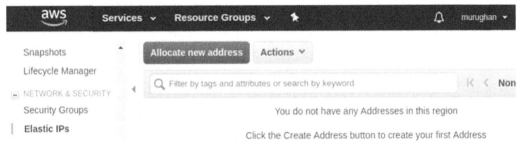

Figure 9.3: Allocate new address

5. Click on **Allocate**.

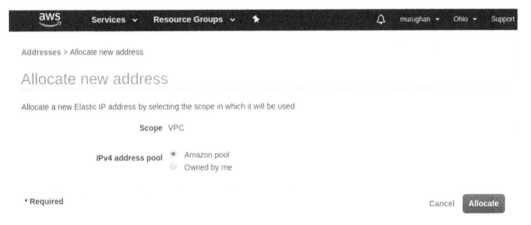

Figure 9.4: Click on Allocate

6. After creating, make a note of the Elastic IP. We will use this IP while creating a public subnet.

Create VPC, one public, and one private Subnet

Virtual Private Cloud (VPC) allows us to create private networks and resources that are logically isolated AWS cloud. Here we will create a VPC with one public and one private subnet.

Steps to create VPC, one public, and one private Subnet are as follows:

1. Select **Ohio (us-east-2a)** region.
2. Select **Launch VPC Wizard** from **https://console.aws.amazon.com/vpc/**.
3. In *Step 1*: Select a **VPC Configuration** option, select **VPC with Public and Private Subnets**.

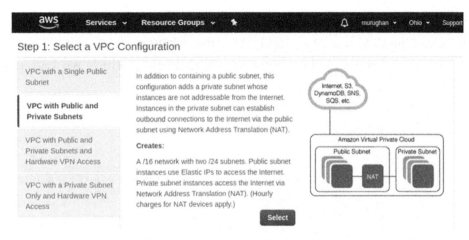

Figure 9.5: *Select a VPC Configuration*

4. Give values for the **VPC Name**, **Public subnet name**, **Private subnet name**. Select **Availability Zone** as the **Ohio (us-east-2a)** region for this configuration. Select the Elastic IP (which we have created in the previous step) as the following screenshot. This will create the VPC with one public and one private subnet:

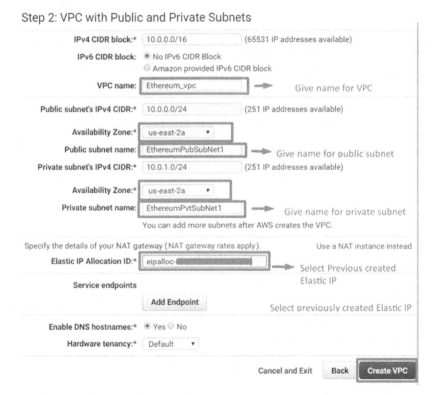

Figure 9.6: *Provide required values*

5. After providing all the values, click on the **Create VPC** button.

6. Once the VPC is created, Navigate to the **Subnets**.

7. Select the public subnet **EthereumPubSubNet1,** which we had created earlier.

8. Note down Root Table id for later use.

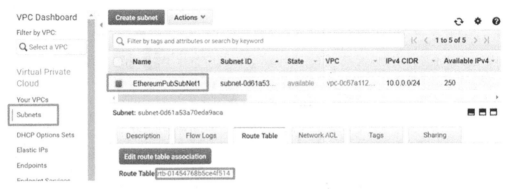

Figure 9.7: Note down Root Table id

9. This Root Table id will be used while creating second public subnet **EthereumPubSubNet2**.

Create a second public subnet in different Availability zone

In the previous step we have created subnets in us-east-2a zone. In this step, we will be creating a public subnet in us-east-2b availability zone.

Steps to create a second public Subnet are as follows:

1. Navigate to **Subnets**.

2. Click on **Create subnet**.

3. Fill the value for thefollowing:

   a) **Name Tag**: EthereumPubSubNet2

   b) **VPC**: Select **Ethereum_vpc**

   c) **Availability Zone**: us-east-2b

   d) **IPv4 CIDR block**: 10.0.2.0/24

4. Click on **Create** to create the second subnet.

Create subnet

Specify your subnet's IP address block in CIDR format; for example, 10.0.0.0/24. IPv4 block sizes must be between a /16 netmask and /28 netmask, and can be the same size as your VPC. An IPv6 CIDR block must be a /64 CIDR block.

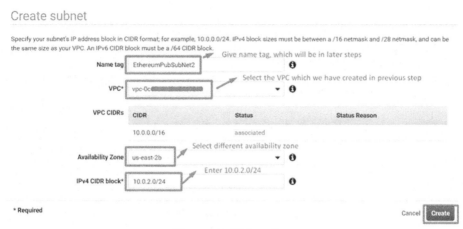

Give name tag, which will be in later steps

Name tag EthereumPubSubNet2 ⓘ

Select the VPC which we have created in previous step

VPC* vpc-0c⬛⬛⬛⬛⬛⬛⬛⬛⬛ ▾ ⓘ

VPC CIDRs

CIDR	Status	Status Reason
10.0.0.0/16	associated	

Select different availability zone

Availability Zone us-east-2b ▾ ⓘ

Enter 10.0.2.0/24

IPv4 CIDR block* 10.0.2.0/24 ⓘ

* Required   Cancel **Create**

Figure 9.8: Click on Create

5. Modify auto-assign Ip:

   a) Select **EthereumPubSubNet2** subnet.

   b) Under **Actions** button.

   c) Select **Modify auto-assign IP settings**.

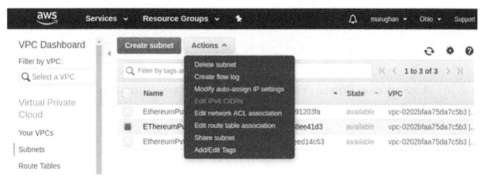

Figure 9.9: Modify auto-assign Ip

   d) Select **Auto-assign IPV4** and save these settings.

Subnets > Modify auto-assign IP settings

Modify auto-assign IP settings

Enable the auto-assign IP address setting to automatically request a public IPv4 or IPv6 address for an instance launched in this subnet. You can override the auto-assign IP settings for an instance at launch time.

Subnet ID subnet-019238d3c435a3366

Auto-assign IPv4 ☑ Enable auto-assign public IPv4 address ⓘ

* Required   Cancel **Save**

Figure 9.10: Auto-assign IPV4

6. Edit Root Table

 a) Select public Subnet **EthereumPubSubNet2**.

 b) Navigate to **Route Tables** tab.

 c) Click on **Edit route table association**.

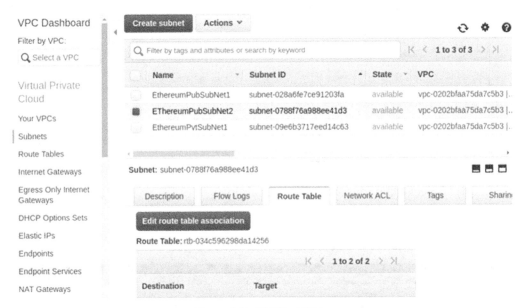

Figure 9.11: Edit Root Table

 d) Change the **Route Table ID** to the one we copied in the earlier step.

Subnets > Edit route table association

Edit route table association

Subnet ID subnet-019238d3c435a3366

Route Table ID* rtb-01454768b5ce4f514   ▼ C

	K < 1 to 2 of 2 > >|
Destination	**Target**
10 0 0 0/16	local
0 0 0 0/0	igw-06a00a30a12da61b8

* Required   Cancel   Save

Figure 9.12: Change the Route Table ID

We have created VPC, two public subnets, and one private subnet. You should have something like this:

Figure 9.13: *Verify*

This completes creating VPC and Subnets. In the next step, we will create security groups.

Create security groups

Security groups in AWS control the inbound and outbound traffic, we will be creating two security groups in AWS. One to control traffic to EC2 instance and second to control traffic to load balancer. Each security group has rules associated with them.

These security groups will also add rules for Ethereum nodes to communicate with other nodes in the network.

Creating a security group for EC2 instance

We will be creating the security group for the EC2 instance to control the traffic flow to our network.

Steps to create a security group for EC2 instance as follows:

1. Open the EC2 page.

2. Navigate to **Security Groups**.

3. Select **Create Security Group**.

4. Give details for the following:

    a) **Security group name**: **EthereumEC2-SG**

    b) **Description**: **Security group for Ethereum template EC2 instance**

c) **VPC**: Select `Ethereum_vpc`

d) Click on **Create**.

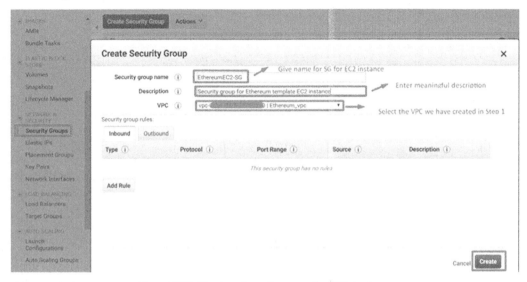

Figure 9.14: Create a Security group for EC2 instance

Inbound and **Outbound** rules will be added in the later steps.

Creating a Security Group for Load Balancer

In this step, we will be creating a security group to control external traffic to the LoadBalancer and a bastion host.

Steps to create a security group for load balancer are as follows:

1. Open the EC2 page

2. Navigate to `Security Groups`

3. Select `Create Security Group`

4. Give details for the following:

   a) `Security group name`: `EthereumELB-SG`

   b) `Description`: `Security group for Ethereum template load balancer`

   c) **VPC**: Select `Ethereum_vpc`

   d) Click on **Create**

Security Groups > Create security group

Create security group

A security group acts as a virtual firewall for your instance to control inbound and outbound traffic. To create a new security group fill in the fields below.

Security group name* EthereumELB-SG

ⓘ

Description* Security group for Ethereum template load balancer

ⓘ

VPC vpc-▓▓▓▓▓▓▓▓▓▓▓▓▓ ▼

ⓘ

* Required   Cancel   **Create**

Figure 9.15: Create a Security group for load balancer

Inbound and Outbound rules will be added in the later steps.

Adding Inbound rules for an EC2 security group

Inbound rules allow us to control the allow or block incoming requests from specific sources. We will add one rule to establish communication between Load Balancer and the EC2 instance and another rule to make communication across all the resources in EC2 instances.

Steps to create add inbound rules to the EC2 Security group are as follows:

1. Navigate to **Security Groups**.

2. Select the Security Group **EthereumEC2-SG,** which we have created in theprevious step.

3. Click on **Inbound**.

4. Select **Edit** option.

5. Add two rules as shown in the following screenshot:

    a) **Rule1**: Select **EthereumEC2-SG**

    b) **Rule2**: Select **EthereumELB-SG**

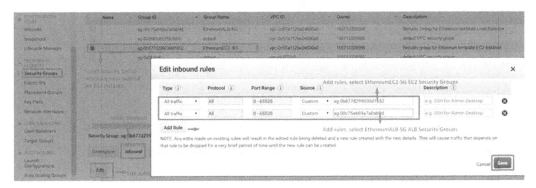

Figure 9.16: Add inbound rules to EC2 Security group

6. Click on **Save** after adding rules.

Editing outbound rules for Load Balancersecurity group

Outbound rules allow outbound connections to EC2 from Load Balancer and the Bastion host. Load Balancer talks to itself and to the Bastion host.

Steps to add outbound rules to load balancer Security group are as follows:

1. Select **EtherumELB-SG** security group.
2. Click on the**Outbound** tab.
3. Select **Edit**.
4. Delete the default rules.
5. Add the followingrules:

   Rule1: Select **EthereumEC2-SG**

   Rule2: Select **EthereumELB-SG**

Create an IAM Role

Access to AWS resources is controlled through **identity and access management(IAM)** resources. The IAM roles are associated with policies. We will create IAM roles with the permission policy, which will be used while provisioning the Ethereum network. We will create an IAM Role for Amazon ECS and an EC2 instance profile.

Creating IAM role for ECS

We will be creating an ECS role to allow Elastic container service to access other AWS resources. This role allows ECS to create and manage AWS resources on our behalf.

Steps to create an IAM role for ECS are as follows:

1. Open **https://console.aws.amazon.com/iam/.**

2. Navigate to **Roles**.

3. Select **Create Role**.

4. Under Select, type of trusted entity, choose **Elastic Container Service**.

5. Under Select your use case, choose **Elastic Container Service**.

6. Click on **Next:Permissions**.

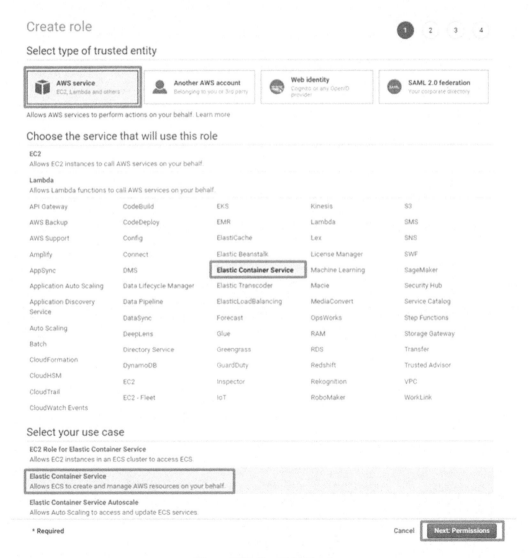

Figure 9.17: Creat3 IAM role

7. On clicking **Next: Permissions**, the consecutive options we can leave it default.

8. On **Review** page, give the following detail:

    Role name: EthereumECSRole

    Role Description: Allows ECS to create and manage AWS resources on your behalf

9. Click on **Create role**.

Figure 9.18: Create role

10. After the role is created, in the **Summary** tab, copy the **Role ARN** as shown in the following screenshot:

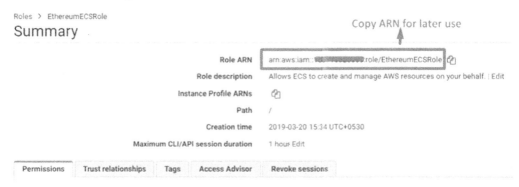

Figure 9.19: Copy the Role ARN

We will be using Role ARN while provisioning Ethereum network.

Creating an EC2 instance profile

We will be creating a role which allow EC2 instances that run our private Ethereum network to access other AWS resources.

Creating a policy

Now we will create a policy that will contain the permissions associated with this role.

Steps to create a policyare as follows:

1. Got to the IAM page.

2. Navigate to **Policies**.

3. Select **Create Policy**.

4. Select **JSON** option from the tab, add below JSON setting the following code that gives access to Ethereum node permission to access container registry, DynamoDB, and logs:

```
{
    "Version": "2012-10-17",
    "Statement": [
        {
            "Effect": "Allow",
            "Action": [
                "ecs:CreateCluster",
                "ecs:DeregisterContainerInstance",
                "ecs:DiscoverPollEndpoint",
                "ecs:Poll",
                "ecs:RegisterContainerInstance",
                "ecs:StartTelemetrySession",
                "ecs:Submit*",
                "ecr:GetAuthorizationToken",
                "ecr:BatchCheckLayerAvailability",
                "ecr:GetDownloadUrlForLayer",
                "ecr:BatchGetImage",
                "logs:CreateLogStream",
                "logs:PutLogEvents",
```

```
                    "dynamodb:BatchGetItem",
                    "dynamodb:BatchWriteItem",
                    "dynamodb:PutItem",
                    "dynamodb:DeleteItem",
        "dynamodb:GetItem",
                    "dynamodb:Scan",
                    "dynamodb:Query",
                    "dynamodb:UpdateItem"
                ],
                "Resource": "*"
            }
        ]
}
```

5. After pasting this JSON configuration, click on **Review policy**.

6. Give the following details:

   Name: **EthereumPolicyEC2**

7. Click on **Create policy**.

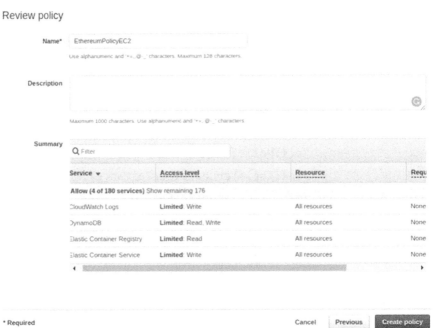

Figure 9.20: Create policy

This will create the policy for an EC2 instance.

Creating a role

We will be creating a role for the EC2 instance and attaching the EthereumPolicyEC2 to this role.

Steps to create a role are as follows:

1. Select **Roles.**

2. Click on **Create Role**.

3. Select **AWS service**.

4. Choose **EC2** under **Choose the service that will use this role**.

5. Choose **EC2** under **Select your use case**.

6. Click on **Next: permissions**.

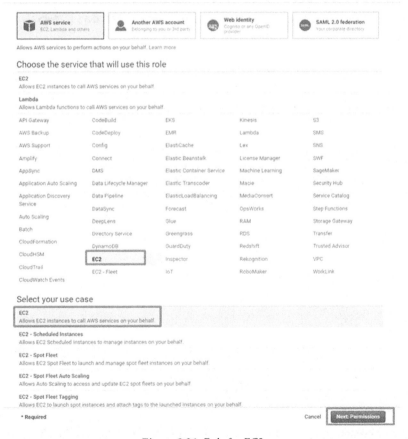

Figure 9.21: Role for EC2

7. In the Search field, select the policy name as **EthereumPolicyEC2,** which we have created in the last step.

Figure 9.22: Set permission

8. Give the following details:

   Role name: EthereumEC2Role

   Role Description: Allow EC2 instances to call AWS services on yourbehalf.

Figure 9.23: Create role

9. Click on **Create role**.

10. After creating, in the summary tab, copy the **Instance Profile ARN** for later use.

Figure 9.24: Instance profile ARN

So far, we have created ElasticIP, VPC, Subnets, and IAM Roles. In the next section, we will be creating a Bastion host.

Creating Bastion host

The Ethereum network that we will be creating is a private network, so we need to create a Bastion host with a public subnet that accepts requests from outside our VPC. Bastion host forwards SSH traffic to the Ethereum network. A Bastion host is an Ec2 instance used toconnect to the web interfaces and instances in your Ethereum network.

A Bastion host has IP which is accessed from outside the VPC. Launch Bastion host in second public subnet which we have created earlier, and is also associated with the load balancer security group.

Creating Linux instance

Here we will create a Linux EC2 instance for the Bastion host.

Steps to create Linux instance are as follows:

1. Open **https://console.aws.amazon.com/ec2/**.

2. Choose **Launch Instance**.

3. Select free tier AMI as **Amazon Linux 2**.

4. Select **t2.micro**.

5. Choose **Edit Instance Details**.

6. Under **Network** choose the **Ethereum_vpc**.

7. Under **Subnet**, select second public subnet **EthereumPubSubNet2** as shown in following screenshot:

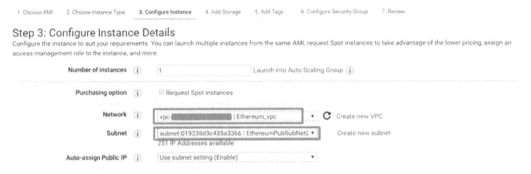

Figure 9.25: Configure public subnet

8. Select default values till **Configure Security Group**.

9. Go to **Configure Security Group** section.

10. Under **Assign a security group** selects the option **Select an existing security group**.

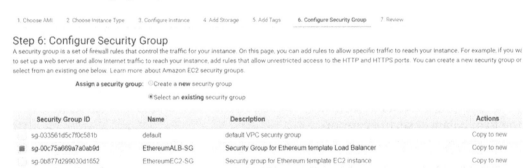

Figure 9.26: Security group configuration

11. Select **EthereumELB-SG**.

12. Verify everything once again and click on **Review** and **Launch**.

Once the instance is provisioned, make a note of the Public address of this instance for later use.

Provision private Ethereum network

So far, we have created all the pre-requisites to create our private Ethereum network. In this step, we will create a private Ethereum network by passing the required parameter to AWS Blockchain CloudFormation template.

Step 1: Launching the Cloud Formation template

1. Visit **https://us-east2.console.aws.amazon.com/cloudformation/ home?region=us-east-2#/stacks/quickcreate?templateURL=https://aws-blockchain-templates-us-east-2.s3.us-east-2.amazonaws.com/ethereum/ templates/latest/ethereum-network.template.yaml.**

2. This will launch **CloudFormation** stack. Enter the name of the stack in the **Stack name** textbox. This name will be used for all the resources in the stack.

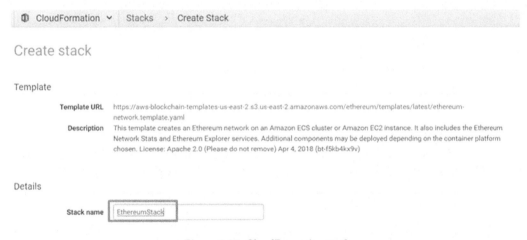

Figure 9.27: CloudFormation stack

This name will be used by CloudFormation all the resources it provisions.

Step2: Entering the network details

In this step, we will pass all the necessary parameters for the Ethereum network.

Keep all the values to default for the following fields:

- **Ethereum Network ID: 1234** (use number apart from 1 to 4)

- **Gas Price floor: 0**

- **Ethereum Node Log Level**: Info

- **Target Block Gas Limit**: 8000000

Parameters

Parameters are defined in your template and allow you to input custom values when you create or update a stack.

Ethereum network parameters

Ethereum Network ID

The ID of the Ethereum network. An ID between 1 and 4 specifies public Ethereum networks. Public networks do not require private Ethereum network parameters, which are used in the genesis block.

```
1234
```

Gas Price Floor

The minimum gas price for a transaction that the miners accept to include a transaction in a block in WEI.

```
0
```

Ethereum Node Log Level

The log level of the Ethereum node

```
Info                                                                          ▼
```

Target Block Gas Limit

The limit on the total amount of gas that can be spent for transactions in a block. This is the target block gas limit for the miner, not the starting block gas limit set in the genesis block.

```
8000000
```

Figure 9.28: Network details

Step3: Entering the Private Ethereum network parameters

1. Copy the MetaMask account address, which you have created in the previous chapter. If not, please create a new account, and copy the address.

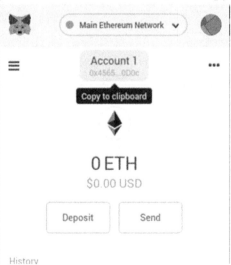

Figure 9.29: Copy the MetaMask account address

2. Paste the address in the **Initial List of Accounts** and **Miner Account Address**, and leave the other fields to the default value.

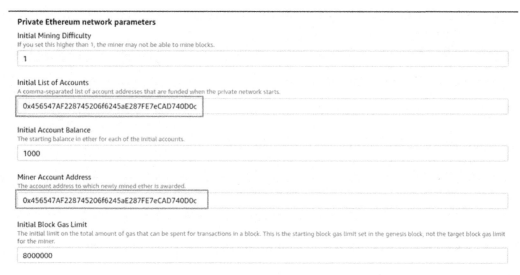

Figure 9.30: *Initial List of Accounts and Miner Account Address*

This will allocate 1000 Ether for this Ethereum account.

Step4: Entering the AWS Platform Specific configuration

1. **`Container Platform`: `ecs`**

2. **EC2 instance type**: You can select different instances based on your needs.

Figure 9.31: *Enter the AWS Platform Specific configuration*

Step5: Entering the EC2 Configurations

Select the following value for each field:

- **`EC2 Key Pair`**: Select the key pair created at the beginning of this chapter.

- **`EC2 Security Group`**: Select **`EthereumEC2-SG`**.

- **EC2 Instance Profile ARN**: Paste **Instance Profile ARN** which you copied while creatingthe EC2 role.

Figure 9.32: Paste Instance Profile ARN

Step6: Selecting the VPC network configuration

Select the following value for each field:

- VPC ID: Select **Ehereum_vpc**.

- Ethereum Network Subnet IDs: Select **EthereumPvtSubNet1** (private subnet).

Figure 9.33: Select the VPC network configuration

Step7: Entering the ECS cluster configuration

Leave the values to default and if you need more nodes, you can modify here.

Figure 9.34: Enter the ECS cluster configuration

Step8: Selecting the Application Load Balancer configuration (ECS only)

Select the following value for each field:

- **Application Load Balancer Subnet IDs**: Select **EthereumPubSubNet1**and **EthereumPubSubNet2** (two public subnets).

- **Application Load Balancer Security Group**: Select **EthereumALB-SG** securitygroup

- **IAM Role**: Paste the ARN copied while creating an ECS IAM role.

Application Load Balancer configuration (ECS only)

Application Load Balancer Subnet IDs	subnet-019238d3c435a3366 (10.0.2.0/24) (EthereumPubSubNet2) ✕
	subnet-0d61a53a70eda9aca (10.0.0.0/24) (EthereumPubSubNet1) ✕
	The IDs of at least two subnets into which the Application Load Balancer is launched. These should be in different Availability Zones.
Application Load Balancer Security Group	EthereumALB-SG (sg-00c75a669a7a0ab... ▾
	The name of an existing security group to assign to the Application Load Balancer in the stack.
IAM Role	arn:aws:iam::155713328566:role/EthereumEC The ARN of the role that ECS uses to interact with Application Load Balancers.

Figure 9.35: Set Application Load Balancer configuration

Make sure you are selecting the right Subnets and entering the IAM of the CES role.

Step 9: Entering the EthStats and the EthExplorer password

Enter the password to provision the Ethstats monitoring tool to check the health of the Blockchain network.

Step 10: Validating all the details and submitting the request.

It will take some time to provision, if anything fails, please verify the steps again and relaunch.

Once the **CloudFormation** is successfully provisioned, you should get the status as
`CREATE_COMPLETE`.

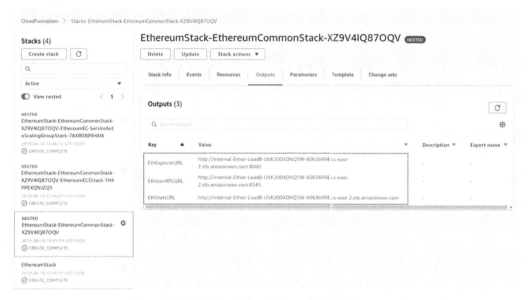

Figure 9.36: Validate all the details and Submit the request

With these steps, we have created the Ethereum private network in AWS. In the next
step, we will connect to the Ethereum network, EthStats, and EthExplorer.

Connecting to EthStats and EthExplorer using the Bastion host

We will connect to Ethereum RPC, EthStats, and EthExplorer through Bastion host
and then set up the SSH tunneling.

Steps to establishing a connection from your computer are as follows:

1. Get the Bastion host IP address.
2. Connect to Bastion host.
3. Configure FoxyProxy.
4. Access EthStat and EthExplorer with FoxyProxy.

Step1: Get Bastion host IP address

- Open EC2 page
- Navigate to Instances
- Select **Bastion Host** and copy the IP address

Figure 9.37: *Get Bastion host IP address*

Step 2: Connect to the Bastion host

The following step is for Mac and Linux:

1. Open your terminal.

2. Change directory to the path where you have saved the .pem file.

3. Enter the following command by changing your .pem file name and your bastion host IP.

   ```
   $ssh -i xxxx.pem ec2-user@ip-address-of-Bastionhost -D 9001
   ```

4. You should be able to SSH successfully to bastion host as shown in the following screenshot:

```
murughan@murughan-Inspiron-5570:~/Downloads$ ssh -i murughan.pem  ec2-user@18.21
6.172.99 -D 9001
Last login: Mon Jun 10 16:19:00 2019 from 27.7.30.21

       __|  __|_  )
       _|  (     /   Amazon Linux 2 AMI
      ___|\___|___|

https://aws.amazon.com/amazon-linux-2/
[ec2-user@ip-10-0-2-89 ~]$ 
```

Figure 9.38: *Connect to the Bastion host*

The following steps are for Windows:

1. Generate key through PuttyGen. Download PuttyGen for Windows from **https://the.earth.li/~sgtatham/putty/0.71/w64/puttygen.exe** and install it in your computer.

2. Then, open PuttyGen, and load the Private key which we have created in the previous steps.

Figure 9.39: Connect Bastion host

3. Next, load the Private Key that we have created in AWS earlier.

4. Save the private key as the same name without an extension like murughan.

5. Connect to Bastion host through SSH forwarding.

6. Download Putty for Windows from **https://www.putty.org/**.

7. Open Putty, enter the Host name and the Hostname details from AWS instance in this format ec2-user@public-id.

8. Expand **Connection**, expand **SSH,** and under **Auth** option, load the key that we have created through **puttyGen** tool in the previous step.

9. Under **Tunnels**, enter **Source port** as **9001**, select **Dynamic** and click on **Open**.

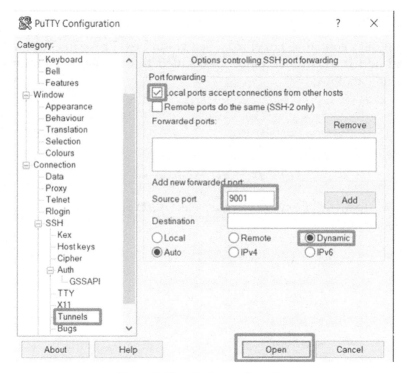

Figure 9.40: puttyGen configuration

10. You should be able to SSH successfully to bastion host as shown in the following screenshot:

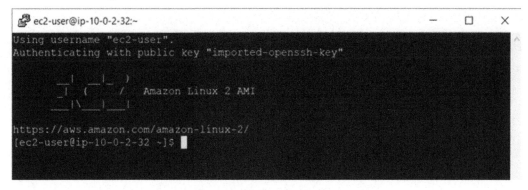

Figure 9.41: ssh to bastion host

11.   If the connection is failing, then validate the steps and try again.

Step3: Configure FoxyProxy

1. Now, let's configure FoxyProxy. Search for FoxyProxy in Chrome extension, and add it to chrome. Once it is added to Chrome, it will appear in the chrome toolbox.

Figure 9.42: FoxyProxy chrome extension

2. Now, open the FoxyProxy and select **Options** as seen in the following screenshot:

Figure 9.43: Options

3. Click on **Add New Proxy** and add localhost under **Host or IP Address**.Port **9001** and save the details.

Figure 9.44: Adding New Proxy

4. Add the **URL Pattern**, and save the changes.

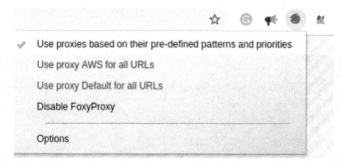

Figure 9.45: Adding URL Pattern

5. Select **Use proxies based on their pre-defined patterns and priorities**, and it will redirect the requests through the bastion host.

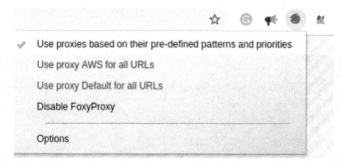

Figure 9.46: Use proxies

6. Make sure your Terminal/Putty connection to bastion host is still connected.

Step4: Access EthStat with FoxyProxy

Now, let's connect to EthStats. Once the connection is successful and FoxyProxy is set up, go to your Cloudformation stack output, and click on the **EthStatsURL** link.

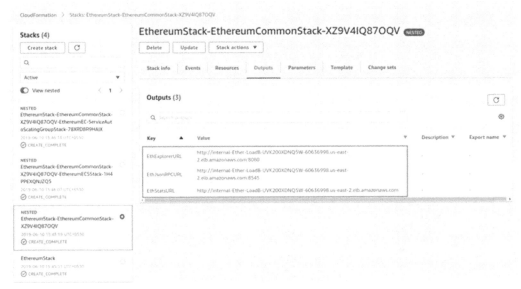

Figure 9.47: EthStatsURL link

Navigate to **EthStatsURL** in the chrome browser and make sure to use proxies based on their pre-defined patterns. Priority is selected under FoxyProxy chrome extension.

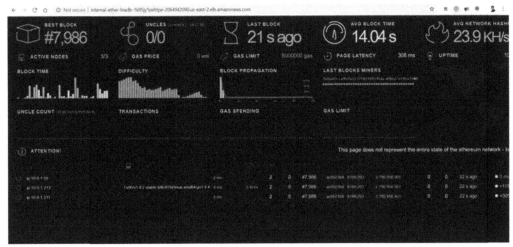

Figure 9.48: EthStatsURL

Next, let's connect to the EthExplorer. From the Cloud Formation output, Open the **EthExplorerURL** link in Chrome browser, and make sure to use proxies based on their pre-defined patterns, and priorities is selected under FoxyProxy chrome extension. You should see a screen like the following screenshot:

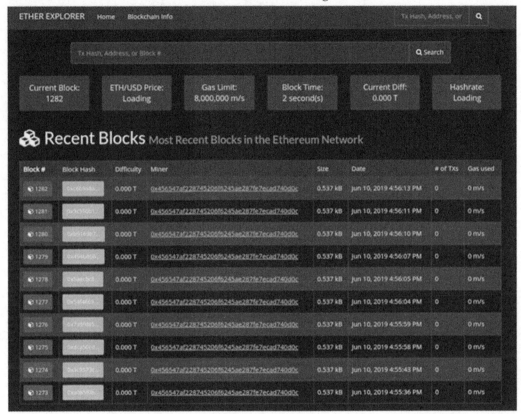

Figure 9.49: EthExplorer

Here you can explore each block details, as and when transaction is happening, and this will reflect the latest changes.

Connecting to AWS Ethereum network with Metamask

We will be using MetaMask to interact with our private Ethereum networks.

Steps to connect to RPC URL are as follows:

1. Copy the **EthJsonRPCURL** from Cloud Formation stack output.
2. Open MetaMask, Select **Custom RPC** under **Network**.

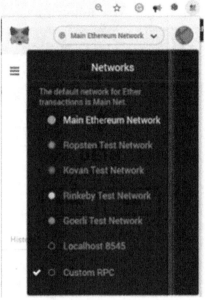

Figure 9.50: Select Custom RPC

3. Paste the copied **EthJsonRPCURL** under the **New RPC URL**.

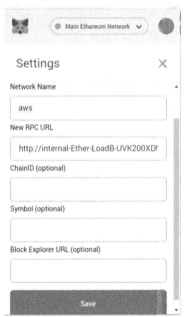

Figure 9.51: EthJsonRPCURL

4. Enter **Network Name**: **aws**.

5. You should be able to see your account with **1000 ETH** and connected to AWSEthereum private network.

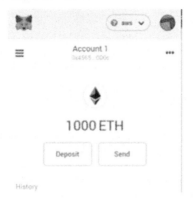

Figure 9.52: *AWS Ethereum private network connection*

We have successfully connected to the AWS Ethereum network with MetaMask.

Conclusion

We have created our Ethereum network in the Ohio region through AWS blockchain templates.

You have learned to provision VPC, Elastic IP, Subnet, roles, and many other AWS resources. We learned to create our own Ethereum private network through AWSblockchain templates. We have learned to create a Bastion host to accept requests outside the VPC to interact withour private Ethereum network. Also, we have learned to use MetaMask to connect to our network.

In the next chapter, we will write a smart Asset Management smart contract with Solidity and deploy it to this network.

Points to remember

- AWS blockchain templates provide a fast and easy way to create and deploy blockchain networks on AWS for Ethereum and Hyperledger Fabric. You can create both private andpublic Ethereum networks with AWS.

- You can connect to AWS Ethereum private network through MetaMask.

Multiple choice questions

1. AWS blockchain templates are available for:

   a) Ethereum

   b) Hyperledger Fabric

   c) All the above

Answer

1. c

Questions

1. What is AWS blockchain template?

2. Create Ethereum private network for healthcare supply chain.

Key Terms

AWS Blockchain Templates: AWS blockchain templates provide a fast and easy way to create and deploy blockchain networks on AWS for Ethereum and Hyperledger Fabric. You can create both private and public Ethereum network with AWS. AWS provides certified Cloud Formation template to create a blockchain network. AWS Cloud Formation allows us to model our complete infrastructure in a text file to provision the resources in an automated way, and this file serves as a single source of truth and helps us to treat the infrastructure as code.

CHAPTER 10

Solidity Smart Contract Language

In the previous chapter, we have understood how Ethereum works and we have also built an Ethereum network in AWS. In this chapter, we will learn the language solidity to write smart contracts.

Structure

In this chapter, we will discuss the following topics:

- What is a smart contract?
- How smart contract works within Ethereum
- Solidity—language to write a smart contract
- Solidity compiler and solidity files
- Structure of a contract
- Data types, functions, modifiers
- Conditional statements and loops
- Constructors, inheritance, and polymorphism
- Abstract contract and interface
- Libraries
- Exceptions, events, and logging

Objectives

After studying this unit, you should be able to:

- Understand what is a smart contract
- Understand solidity language
- Writesmart contract

Understanding smart contract

In this section, we will understand what is a smart contract, why is it important, and when we should create smart contracts.

Smart contract

A smart contract is a computer code which has a set of business rules between two parties in a business. Smart contracts are deployed into the Ethereum blockchain and run on it as a self-operating computer program that automatically executes while specific conditions are met or executed based on the event. Once the contract executes a particular action, it makes an entry into the blockchain ledger as an immutable record.

A smart contract is immutable which means it's tamper-proof. It's automation in the decentralized world and executes automatically when the condition is met, and smart contract governs the behavior of the Ethereum accounts in the network.

For example, consider that Alice and Bob have a business. In the traditional business model, Alice and Bob will involve a bank as a middleman, and create paper agreements to smoothly run the business. However, this model is having a few downsides such as delay in payment processing, chances of fraud are high, transactions are stored in traditional databases which leads to data tampering.

With blockchain, Alice and Bob can do business together as all the business rules are written in the smart contract as a program and deployed over the Ethereum network. Smart contract releases/stops the fund transfer based on the business rules. This automates the entire process, doesn't require any third party, payments happen faster, and the important thing is that you can do business with anyone in the world without any paperwork and this enables a trustless trust system.

Where to use smart contract

Smart contracts revolutionize the way we run a business. We can write a smart contract for various industries and multiple business use-cases. The following are some of the use-cases where you can write a smart contract:

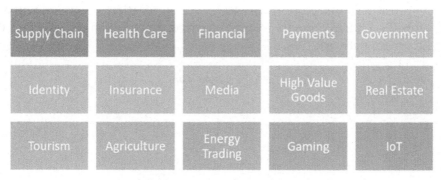

Figure 10.1: use-cases of a smart contract

For example, in the case of a supply chain, all the parties/participants in the supply chain agree to common business rules in the way they want to transact. These rules are coded into the system as a smart contract and the smart contract executes when certain rules are met.

Solidity - a smart contract language for Ethereum

Solidity is the language used to write smart contracts within the Ethereum network and runs on **Ethereum Virtual Machine (EVM)**. It is an object-oriented, high-level language and the syntax of the solidity language is like JavaScript. Solidity is statically typed and contract-oriented language. Solidity also supports inheritance, polymorphism, libraries, and user-defined types.

Solidity files and compiler

Solidity files are written with the .sol extension. The code written in the .sol file has the program definitions; this code will be fed into the solidity compiler which then compiles the code and creates two separate outputs as follows:

- **Byte code:** It will be deployed onto the Ethereum network.

- **Application binary interface (ABI)**: Our application's frontend will interact with the ABI to connect to our smart contract which is deployed on the Ethereum network.

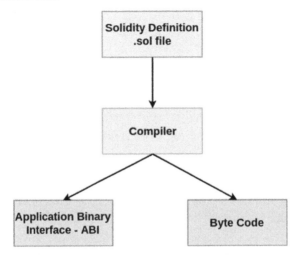

Figure 10.2:Solidity files and compiler

Solidity editor - Remix

Solidity smart contracts can be written and compiled in multiple ways as follows:

1. Remix - online editor

2. solc compiler in Visual Studio Code IDE

3. Truffle

In this chapter, we will use Remix the online editor to create, compile, and test oursmart contracts.

Create, compile, deploy and run your first smart contract

Let's write a simple contract to understand the structure of a solidity program, this program returns a welcome message to the user who calls this contract's function.

The steps to write our first smart contract are as follows:

1. Open the Remix online editor with this link **https://remix.Ethereum.org.**

2. Create a new file called Welcome.sol in Remix editor as shown in the following screenshot:

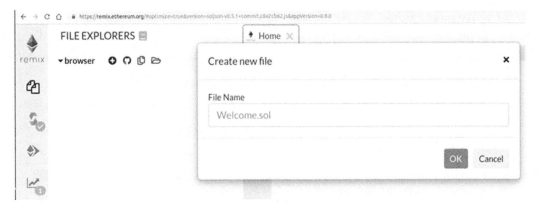

Figure 10.3: File creation

3. Mention the solidity compiler version to the `Welcome.sol` file, copy the following code:

```
pragma solidity >=0.4.25 <0.6.0;
```

The first line of the preceding contract which is `pragma solidity >=0.4.25 <0.6.0;` implies that the code can be executed by any solidity version above **0.4.25** and below **0.6.0**.

4. Create a contract called `Welcome` and add the following code to the `Welcome.sol` file. Here the `contract` is the keyword to create a new smart contract and `Welcome` is the name of the contract. Also, you can create any number of contracts in the same file.

```
contract Welcome
{
}
```

5. Create a variable—smart contracts can have any number of variables. Here we will create a variable called a `message` to hold a welcome message and add the following code to the `Welcome.sol` file:

```
string private message = "Welcome to Blockchain on AWS";
```

6. Create a function to return a welcome message—smart contracts can have any number of functions with a relevant access specifier. Here, we will create a function called `WelcomeMessage()` which is a public method. This means anyone can call this function and return the welcome message. Copy the following code to the `Welcome.sol` file:

```
function WelcomeMessage() public view returns (string memory){
        return message;
    }
```

7. We have created our first smart contract. Let's verify our code, it should look like the following screenshot:

Figure 10.4: Verifying the code

8. Compiling the Welcome contract.

   a) Navigate to the **Compile** tab in Remix

   b) Select the right **Compiler** version, here, select solidity 0.5.1version

   c) Select the **Auto compile** option

   d) If there are no errors in the code, you should see Welcome.sol in the **Contract** dropdown

Figure 10.5: Compile the Welcome contract

9. Once the contract is compiled successfully, it's time to deploy the contract to the inbuilt blockchain in the Chrome browser.

   a) Navigate to the **Run** tab

   b) Select JavaScript VM under the **Environment** dropdown, which means we are deploying smart contract to the Ethereum blockchain network inside Chrome.

   c) JavaScript VM comes with free Ethereum accounts, so the first account will be used to deploy our contract. Select the first account under the **Account** dropdown.

d) Select the **Welcome** contract in the **contract** dropdown.

e) Click on the **Deploy** button which will deploy our contract to Ethereum blockchain inbuilt in the browser.

Figure 10.6: Deploy the contract

10. Running Welcome smart contract.

a) Once the Welcome contract is deployed, you will get the option to invoke the contract function.

b) Click on the **WelcomeMessage** button to invoke our contract function which will return the output as per the program.

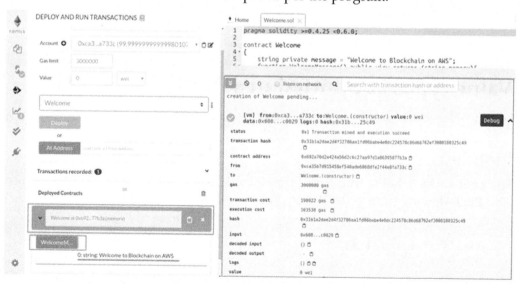

Figure 10.7: Run Welcome smart contract

Our Welcome contract has been successfully compiled, deployed, and tested for the expected behavior.

> Note: We will be following the same approach as above to write, compile, deploy and run all our smart contracts in this chapter.

Exploring data types

Variable created in solidity should mention the state and location. Based on the way variables are assigned and stored in EVM, they are broadly classified as value types and reference types.

Value types

Variables created as a value type directly contain their data and these variables are always passed by the value. Each variable has its own copy of the data within its own memoryspace.

Let's create a new contract in Remix to understand value types:

1. Open the Remix online editor with this link **https://remix.Ethereum.org.**
2. Create a new file called `ValueTypes.sol` in Remix editor.
3. Create a contract called ValueTypes, add the following code to the `ValueTypes.sol` file in Remix editor.

```
pragma solidity >=0.4.25 <0.6.0;

contract ValueTypes {


}
```

Value types supported in solidity

Let's now have a look at the various value types supported in solidity.

boolean

The **bool** variable holds true=1 or false=0 value. The default value for bool is false. Add the following code to the `ValueTypes.sol` file in the Remix editor:

```
bool isTrue = false;


function getBooleanVariable() public view returns (bool) {
    return isTrue;
}
```

int

Solidity provides signed and unsigned integers to store numbers for different sizes from 8 bit to 256 bits. A signed integer can hold both negative and positive values. On the other hand, an unsigned integer can hold only positive values and zero.

```solidity
int item4 = -1;
    int item5 = -6535;

    function getInt() public view returns (int) {
        return item5;
    }

uint item = 5;
    uint8 item2 = 255;
    uint16 item3 = 65535;

    function getUInt() public returns (uint, uint8, uint16) {
        item = 20;
        return (item, item2, item3);
    }
```

address

Special type in solidity to hold an address of smart contracts and accounts, which is of 20 bytes data type. The address has the **balance** property to hold the balance of an account. Address data type provides transfer and sends functions to transfer Ether.

```solidity
address owner;
    address payable owner2;

    function getAddress() public returns (address) {
        owner = msg.sender; //Assign user address to owner variable
        return owner;
    }
    function transferEther() public {
        if (owner2.balance < 30 &&owner.balance>= 30) {
            owner2.transfer(30);
```

```
        }
    }
```

bytes

This is used to store information in binary format, it represents fixed size a byte array. Provides ranges from bytes1 to bytes32. The default value for the byte is 0x00.

```
function getBytes() public pure returns (bytes1, uint) {
        bytes1 byteVar = 0x65;
uintitemInt;


        assembly {
itemInt := byte(0, byteVar)
        }
        return (byteVar, itemInt);
    }
```

enums

Enumerations that can hold predefined constant values where we want to store a list of items, for example, gender as shown in the following code:

```
enum gender {male, female, others}


    function getEnums() public pure returns(gender) {
        return gender.female;
    }
```

Compile and run the preceding contract in the Remix editor:

Referencetypes

Unlike value type, a reference type doesn't store its value directly. Instead, reference types store address to their data. Here multiple variables can reference the same data.

Let's create a new contract in Remix to understand reference types:

1. Create a new file called `ReferenceTypes.sol` in the Remix editor.
2. Create a contract called `ReferenceTypes` and add the following code to the `ReferenceTypes.sol` file in the Remix editor.

   ```
   pragma solidity >=0.4.25 <0.6.0;
   ```

```
contract ReferenceTypes {

}
```

The various reference types supported in solidity are covered in the next sections.

array

An array is a data structure that can hold other data types. A group of values of the same datatypes is stored in an array and it helps to iterate through the data list. Arrays can be of fixed or dynamic length.

```
uint[5] fixedNumbers;

uint[] dynamicNumbers = [1,2,3,4,5];


    function arrays() public returns(uint, uint) {
dynamicNumbers.push(6);
        return ( fixedNumbers.length, dynamicNumbers[3]);
    }
```

string

string literal stores sequence of characters, string can store long sentences as well and uses quotes to add values:

```
string name = "Murughan";

    string country = 'India';
```

mapping

Mapping is used to store key-value pairs such as hash tables ordictionaries. The values are retrieved from mapping based on the key.

```
mapping (uint => address) accounts;

uint counter;


    function addAccounts(address account) public returns (uint) {
        counter++;
        accounts[counter] = account;
        return counter;
    }
    function getAccounts(uint id) public view returns (address) {
```

```
    return accounts[id];
 }
```

struct

Structs are custom defined types, they are used to define user-defined structures.

```
    struct Funder {
address addr;
uint amount;
 }
```

```
    Funder = Funder(msg.sender, 10);
```

Compile and run the preceding contract in the Remix editor.

Functions

Smart contract business logics are written inside functions within the solidity files. Functions are the executable units of code. Using the function, we can read and write to the blockchain ledger which changes the state of a variable in the blockchain ledger. Functions accept parameters and return values.

The visibility of the function is defined through function types.

Let's create a new contract in Remix to understand functions:

Create a new file called `Functions.sol` in the Remix editor, create a contract called `Functions`, add the following code to the `Functions.sol` file in the Remixeditor:

```
pragma solidity >=0.4.25 <0.6.0;

contract Functions {


}
```

Solidity supports function types following:

Public

Anyone with an Ethereum account can call this function.

Private

Functions within the contract can access private functions.

Internal

Only derived contracts and those within a contract can call this function.

External

External functions can be called from other contracts.

View

This function type returns data and does not modify the contract's data.

```
string private message = "Welcome to Blockchain on AWS";
    function ViewFunctionType() public view returns(string memory) {
        return message;
    }
```

Pure

This neither modifies the contract data nor reads it.

```
    function PureFunctionType() public pure returns(string memory) {
        return "Welcome to Blockchain on AWS";
    }
```

Payable

This enables the function to accept Ether while executing the function. The function of payable types can transfer the Ether.

```
    function GetBalance() public payable returns(uint) {
        return msg.sender.balance;
    }
```

Calling the preceding function from different contract.

Let's create one more contract called `Caller` in the `Function.sol` file which will invoke the preceding functions. Add the following code to the `Functions.sol` file in the Remix editor:

```
contract Caller {
    Functions func = new Functions();
    function functionCall() public view returns (string memory) {
        return func.ViewFunctionType();
    }
}
```

This `Caller` contract creates an object of type Functions contract and uses the func object to invoke `ViewFunctionType()`.

Compile and run the preceding contract in the Remix editor.

Function modifiers

Modifiers help in changing the behavior of the function and are used to check the condition prior to executing the function. You can also have multiple modifiers for one function and each modifier is executed and validated sequentially.

Let's create a new contract in Remix to understand function modifiers:

1. Create a new file called `FunctionModifier.sol` in the Remix editor.

2. Create a contract called `FunctionModifier`

3. Add the following code to the `FunctionModifier.sol` file in the Remix editor:

```
pragma solidity >=0.4.25 <0.6.0;

contract FunctionModifier {


}
```

Add all the following code inside the `FunctionModifier` contract and create the `onlyOwner()` modifier which verifies whether the sender is an owner or not.

```
    address payable owner;


    //Constructor for initialization
constructor() public {
        //Get account address
        owner = msg.sender;
    }
    //Modifier verifies whether the sender is the owner or not
    modifier onlyOwner {
if(msg.sender == owner) {

            _;
        }
    }
```

Calling the `selfdestruct` function—the `close()` function will be executed only by the contract owner, before executing the `close()` function it validates against the `onlyOwner()` modifier if this condition whether the sender is the owner or not satisfies only then the `close()` function will be executed.

```
function Close() public onlyOwner {
        //Below statement will be executed only if the user is owner.
    selfdestruct(owner);
        }
```

Compile and run the above contract in Remix editor.

Conditional statements

Solidity supports regular control structures available in other languages like C and JavaScript.

If else decision control

Using if and else, we can write conditional statements.

Let's understand this through code, create a solidity file called `Conditional Statements.sol` in Remix and add the following code:

```
pragma solidity >=0.4.25 <0.6.0;

contract ConditionalStatements {
    function Eligibility(int age) public pure returns(string memory) {

        if (age < 21)
            return "Not Eligible";

        else if(age >= 21 && age <= 60)
            return "Eligible";

        else
            return "Not Eligible";
    }
}
```

Compile and run the preceding contract in the Remix editor.

Loops

Solidity supports while, do-while, and for loop. Let's understand how each one works.

Let's create a new contract in Remix to understand loops:

Create a new file called `Loops.sol` in the Remix editor, create a contract called `Loops`, add the following code to the `Loops.sol` file in the Remix editor:

```solidity
pragma solidity >=0.4.25 <0.6.0;

contract Loops {

uint private counter = 2;

uint private index = 0;

    mapping (uint =>uint) numbers;

}
```

Add all the following code inside the `Loops` contract.

while

While is used when we need to execute statements repeatedly based on a condition. The **while** keyword evaluates the expression, if the evaluation is true then it executes the code until the evaluation false.

```solidity
    function WhileLoop() public {

while (index < counter) {

        index++;

    }

    }
```

for

The **for** keyword enables to loop through the code for n number of times. In each iteration, it increments and executes for the next index.

```solidity
    function ForLoop() public {

for (index = 0; index < counter; index++) {

        numbers[index] = counter;

    }

    }
```

do while

The **do-while** keyword works the same as the **while** loop, the only difference is instructions in the **while** loop will not execute if the condition is false, whereas, in **do while**, the instructions are executed at least once.

```
function DoWhileLoop() public {
    do {
        index++;
    } while (index < counter);
}
```

break

The **break** keyword will exit the loop and execute the next statements outside the loop when the condition is met.

```
function Break() public {
for (index = 0; index < counter; index++) {
    if (index == 1)
        break;
    numbers[index] = counter;
    }
}
```

continue

The **continue** keyword will stop the current iteration and move to the next element in the iteration.

```
function Continue() public {
for (index = 0;index< counter; index++) {
    if (index > 1)
        continue;
    numbers[index] = counter;
    }
}
```

Compile and run the preceding contract in the Remix editor.

Constructors

Constructors are used to initialize the contract's state variables. Constructors are optionaland the compiler induces the default constructor when a constructor is not declared. A constructor iscreated using the **constructor** keyword or the same name as that of the contract. You can have more than one constructor; a constructor is executed while deploying the contract and the initial values tothe constructor should be passed while deploying the contract.

Let's understand this through code, create a solidity file called `Constructor.sol` and add the following code:

```
pragma solidity >=0.4.25 <0.6.0;


contract Constructor {
    string private accountName;
    address payable private owner;


constructor(string memory name) public {
accountName = name;
        owner = msg.sender;

    }
}
```

When you create an object of the preceding contract `Constructor`, contract initialization takes place. Here, it will initiate the `accountName` and `owner` value based on the input.

Inheritance

Within heritance, we can reuse the properties and methods of other classes, contracts can inherit state variables and functions from other contracts. When the child contract is deployed, the code from all the base contracts is compiled and a single contract is created on blockchain. Also, solidity supports multiple inheritances.

The use keyword that inherits from another contract, a contract can access all non-private state variables and functions. Use comma to inherit multiple contracts.

Let's create a new contract in Remix to understand inheritance:

Create a new file called `Inheritance.sol` in the Remix editor. Create a contract called `Inheritance` and add the following code to the `Inheritance.sol` file in the Remix editor:

```
pragma solidity >=0.4.25 <0.6.0;
contract Inheritance {
}
```

Add all the following code inside the `Inheritance` contract.

Create a `Parent` contract with one public function.

```
contract Parent {
uint internal value;

  function SetValue(uint input) public {
    value = input;
  }
}
```

Create a `Child` contract that inherits from the `Parent` contract.

```
contract Child is Parent {
  bool private isValid;

  function GetValue() public view returns (uint) {
    return value;
  }
}
```

Invoke the `Parent` contract function `callInheritedFunctions()` through the `Child` contract.

```
contract Client {
  Child child = new Child();
  function callInheritedFunctions() public returns (uint) {
      //Invoke Parent contract
child.SetValue(10);
      //Invoke Child contract
      return child.GetValue();
  }
```

Create a `Parent2` contract with one variable of internal visibility.

```
contract Parent2 {
```

```
    bool internal eligible;
}
```

Create the `Derived` contract to achieve multiple inheritances, here `Derived` contract can call `Parent` and `Parent2` contract variables and functions.

```
contract Derived is Parent2, Parent {
bool private isValid;

    function GetValue() public view returns (uint) {
      return value;
    }
}
```

Compile and run the preceding contract in the Remix editor.

Polymorphism

Polymorphism allows us to create multiple forms of the function with the same name and difference in parameters. We can achieve both functional overloading and contract overloading.

Contract overloading refers to using multiple contract instances interchangeably when the contracts are related to each other through inheritance. Contract polymorphism helps ininvoking derived contract functions using a base contract instance.

Let's create a new contract in Remix to understand `Polymorphism`:

1. Create a new file called `Polymorphism.sol` in the Remix editor.
2. Create a contract called `Polymorphism`
3. Add the following code to the `Polymorphism.sol` file in the Remix editor:

   ```
   pragma solidity >=0.4.25 <0.6.0;
   contract Polymorphism {
   }
   ```

   Add all the following code inside `Polymorphism` contract.

   Create a function named `Details()` which accepts `uint` as input:

   ```
   function Details(uint age) public pure returns(uint) {
           return age;
       }
   ```

Create a function with the same name as `Details()` but this function accepts two parameters `uint` and `string` as input. This way you can achieve polymorphism in solidity.

```
    function Details(uint age, string memory name) public pure

returns(uint, string memory) {

return (age, name);

    }
```

Compile and run the preceding contract in the Remix editor.

Abstract contracts

Abstract contracts are usually base contracts that have common behaviors and properties which can be used in derived contracts. An abstract contract cannot be instantiated it has to be inherited. The abstract class will have partial functionality and the contract becomes abstract if the functions inside it don't have the implementation.

Let's create a new contract in Remix to understand `AbstractContract`:

Create a new file called `AbstractContract.sol` in the Remix editor and add the following code to the `AbstractContract.sol` file in the Remix editor:

```
pragma solidity >=0.4.25 <0.6.0;
```

Add all the following code inside the `AbstractContract.sol` file.

Create an abstract contract called `AbstractContract` with the setter and getter function.

```
contract AbstractContract {

uint private value = 10;

    function SetValue(uint input) public;

    function GetValue() public view returns (uint) {

        return value;

    }

}
```

Inheriting `AbstractContract` in `Child` contract.

```
contract Child is AbstractContract {

uint private value;


  function SetValue(uint input) public {

  value = input;
```

```
    }
}
```

Since abstract contract cannot be instantiated directly, we will instantiate it with the `Child` contract. Here, with the `child` object `abstractContract` we are able to access the `SetValue()` and `GetValue()` functions.

```
contract Client {

AbstractContractabstractContract;


constructor() public {
abstractContract = new Child();
    }


    function callInheritedFunctions() public returns (uint) {
abstractContract.SetValue(10);
        return abstractContract.GetValue();//Output - 10
    }
}
```

Compile and run the preceding contract in the Remix editor.

Interfaces

Interfaces work like abstract contracts except that interfaces cannot have function definition and it holds only function declarations, derived contracts should implement the functions. Interfaces will not consist of any state variables, interfaces cannot inherit from other contracts, but interfaces can inherit from other interfaces.

Let's create a new contract in Remix to understand interfaces:

1. Create a new file called `Interface.sol` in the Remix editor
2. Add all the following code inside `Interface.sol` file.

   ```
   pragma solidity >=0.4.25 <0.6.0;


   interface IBase {
       function SetValue(uint input) external;
       function GetValue() external view returns (uint);
   }
   ```

Create an interface called `IBase` with two public function declarations `SetValue()` and `GetValue()`, these functions don't have the implementation.

Inherit the `IBase` interface in the `Child` contract and implement the interface methods.

```
contract Child is IBase {
uint private value;

  function SetValue(uint input) public {
   value = input;
}

  function GetValue() public view returns (uint){
   return value;
  }
}
```

Invoke the interface function with `Child` contract. Create a `Child` object through `IBaseinterface` and invoke the `Child` contract functions.

```
contract Client {
IBase obj;

constructor() public {
   obj = new Child();
  }

  function callInheritedFunctions() public returns (uint) {
obj.SetValue(10);
    return obj.GetValue();
   }
}
```

Compile and run the preceding contract in the Remix editor.

Libraries

Libraries help to create and deploy smart contract code once and reuse it in another contract through the DELEGATECALL feature of the EVM. We can even call the library functions without DELEGATECALL for view and pure function types. When the `library` function is called from the contract, it executes in the context of the calling contract.

Let's create a new contract in Remix to understand libraries:

1. Create a new file called `CalculatorLibrary.sol` in Remix editor.
2. Add all the following code inside the `CalculatorLibrary.sol` file.

```solidity
pragma solidity >=0.4.25 <0.6.0;


library Calculator {


    function Add(uint a, uint b) public pure returns (uint) {
        return a + b;
    }
    function Subtract(uint a, uint b) public pure returns (uint) {
        return a - b;
    }
}
```

Create the second solidity file called `UseLibrary.sol` to make use of the preceding `Calculator` library and add the following code to the `UseLibrary.sol` file. With the **import** keyword, we will be able toaccess library contract functions and variables.

```solidity
pragma solidity >=0.4.25 <0.6.0;


import "browser/CalculatorLibrary.sol";


contract UseLibrary {
    using Calculator for uint;
    function Add(uint a, uint b) public pure returns (uint) {
        return Calculator.Add(a,b);
    }
}
```

Error handling

Exceptions can occur for many reasons like out-of-gas error, our contract should handle exceptions very well. Solidity uses state-reverting exception handling through which if any exceptions occur then it will revert the state to the original. There is no try and catch to handle an exception, solidity uses require and assert to do this.

Let's create a new contract in Remix to understand error handling:

1. Create a new file called `ErrorHandling.sol` in the Remix editor.
2. Create a contract called `ErrorHandling`
3. Add the following code to the `toErrorHandling.sol` file in the Remix editor.

```
pragma solidity >=0.4.25 <0.6.0;

contract ErrorHandling {



}
```

Add all the following code inside the `ErrorHandling` contract.

require

The **require** function allows us to put prerequisites for running the function, we can add constraints through the **require** function. The statements inside the **require** function should satisfy, only then the next statement will be executed. We can use this to validate the incoming values of arguments and parameters, validate return data, require will throw anexception if the condition fails.

```
    function Require() public pure {
require(10 > 20);
    }
```

assert

The **assert** function is used to check the internal errors and to check variants. It evaluates the condition, if it's true, it executes the next statement and if the condition fails, then it throws an error. The `Assert` function will revert the changes to previous when an exception occurs. It can also throw an error with a custom message on the exception, assert should be used to validate the current state.

```
    function Assert() public pure {
assert(10 == 20);
    }
```

revert

The **revert** function is like the **require** function, but it does not evaluate any statement. Revert means that the exception is thrown and it reverts to the previous state.

```
    function Revert() public pure {
revert();
    }
```

Events and logging

Events are the changes in the contract. When you call the events, the arguments will be stored in the transaction log into blockchain. These logs are associated with the contract address and cannot be accessed from within contracts. Applications can subscribe and listen to these events through the RPC interface.

Let's create a new contract in Remix to understand `EventsandLogging`:

1. Create a new file called `EventsAndLogging.sol` in the Remix editor.
2. Create a contract called `EventsAndLogging`
3. Add the following code to the `toEventsAndLogging.sol` file in the Remix editor:

```
pragma solidity >=0.4.25 <0.6.0;


contract EventsAndLogging {


}
```

Add all the following code inside the `ErrorHandling` contract.

Create an event to log the sender's address:

```
event LogSenderAddress(address);
```

Invoke the `LogSenderAddress` event to store/log the sender account address:

```
address private owner;
constructor() public {
        owner = msg.sender;
    }
    function () payable external {
        emit LogSenderAddress(msg.sender);
    }
```

With this, we have written solidity smart contracts to learn the language specifics.

Conclusion

A smart contract is immutable which means it's tamper-proof. It's the automation in the decentralized world and executes automatically when the condition is met, and smart contract governs the behavior of Ethereum accounts in the network.

In this chapter, we have learned to write smart contracts with solidity, the Remix tool, and MetaMask usage. With this understanding, you are now ready to write smart contracts for real use-cases.

In the next chapter, we will write a smart contract for the AssetTracking application and we will also deploy it to the AWS Ethereum network.

Points to remember

- A smart contract is a computer code having a set of business rules between two parties in the business. Smart contracts are deployed into the Ethereum blockchain and run on Ethereum blockchain as a self-operating computer program. This program automatically executes while specific conditions are met or executed based on the event. Once the contract executes particular action, it makes an entry to blockchain ledger as an immutable record.

- Solidity is the language used to write smart contracts within the Ethereum network and it runs on EVM. It is an object-oriented, high-level language and the syntax of solidity language is similar to that of JavaScript. Solidity is statically-typed unlike JavaScript which is dynamically typed and contract-oriented language. Solidity also supports inheritance, polymorphism, libraries, and user-defined types.

- Solidity files are written with the `.sol` extension.

- Solidity smart contracts can be written and compiled in multiple ways as follows:
    - o Remix—online editor
    - o Solc compiler in Visual Studio Code IDE
    - o Truffle

Multiple-choice questions

1. Smart contracts are centralized:
    - a) Yes
    - b) No
2. List all the value types:
    - a) Boolean
    - b) Int
    - c) Array
    - d) Address
    - e) String

Answer

1. a

2. a, b, d,

Questions

1. What is asmart contract?

2. Write a smart contract for the healthcare supply chain with solidity.

Key terms

1. **Solidity**: Solidity is the language used to write smart contracts within the Ethereum network and runs on EVM. It is an object-oriented, high-level language and the syntax of solidity language is like JavaScript.

2. `.sol`: Solidity files are written with the `.sol` extension.

3. **Application binary interface (ABI)**: Our application frontend will interact with the ABI to connect to our smart contract which is deployed on the Ethereum network.

4. **Remix**: Online smart contract editor.

CHAPTER 11
Create and Deploy Asset Tracker Contract on AWS

We have explored Solidity - smart contract language, written a few smart contracts, and explored the solidity language. With this knowledge, let us write a smartcontract for the asset tracker application, and deploy it to Ethereum Private blockchain, that we have created in *Chapter 9* AWS Blockchain Template to Create Private Ethereum.

Structure

In this chapter, we will discuss the following topics:

- What is an asset management?
- What are assets?
- Challenges with asset tracking in the real world
- Asset tracker use case
- Local Blockchain network with Ganache
- Truffle framework
- Web3.js
- Identify participants in the asset tracker application
- Creating a participant contract and an asset contract
- Building an asset tracker smart contract with Solidity

- Deploy an AssetTracker smart contact to AWS Ethereum private network

Objectives

After studying this unit, you should be able to:

- Write a smart contract for real-world use case asset management
- Learning Truffle and Web3.js framework
- Deploy AssetTracker smart contract to AWS Ethereum private network

Pre-requisites for this chapter

In this chapter, we are writing AssetTracker smart contract with Solidity language. Please go through the *Chapter 10* Solidity Smart Contract Language before starting this chapter.

You need to complete the following steps before we proceed with this chapter:

1. Ethereum private network should be deployed on AWS as mentioned in the *Chapter 9* AWS Blockchain Template to Create Private Ethereum
2. IDE - You can use any of your preferred IDE; I will be using Visual Studio code
3. Solidity Compiler - Solidity extension to Visual Studio code
4. Chrome browser
5. MetaMask wallet extension in the Chrome browser
6. node.js and npm
7. Solidity compiler for node.js: `npm install -g solc`

Make sure all the pre-requisites are in place before you start the chapter.

Asset Management

Asset management refers to asystematic approach to the governance and realization of value from the things that a group or entity is responsible for, over their entire life cycles. Asset management is a systematic process of developing, operating, maintaining, upgrading, and disposing of assets in the most cost-effective manner (including all costs, risks, and performance attributes) -Wikipedia.

Asset

An asset is something that has potential or actual value to an organization. An asset can be tangible or intangible. Tangible assets (assets thatcan be touchable) include buildings, materials, vehicles, properties, and equipment among others. On the other hand, intangible assets (assets that are not touchable) like copyrights, patents, software, and so on.

Asset management is not new, people have been managing assets for years. Over the years, managing assets is getting better and easier through adopting technology solutions. However, current asset management process is not efficient and optimized..

Challenges with current asset management solutions

Asset management is the biggest area in many supply chain industries. Current asset management solutions are facing the following challenges:

- **KYC:** Knowing participant's history and behaviors helps to predict the business outcome accurately. Participants/parties identity within the supply chain is still manual and involves paperwork. Some participants have a digital identity, but lacks trust as it is built on a centralized platform.

- **Provenance and authenticity:** Unable to trace the asset to its origin and provenance. It is very difficult/impossible/costly to trace an asset in the asset lifecycle.

- **Agreement and Paperwork:** A lot of parties in the supply chain still follow paperwork to create a contract, and record the transactions.

- **Ownership in case ofasset damage:** Asset gets exchange multiple hands in the supply chain when something goes wrong with the asset. It's impossible to find out where it went wrong.

- **Cost:** Companies spending millions to billions of dollars every year to manage assets better.

- **Multiple parties involved:** Too many people involved and each of them operates in their own way.

Apart from the above challenges, current asset management solutions are non-auditable and nontraceable with a very high fraud rate.

Advantages of building asset management in blockchain

Designing an asset management system with blockchain overcomes above challenges, and has the following advantages:

- **Traceability and auditing:** State of assets and all the transactions from manufacturer to the buyer isrecorded in the immutable ledger. For example metrics like temperature, condition of the asset, and so on through IoT devices are stored in blockchain. Blockchain tracks information like geolocation which makes it easy to trace assets. This makes blockchain a single source of truth.

- **Consensus:** Each transaction will be validated by the participant in the network, which makes the transactions trustable.

- **Smart contracts:** Makes business rules and contracts programmable, automates the processes and eliminates the waits in the life cycle.

- **Security:** Private blockchains mitigatemuch of this operational risk, eliminates fraud, and data tampering.

- **Decentralized:** No one in the supply chain controls the data, which means that the data can be trusted. Every participant in the network will have a copy of the ledger, which makes the system consistent, highly available, and fault tolerance.

- **Auto payments:** Based on asset arrival and condition through crypto or off-chain payment system.

- **Eliminates middlemen:** Eliminate transfer agents, broker-dealers, and so on. Reduces operational cost.

Apart from the above advantages, blockchain provides efficient processing and real-time access to information.

Asset tracker project

Blockchain is the right fit for asset management, which brings trust and traceability alongside eliminating fraud, reducing cost, and offering a decentralized infrastructure.

The following are the asset tracking use cases, where blockchain is aright fit:

- Tracking of high-value goods like Rolex watches, diamonds, jewelry, and so on

- Tracking machinery from manufacturer till the disposal

- Tracking computer equipment in an office

- Tracking intellectual properties

- Tracking vehicles start from manufacturing to recycling/disposal and so on

In this chapter, we will be building an asset tracking application that tracks vehicle assets from manufacturing to the buyer.

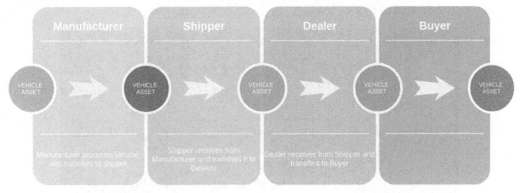

Figure 11.1: *Asset tracker project workflow diagram*

In the above picture, we can see that we are considering only four participants mainly Manufacturer, Shipper, Dealer, and Buyer for this sample. In real-lifesupply chain, you will have more participants. The same smart contract can be extended to include more participants.

Ganache - setup local blockchain network

Ganache makes the development of smart contracts faster and easier. Instead of using a live / test blockchain network for Ethereum development, you can use Ganache to create a local blockchain network to deploy contracts, develop applications, and run tests.

Installing Ganache

Now that we have a fair idea of what Ganache is and how it assists in smart contract development, let us walk through the installation process of this tool.

Steps to install the Ganache are as follows:

1. Navigate to **https://truffleframework.com/ganache** and download Ganache for your respective OS (Windows: Ganache-*.appx, Mac: Ganache-*.dmg, Linux:Ganache-*.AppImage) and install on your local machine.

2. Post-installation, open Ganache. In the home screen, you are prompted to load an existing workspace (if any exist) or create a new custom workspace. Click on **QUICKSTART** to start the local Ethereum blockchain.

Figure 11.2: Start the local Ethereum blockchain

3. Ganache starts the network with default Ethereum accounts, each account having 100 Ether.

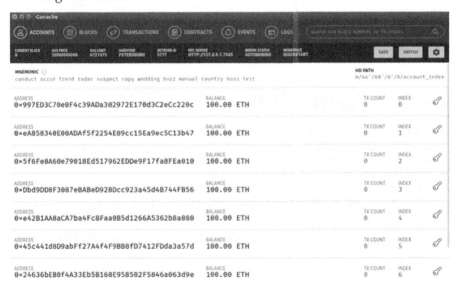

Figure 11.3: Default Ethereum accounts

We can see in the above screen that the default accounts are listed with balance; these accounts will be used to interact with smart contract:

Also, look at other fields in Ganache:

- **CURRENT BLOCK** is **0** (since this blockchain network is new, no blocks added yet)
- **GAS PRICE** is **20000000000**
- **GAS LIMIT** is **6721975**
- **HARDFORK** is **PETERSBURG**
- **NETWORK ID** of **5777**
- **RPC SERVER** is **HTTP://127.0.0.1:7545**
- **MINING STATUS** is **AUTOMINING**

There are other tabs to explore such as **BLOCKS**, **TRANSACTIONS**, **CONTRACTS**, **EVENTS**, and **LOGS**.

We will explore these tabs later in the chapter.

Truffle framework - setup asset tracker project

Truffle is the development framework to build Ethereum blockchain applications. It aims to make the life of a developer easy.

The following are some of the advantages of usingTruffle:

- Truffle helps in building, compiling, and deploying solidity smart contracts to any Ethereum network (local, Test net, private network, and main network).
- Creates a pipeline for blockchain using EVM.
- Automated contract testing for rapid development.
- Scriptable, extensible deployment and migrations framework.
- Package management with the EthPM and NPM, using theERC190 standard.
- Interactive console for direct contract communication.

Truffle makes it easy to start with basic project templates.

Installing Truffle

Before installing truffle makes sure *NodeJS v8.9.4* or later is installed. Once that isdone, follow the steps to install Truffle:

1. Truffle can be installed through **npm** by entering the following command:

```
$ npm install -g truffle
```

2. After the installation, verify the installation with the following command:

```
$ truffle version
```

3. The output will look like the following:

```
//Output


Truffle v5.0.19 (core: 5.0.19)
Solidity v0.5.0 (solc-js)
Node v8.16.0
```

Truffle provides the following commands to interact with smart contracts.

```
murughan@murughan-Inspiron-5570:~/projects/AssetTracker$ truffle
Truffle v5.0.19 - a development framework for Ethereum

Usage: truffle <command> [options]

Commands:
  build      Execute build pipeline (if configuration present)
  compile    Compile contract source files
  config     Set user-level configuration options
  console    Run a console with contract abstractions and commands available
  create     Helper to create new contracts, migrations and tests
  debug      Interactively debug any transaction on the blockchain (experimental)
  deploy     (alias for migrate)
  develop    Open a console with a local development blockchain
  exec       Execute a JS module within this Truffle environment
  help       List all commands or provide information about a specific command
  init       Initialize new and empty Ethereum project
  install    Install a package from the Ethereum Package Registry
  migrate    Run migrations to deploy contracts
  networks   Show addresses for deployed contracts on each network
  obtain     Fetch and cache a specified compiler
  opcode     Print the compiled opcodes for a given contract
  publish    Publish a package to the Ethereum Package Registry
  run        Run a third-party command
  test       Run JavaScript and Solidity tests
  unbox      Download a Truffle Box, a pre-built Truffle project
  version    Show version number and exit
  watch      Watch filesystem for changes and rebuild the project automatically

See more at http://truffleframework.com/docs
```

Figure 11.4: Truffle command

We will use Truffle compile, develop, console, and migrate commands in this chapter.

Creating AssetTracker project

In this section, we will create an **AssetTacker** project through Truffle.

The following are step by step instructions forcreating an **AssetTracker** project:

1. Create a new folder called the **AssetTracker**.

```
$ mkdir AssetTracker
```

2. Change directory to the **AssetTracker**

```
$ cd AssetTracker
```

3. Enter the following command to create an empty project with basic files:

```
$ truffle init
```

This is what it'd look like:

```
murughan@murughan-Inspiron-5570:~/projects/AssetTracker$ truffle init

✔ Preparing to download
✔ Downloading
✔ Cleaning up temporary files
✔ Setting up box

Unbox successful. Sweet!

Commands:

  Compile:        truffle compile
  Migrate:        truffle migrate
  Test contracts: truffle test
```

Figure 11.5: Initialize

4. Open this project in Visual Studio code, you should see the default files.

   a) Truffle created a **contracts** folder; this is where we will keep smart contracts forour application.

   b) migrations folder store scripts to deploy smart contracts.

   c) test folder consists of unit tests.

   d) truffle-config.js to application configuration.

Figure 11.6: Explore project

We will use this as a base template and start building an **AssetTracker** application on top of this.

Web3.js - Ethereum JavaScript API

web3.js is a collection of libraries that allows you to interact with a local or remote Ethereum node, using an HTTP, WebSocket or IPC connection.

Installing web3.js

Web3.js can be installed through **npm** package manager. Enter the following command inside the **AssetTracker** directory to install web3.

```
$ npm install web3
```

It will look like the following screenshot:

```
murughan@murughan-Inspiron-5570:~/projects$ cd AssetTracker
murughan@murughan-Inspiron-5570:~/projects/AssetTracker$ npm install web3

> keccak@1.4.0 install /home/murughan/projects/AssetTracker/node_modules/keccak
> npm run rebuild || echo "Keccak bindings compilation fail. Pure JS implementat
ion will be used."
```

Figure 11.7: Install web3.js

We shall explore Web3.js in a more detailed way in the next chapter. In this chapter, we will be using very minimal functionalities of web3.js

Creating participants contracts

There are multiple parties involved in vehicle transfer start from supplier to disposal. For this sample, we have identified four players/participants namely:

1. Manufacturer - Producer of the vehicle asset
2. Shipper - Ships vehicle asset to the dealers
3. Dealer – Sells the vehicle to a consumer
4. Buyer - Buys from seller

We need to track afew details of these participants and transactions into the blockchain. We will write a smart contract to track assets.

Creating a manufacturer contract

Our first contract will be for the manufacturer, which will store the manufacturer name, account address, and location onto the blockchain. If you want to track more attributes (QR Code, and so on.) you can add them, but for now, let us stick to three properties for simplicity.

Now, will create a new file called **Manufacturer.sol** under contracts folder by adding the following code:

```solidity
pragma solidity >=0.4.25 <0.6.0;
contract Manufacturer
{
    string public name;
    address public manufacturer_address;
    string public location;
    constructor ( string memory manufacturerName, address
manufacturerAddress,
                string memory manufacturerLocation) public {
        name = manufacturerName;
        manufacturer_address = manufacturerAddress;
        location = manufacturerLocation;
    }
}
```

Here we are creating a contract called **Manufacturer**. There are three public properties namely, the **manufacturer_address**, location, and a constructor that will be executed while initiating this contract.

Creating a shipper contract

Our second contract will be for **Shipper** - which stores shipper name, shipper account address, and shipper location onto the blockchain. This can be done by creating a new file called **Shipper.sol** under the contracts folder, and adding the following code :

```solidity
pragma solidity >=0.4.25 <0.6.0;
contract Shipper
{
    string public name;
    address public shipper_address;
    string public location;
    constructor (string memory shipperName, address shipperAddress,
                string memory shipperLocation) public {
        name = shipperName;
        shipper_address = shipperAddress;
        location = shipperLocation;
```

```
        }
}
```

Here we are creating a contract called **Shipper**. There are three public properties name, the **shipper_address**, location, and a constructor, which will be executed while initiating this contract.

Creating a dealer contract

Our third contract will be for **Dealer** that stores the dealer name, dealer account address, and the dealer location onto the blockchain. To get started, create a new file called **Dealer.sol** under the contracts folder and add the following code:

```solidity
pragma solidity >=0.4.25 <0.6.0;

contract Dealer
{
    string public name;
    address public dealer_address;
    string public location;
    constructor (string memory dealerName, address dealerAddress,
    string memory dealerLocation) public
    {
        name = dealerName;
        dealer_address = dealerAddress;
        location = dealerLocation;
    }
}
```

Here we are creating a contract called **Dealer**. There are three public properties name, **dealer_address**, location, and a constructor, which will be executed while initiating this contract.

Creating a buyer contract

Our fourth contract will be for **Buyer**, which stores buyer name, buyer account address, and buyer location onto the blockchain. This can be done by creating a new file called **Buyer.sol** under the contracts folder adding the following code:

```solidity
pragma solidity >=0.4.25 <0.6.0;

contract Buyer
{
```

```
    string public name;
    address public buyer_address;
    string public location;
    constructor(string memory buyerName, address buyerAddress,
    string memory buyerLocation) public
    {
        name = buyerName;
        buyer_address = buyerAddress;
        location = buyerLocation;
    }
}
```

Here we are creating a contract called **Buyer**, three public properties name, **buyer_address**, location, and a constructor, which will be executed while initiating this contract.

Creating asset contract

An asset is something that adds potential or actual value to an organization. In this application vehicle is our asset, we will an create asset contract with public properties and functions.

Now, let us create a smart contract for **Asset**. Keep in mind that we would like to have a unique id for each asset, name of the asset, the current owner, and asset current location that will be useful to track when the vehicle is under shipment.

Create a new file called **Asset.sol** under contracts folder, and add the following code:

```
pragma solidity >=0.4.25 <0.6.0;
contract Asset {
    int public id;
    string public name;
    address public owner;
    string public asset_location;
    enum StateType { Manufacturer, Shipper, Dealer, Buyer }
    StateType public state;
    constructor (int assetId, string memory assetName, address assetOwner)
public
    {
```

```
        id = assetId;
        name = assetName;
        state = StateType.Manufacturer;
        owner = assetOwner;
    }
    function setOwner(address assetOwner) public {
        owner = assetOwner;
    }
    function setState(StateType assetState) public {
        state = assetState;
    }
    function setAssetLocation(string memory assetLocation) public {
        asset_location = assetLocation;
    }
}
```

Here we are creating a contract called **Asset**, five public properties id, name, owner, **asset_location**, state, and a constructor to initialize values.

We have also created the setter function for the owner, state, and location:

- **setOwner()** function to update the current owner.
- **setState()** function to update the current state of the asset.
- **setAssetLocation()** to track the location of the asset which it's in shipment and also with other parties.

Creating the main contract - AssetTracker contract

In the previous steps, we have created smart contracts for all the participants and assets. In this step, we will import all those contracts and create our final contract which will be deployed as a single contract onto the AWS.

This contract is quite big so we will break it down into multiple parts as follows: Create a file called **AssetTracker.sol** under contracts folder. Add the following to **AssetTracker.sol** file:

Step1: Importing participants and asset contract

Importing all the participants and asset contracts (**Manufacturer.sol**, **Shipper. sol**, **Dealer.sol**, **Buyer.sol**, and **Asset.sol**)

```
pragma solidity >=0.4.25 <0.6.0;
import "./Asset.sol";
import "./Manufacturer.sol"; import "./Shipper.sol"; import "./Dealer.
sol"; import "./Buyer.sol";
```

Step2: Creating variables

Creating the **AssetTracker** contract, creating mapping datatype to store key-value pair for all the participants such as manufacturers, shippers, dealers, buyers. It stores account address as a key and participant's details as a value. Creating mapping datatype for assets to store the **assetId** and the asset details.

```
contract AssetTracker
{
    //Participants
mapping (address => Manufacturer) public manufacturers;
    mapping (address => Shipper) public shippers;
    mapping (address => Dealer) public dealers;
    mapping (address => Buyer) public buyers;
    //Asset
    mapping (int => Asset) public assets;
    int public assetId;
}
```

Step3: Creating events

Creating two events, the **AssetCreate(address account, int assetID, string manufacturer)** and the **AssetTransfer(address from, address to, int assetID)** to log all the transactions when the asset is created and when an asset is transferred to others.

```
    //Events
    event AssetCreate(address account, int assetID, string manufacturer);
    event AssetTransfer(address from, address to, int assetID);
```

Step4: Writing functions to create manufacturer

Creating functions the **createManufacturer(string memory manufacturerName, address manufacturerAddress, string memory manufacturerLocation)** to add a new manufacturer.

```
function createManufacturer(string memory manufacturerName, address
manufacturerAddress, string memory manufacturerLocation) public
    {
        Manufacturer = new Manufacturer(manufacturerName,
manufacturerAddress, manufacturerLocation);
manufacturers[manufacturerAddress] = manufacturer;
    }
```

Manufacturer details will be stored in the manufacturer's mapping variable.

Step5: Writing functions to create a **Shipper**

Creating function **createShipper(string memory shipperName, address shipperAddress, string memory shipperLocation)** to add a new shipper.

```
function createShipper(string memory shipperName, address shipperAddress,
string memory shipperLocation) public
    {
      Shipper = new Shipper(shipperName, shipperAddress, shipperLocation);
        shippers[shipperAddress] = shipper;
    }
```

Shipper details will be stored in the buyer's mapping variables.

Step6: Writing functions to create a **Dealer**

Creating function **createDealer(string memory dealerName, address dealerAddress, string memory dealerLocation)** to add a new dealer.

```
    function createDealer(string memory dealerName, address dealerAddress,
string memory dealerLocation) public
    {
        Dealer = new Dealer(dealerName, dealerAddress, dealerLocation);
        dealers[dealerAddress] = dealer;
    }
```

Dealer's details will be stored in the buyer's mapping variables.

Step7: Writing functions to create a **Buyer**

Creating function **createBuyer(string memory buyerName, address buyerAddress, string memory buyerLocation)** to add a new buyer.

```
    function createBuyer(string memory buyerName, address buyerAddress,
string memory buyerLocation) public
```

```
{
    Buyer = new Buyer(buyerName, buyerAddress, buyerLocation);
    buyers[buyerAddress] = buyer;
}
```

Buyer details will be stored in the buyers mapping variables.

Step8: Writing functions to create an **Asset**

Creating **createAsset(string memory assetName)** function to create new asset.

```
//Create Assets
function createAsset(string memory assetName) public returns (int)
{
  //Only manufacturer can create an asset
  if (msg.sender != manufacturers[msg.sender].manufacturer_address())
        revert();
    assetId = assetId + 1;
    Asset = new Asset(assetId, assetName, msg.sender);
    assets[assetId] = asset;
    emit AssetCreate (msg.sender, assetId, manufacturers[msg.sender].
name());
        return assetId;
}
```

Details are stored in the assets mapping variable. While creating a new asset, the asset ownership is assigned to the manufacturer who creates an asset. After the creation of an asset, the **createAsset** event will be fired to log the transaction onto the blockchain. We are incrementing the **AssetId** by 1 for every new asset.

Step9: Writing function to get the current owner of an asset

getCurrentOwner(int assetID) function returns the current owner detail, as and when an asset gets transferred, this function will return the current owner of that asset.

```
function getCurrentOwner(int assetID) public view returns(address) {
    Asset = assets[assetID];
    return asset.owner();
}
```

Step10: Writing function to get the current state of an asset

> **getCurrentState(int assetID)** function return the current state of an asset.

```
    function getCurrentState(int assetID) public view returns(Asset.
StateType) {
        Asset asset = assets[assetID];
        return asset.state();
    }
```

Step11: Writing function to set the current location of an asset

setAssetCurrentLocation(intassetID, string memory assetLocation) function sets the current location of the asset. This function can be executed by the shipper to track the current location of the asset.

```
function setAssetCurrentLocation(int assetID, string memory assetLocation)
public
    {
        //Transfer to Shipper from Manufacturer
        Asset = assets[assetID];
        asset.setAssetLocation(assetLocation);
    }
```

Step12: Writing function to transfer an asset

Our final and important function is the **transferAsset(address to, int assetID)** function, which will be called every time the asset moves from one participant to another. This function validates the current state, and the owner based on that it makes the transfer of ownership. Condition to check the current state **asset.state() == 0** gets the first element in the **enum**, here it returns **Manufacturer**.

```
    function transferAsset(address to, int assetID) public
    {
        //Transfer to Shipper from Manufacturer
        Asset asset = assets[assetID];
      if(int(asset.state()) == 0 && to == shippers[to].shipper_address())
        {
asset.setOwner(to);
        asset.setState(Asset.StateType.Shipper);
        }
        //Transfer to Dealer from Shipper
```

```
        else if(int(asset.state()) == 1 && to == dealers[to].dealer_
address())
    {
        asset.setOwner(to);
        asset.setState(Asset.StateType.Dealer);
    }
    //Transfer to Buyer from Dealer
    else if(int(asset.state()) == 2 && to == buyers[to].buyer_address())
    {
        asset.setOwner(to);
        asset.setState(Asset.StateType.Buyer);
    }
    emit AssetTransfer (msg.sender, to, assetID);
}
```

Compiling all the contract

Let us use Truffle to compile these contracts. Use the following command in the terminal to compile all our contracts:

$ truffle compile

If you have made any mistakes, the truffle will list them out. After fixing the error, rerun the truffle compile command. Once everything is successful, you should see the output like the following screenshot:

```
murughan@murughan-Inspiron-5570:~/projects/AssetTracker$ truffle compile

Compiling your contracts...
===========================
> Compiling ./contracts/Asset.sol
> Compiling ./contracts/AssetTracker.sol
> Compiling ./contracts/Buyer.sol
> Compiling ./contracts/Dealer.sol
> Compiling ./contracts/Manufacturer.sol
> Compiling ./contracts/Migrations.sol
> Compiling ./contracts/Shipper.sol
> Artifacts written to /home/murughan/projects/AssetTracker/build/contracts
> Compiled successfully using:
   - solc: 0.5.0+commit.1d4f565a.Emscripten.clang
```

Figure 11.8: Compile

This command creates a folder called the build stores artifacts and the **application binary interface(ABI)** for each contract.

Configure deployment script

Deployments scripts are placed under the migrations folder, migration and deployment mean the same. To deploy **AssetTracker** contract, add a file called **1_deploy_contracts.js** under the migrations folder and add the following deployment steps:

```
var AssetTracker = artifacts.require("AssetTracker");

module.exports = function (deployer) {

  deployer.deploy(AssetTracker);

};
```

Figure 11.9: Configure deployment script

Make sure ganache is running and then modify the **truffle-config.js** to include local Ethereum network details. Since Ganache is running on **127.0.0.1:7545**, update the configuration accordingly.

```
module.exports = {


  networks: {

    development: {

      host: "127.0.0.1",

      port: 7545,

      network_id: "*",

    }

  }

}
```

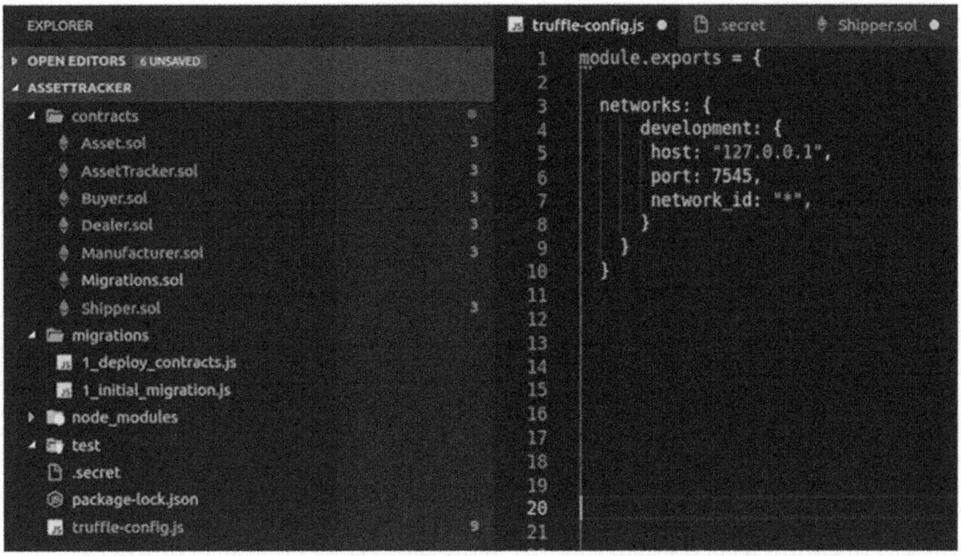

Figure 11.10: *Update the configuration*

Run the following **migrate** command to deploy **AssetTracker** smart contract to the local network:

$ truffle migrate

You should see the output like the following screenshot:

Figure 11.11: *Migrate*

If you make any changes to the contract, then you can use truffle migrate and reset to run all your migrations from the beginning. Verify if the AssetTracker contracts are deployed to the local network in Ganache.

Figure 11.12: Verify the AssetTracker contracts are deployed

Here we can observe that four blocks are created. A block can contain more than one transaction. Click on any block number to see the transactions.

Explore the Blocks for the AssetTracker smart contract, check the smart contract address,This address is used to interact with AssetTracker smart contract.

Figure 11.13: Explore the Blocks

Also, explore the **Transactions** tab which has details of each transaction.

Running the AssetTracker smart contract

Before we deploy the AssetTracker smart contract to AWS. Let us run it locally against the Ganache to check if all the functions are working as expected.

The Truffle provides two easy ways to develop smart contract.

- truffle console
- truffle develop

Truffle develop

truffle develop is an interactive console that also spawns a development blockchain. We will be using truffle develop to validate our contract.

Go to your terminal/command prompt enter the following command:

```
$ truffle develop
```

Figure 11.14: Truffle develop

This command will open a development console, which uses the **localhost:9545** network, and provides Ethereum accounts to interact with smart contract.

Creating a contract instance

Let's create the instance object to hold the **AssetTracker** contract and enter the following command in the terminal to get the contract instance:

```
$ let instance = await AssetTracker.deployed()
```

Enter instance object in the terminal to see full object detail.

```
$ instance
```

Getting Ethereum accounts with web3.js

Use **web3.js** to get Ethereum accounts which are created by Ganache. These accounts will be used to create participants. Enter the following command to assign default accounts to JavaScript variable accounts:

```
$ let accounts = await web3.eth.getAccounts()
```

Enter the accounts variable to see the list of accounts available.

$ accounts

```
truffle(develop)> let accounts = await web3.eth.getAccounts()
undefined
truffle(develop)> accounts
[ '0xF6960e67Ed094Ac1fDD9b22cD84aF81F1cA48a8b',
  '0xc256701A8Aa6F09E59606788c72F087a0D672B42',
  '0xC57b1b4b9b79b87721f25A0ee413e07B388dcC9C',
  '0x8768369ad089690f129d730B868C25F2A3682207',
  '0x09646781509cb8d58115B5abD265741071ecd959',
  '0x57FD8AFAc851489C582BC40Fbb4CFA6C8678A9b3',
  '0xEea8C34e8c2c97a049653A4c8267d19F52394371',
  '0x322776B87ee293d0D47d3A9f272815e256655d0c',
  '0x8B7f205EafC827362cBf8DB2AB87dbD53f4312Ec',
  '0x7f4BC1c8c0D59be64AAceb92cc8735a4e45f1Ef2' ]
```

Figure 11.15: Get Ethereum accounts

Accounts variable stores all these accounts in an array. We shall use these unique addresses to create participants, as each participant will have a unique account address.

Creating participants

Let's create a Manufacturer, Shipper, Dealer, and Buyer by calling the respective contract function.

Execute the **creatManufacturer()** function to create a Manufacturer as follows:

$ instance.createManufacturer("manufacturer1", accounts[0], "AL")

You should get an output like this for successful creation:

```
truffle(develop)> instance.createManufacturer("manufacturer1", accounts[0], "AL")
{ tx: '0x5308e74d88eebe48a9c3e66941dd665f0d27846dea8019ab9ad72a70511af4f3',
  receipt:
   { transactionHash: '0x5308e74d88eebe48a9c3e66941dd665f0d27846dea8019ab9ad72a70511af4f3',
     transactionIndex: 0,
     blockHash: '0x78ee6bedf3c707bfc6c6b4eaacbf9d8dd4893d3b988d117e34811eae9d206572',
     blockNumber: 1,
     from: '0xf6960e67ed094ac1fdd9b22cd84af81f1ca48a8b',
     to: '0x7736a650fc860f245c2806879c6393320f0392ca',
     gasUsed: 24664,
     cumulativeGasUsed: 24664,
     contractAddress: null,
     logs: [],
     status: true,
     logsBloom: '0x000000000000000000000000000000000000000000000000000000000000000000000000000000000000000000000000000000000
0000000000000000000000000000000000000000000000000000000000000000000000000000000000000000000000000000000000000000000000000
00000000000000000000000000000000000000000000000000000000000000000000000000000000000000000000000000000000000000000000000000
00000000000000000000000000000000000000000000000000000000000000000000000000000000000000000000000000000000000000000000000000
0000000000000000000000000',
     v: '0x1c',
     r: '0x7b07fb9ea6e90fcc259c8228f74fe395b57b56e5da19fae8ecd2c9db62acbd45',
     s: '0x620fe651d1892303589af6d1b8de2c1d269428aa18aacf6126b901cb8a50f998',
     rawLogs: [] },
  logs: [] }
```

Figure 11.16: Create participants

Similarly create Shipper, Dealer, and Buyer.

$ instance.createShipper("shipper1", accounts[1], "IL")

```
$ instance.createDealer("dealer1", accounts[2], "CO")
```

```
$ instance.createBuyer("b", accounts[3], "CA")
```

So far, we have successfully created all the participants.

Creating a vehicle asset

Let's create a vehicle asset by executing the **createAsset()** function as shown in following code:

```
$ instance.createAsset("Aston Martin DB11")
```

This creates new asset with ID as 1, to get the **assetId** by calling **assetId** variable function.

```
$ instance.assetId()
```

```
//output = 1
```

Check the current owner, it should be the accounts[0] which is the manufacturer account.

```
$ instance.getCurrentOwner(1)
```

```
Result {
```

```
'0':'0x997ED3C70e0F4c39ADa302972E170d3C2eCc220c',   '1': <BN: 0> }
```

Transfer vehicle

To transfer the vehicle to another participant, we have created the **transferAsset()** function. All these tractions are logged into the blockchain so that we can trace it to their origin. Transfer the vehicle asset from Manufacturer to the Shipper: Enter the following command where **account[1]** is the account of a Shipper and 1 is the id of Vehicle asset - Aston Martin DB11.

```
$ instance.transferAsset(accounts[1], 1)
```

With this operation now, the owner is a shipper account[0].

Transfer the vehicle asset from Shipper to Dealer: Enter the following command where **account[2]** is the account of a Dealer and 1 is the id of Vehicle asset Aston Martin DB11.

```
$ instance.transferAsset(accounts[2], 1)
```

With this operation, now the owner is the Dealer **accounts[2]**.

Transfer vehicle asset from the Dealer to Buyer: Enter following command where **accounts[3]** is the account of a Buyer and 1 is the id of Vehicle asset Aston Martin DB11.

```
$ instance.transferAsset(accounts[3], 1)
```

Now you check the current owner, it should belong to the buyer that is **accounts[3]**.

```
$ instance.getCurrentOwner(1)
Result {
  '0': '0x8768369ad089690f129d730B868C25F2A3682207',
  '1': <BN: 3> }
```

Our smart contract is working as expected and it's time to deploy to AWS.

Deploying AssetTransfer contact to the AWSEthereum private network

In the *Chapter 9* AWS Blockchain Template to Create Private Ethereum, we have provisioned the Ethereum private network. If you have deleted the resources, then please follow the steps to create Ethereum private network and make sure you are able to ssh to the Bastion host and you are abletoview the **EthStatsURL** and the **EthExplorerURL** links from the Cloud formation stack output in the browser.

Figure 11.17: Verify Cloudformation stack output

Once you can view these in the browser, then we can deploy to AWS Ethereum private network.

You can deploy a smart contract to the AWS Ethereum network in two ways:

1. Deploy through Remix online tool
2. Deploy through Truffle

Approach 1 – Deploy AssetTracker contract with Remix online tool

The Remix tool is the easier and faster way to compile, test and deploy contracts to any network. We will be using the Remix tool to deploy smart contract to our AWS Ethereum private network which we have provisioned.

Steps to deploy **AssetTracker** contract with Remix as follows:

1. Verify the connection to the Bastion host and MetaMask connected to AWSEthereum private network

2. Open the **AssetTracker** contract in the Remix online editor.

3. Deploy the **AssetTracker** contract to an AWS Ethereum private network.

4. Interact with **AssetTracker** contract that is deployed on AWS

Step1: Verify the connection to the Bastion host and the MetaMask connected to AWS Ethereum private network.

1. Verify that you can **ssh** to the bastion host as shown in the following screenshot:

```
murughan@murughan-Inspiron-5570:~/Downloads$ ssh -i murughan.pem ec2-user@18.21
6.172.99 -D 9001
Last login: Mon Jun 10 16:19:00 2019 from 27.7.30.21

       __|  __|_  )
       _|  (     /    Amazon Linux 2 AMI
      ___|\___|___|

https://aws.amazon.com/amazon-linux-2/
[ec2-user@ip-10-0-2-89 ~]$ 
```

Figure 11.18: ssh to bastion

2. Verify that you can connect to the EthJsonRPCURL with the MetaMask. If you have not done this, please follow the *Chapter 9* AWS Blockchain Template to Create Private Ethereum.

Figure 11.19: Connect to EthJsonRPCURL

Step2: Open the AssetTracker contract in Remix online editor

1. Open the Remix online editor **https://remix.ethereum.org** in the chrome browser.

2. Open the AssetTracker smart contracts(Assets, Buyer, Dealer, Shipper, and AssetTracker) in the Remix as shown in the following screenshot:

Figure 11.20: Open AssetTracker smart contracts

3. Auto-compile would be enabled in the Remix, if not, then compile the AssetTracker contract. Once the contracts are compiled then we are ready to deploy to an AWS privateEthereum network.

4. Select the **Run** option from left, and select the following values:

   a) **Environment**: **Injected Web3**

   b) **Account**: Metamask the account 1 (select the account used while deploying the AWS private Ethereum)

   c) Select the **AssetTracker** contract to be deployed

   d) In MetaMask

      i. Select the **aws** as network

      ii. Select the **Account 1** (You should be having the balance of 1000 Ether initiated by AWS, you can use this Ether only for this network)

      iii. Verify everything and click on the **Deploybutton**.

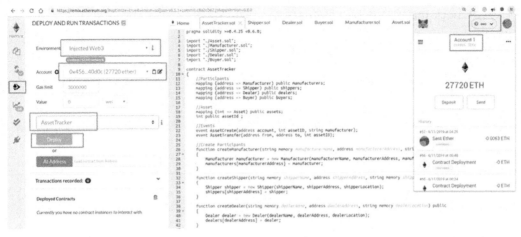

Figure 11.21: Deploy contract

4. This transaction requires an Ether, so confirm in the MetaMask as shown in the following screenshot:

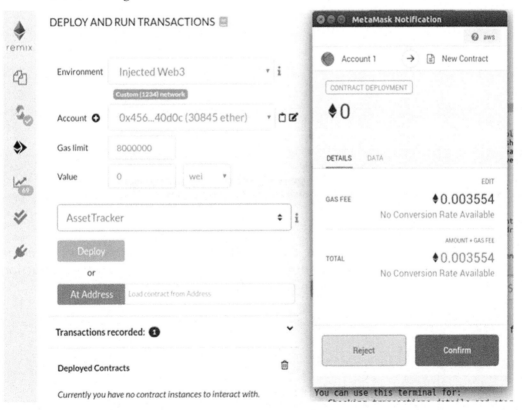

Figure 11.22: Confirm in the Metamask

5. Check the transaction status is the MetaMask.

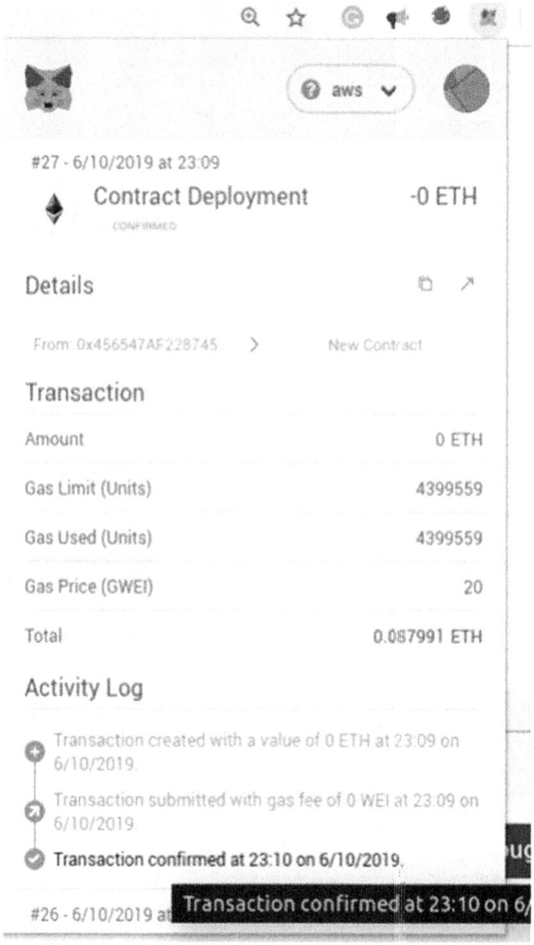

Figure 11.23: Transaction status

6. Click on the **Transaction confirmed** from the above screen result to get the transaction id. This will redirect to the Etherscan, so just copy the transaction id as shown in the following screenshot:

Figure 11.24: View in Etherscan

7. Paste the transaction if in EthExplorer to get details on the transaction.

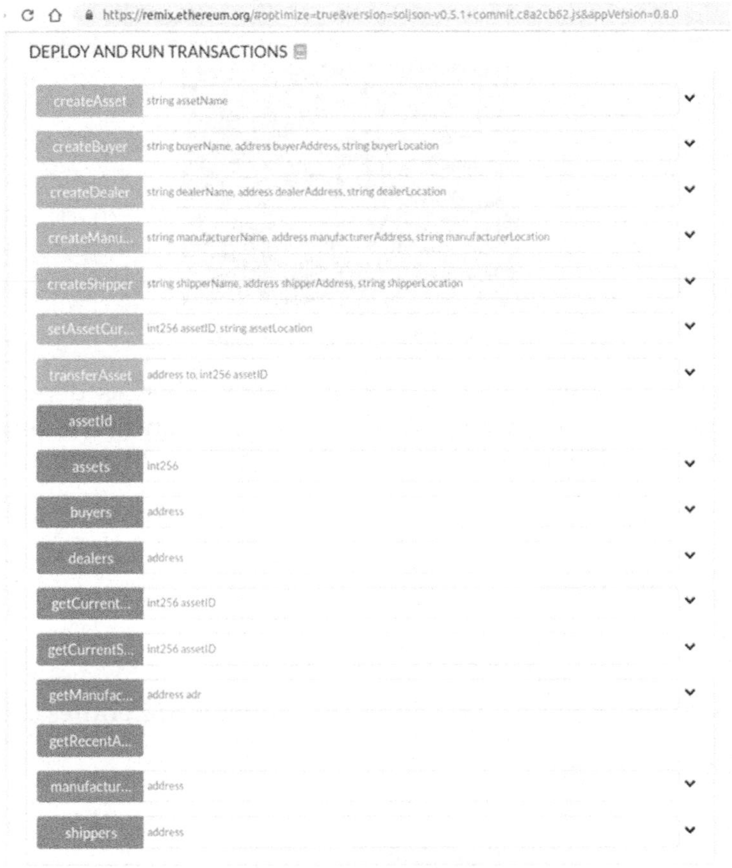

Figure 11.25: EthExplorer

8. Once the AssetTracker is deployed, check the available functions in the Remix.

   a) **Account1** for the Manufacturer

   b) **Account 2** for the Shipper

   c) **Account 3** for the Dealer

d) **Account 4** for the Buyer

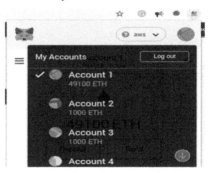

Figure 11.26: Available functions

9. Let's interact with the AssetTracker contract which is deployed on AWS Ethereum private network. Give details for each function in order. Note that transactions will require the Ether to be paid and calls are free.

a. Create Manufacturer, give your Ethereum the account 1 address.

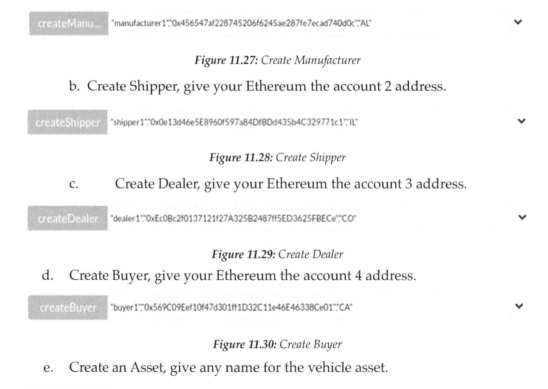

Figure 11.27: Create Manufacturer

b. Create Shipper, give your Ethereum the account 2 address.

Figure 11.28: Create Shipper

c. Create Dealer, give your Ethereum the account 3 address.

Figure 11.29: Create Dealer

d. Create Buyer, give your Ethereum the account 4 address.

Figure 11.30: Create Buyer

e. Create an Asset, give any name for the vehicle asset.

Figure 11.31: Create an Asset

f. Check the **assetId**.

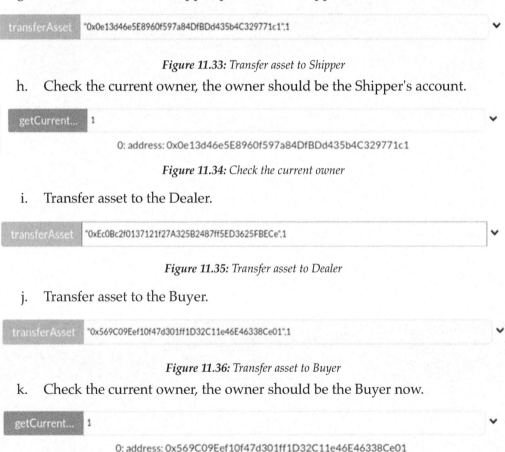

assetId

0: int256: 1

Figure 11.32: Check the AssetId

g. Transfer asset to the Shipper, provide the Shipper Ethereum account address.

transferAsset "0x0e13d46e5E8960f597a84DfBDd435b4C329771c1",1 ⌄

Figure 11.33: Transfer asset to Shipper

h. Check the current owner, the owner should be the Shipper's account.

getCurrent... 1 ⌄

0: address: 0x0e13d46e5E8960f597a84DfBDd435b4C329771c1

Figure 11.34: Check the current owner

i. Transfer asset to the Dealer.

transferAsset "0xEc0Bc2f0137121f27A325B2487ff5ED3625FBECe",1 ⌄

Figure 11.35: Transfer asset to Dealer

j. Transfer asset to the Buyer.

transferAsset "0x569C09Eef10f47d301ff1D32C11e46E46338Ce01",1 ⌄

Figure 11.36: Transfer asset to Buyer

k. Check the current owner, the owner should be the Buyer now.

getCurrent... 1 ⌄

0: address: 0x569C09Eef10f47d301ff1D32C11e46E46338Ce01

Figure 11.37: Check the current owner

You can verify each transaction details in the EthExplorer as shown in the following screenshot:

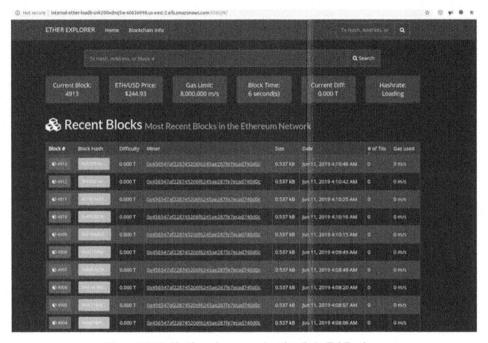

Figure 11.38: Verify each transaction details in EthExplorer

You can verify each transaction details in the EthStat as shown in the following screenshot:

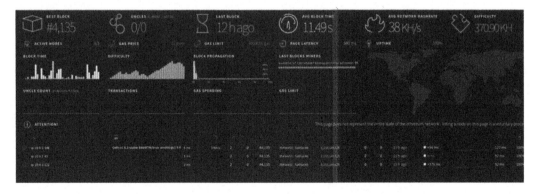

Figure 11.39: Verify each transaction details in EthStat

We have successfully completed deploying the AssetTracker to an AWS Ethereum private network, and interacting with the contract functions.

Approach 2 – Deploy the AsssetTracker contract with Truffle

Truffle provides an option to deploy smart contracts to AWS with the truffle migrate command:

Steps to deploy the AsssetTracker contract with Truffle are as follows:

1. Creating a secret file to store mnemonic
2. Configure the **truffle-config.js** for AWS private network
3. Migrating smart contract to AWS private network with the truffle migrate command

Step1: Creating a secret file to store mnemonic

We have used an Ethereum account from the MetaMask account 1 while provisioning the Ethereum network through CloudFormation template. Use the seed key of this account to connect tothe AWS Ethereum private network.

1. Get the seed for your MetaMask account 1 as shown in the following screenshot:

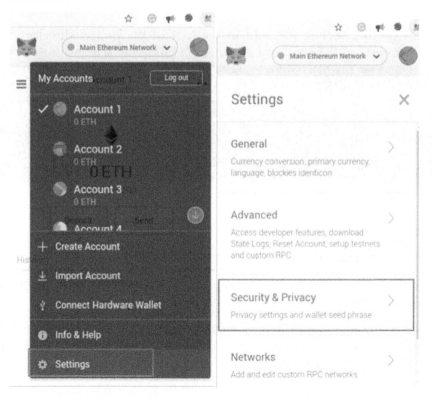

Figure 11.40: *Seed for your Metamask account*

2. Click on the **Reveal Seed Words**:

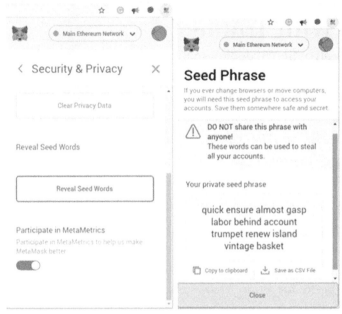

Figure 11.41: Reveal Seed Words

3. Create the **.secret** file, add in the root of the project directory, and add mnemonic of the account 1 as shown in following screenshot:

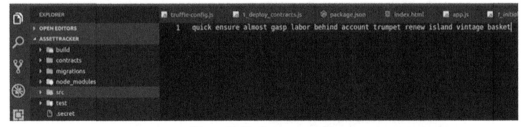

Figure 11.42: Create .secret file

This secret mnemonic will be used to deploy to AWS.

Step2: Configure **truffle-config.js** for the AWS private network

Add the AWS private network configuration to **truffle-config.js** to deploy/ migrate smart contracts.

1. Copy the **EthJsonRPCURL** from the output of CloudFormation Ethereum template, which we have deployed earlier, paste in the **truffle-config.js** file under live configuration.

2. Paste your Metamask Account 1 address from the field in **truffle-config.js** file as shown in the following screenshot:

```
const HDWalletProvider = require('truffle-hdwallet-provider');

const fs = require('fs');

const mnemonic = fs.readFileSync(".secret").toString().trim();

module.exports = {

  networks: {

    development: {

      host: "127.0.0.1",

      port: 7545,

      network_id: "*",

    },

    live: {

      provider: () => new HDWalletProvider(mnemonic,

        `http://ENTER YOUR AWS EthJsonRPCURL:8545`),

      network_id: 1234,

      port: 8545,

      gas: 8000000,

      from: 0x456547af228745206f6245ae287fe7ecad740d0c

    }

  }

}
```

Enter the configurations as follows:

we have two networks - one for development with the ganache network detail, and another one for the Live AWS Ethereum private network details. Please take a look at the following screenshot:

Figure 11.43: Configure network detail

Makes sure you have entered the same details used while provisioning in AWS for the following fields.

- Provider link - EnterEthJsonRPCURL from CloudFormation output
- network_id - Default it is 1234, modify it if you have used a different id
- from - Enter Ethereum account used to provision network in AWS.

Step3: Migrating smart contract to AWS private

Network with the truffle migrate command. If all the configurations are rightly entered then the fire below truffle migrate command, which will deploy **AssetTransfer** contract to AWS.

```
$ truffle migrate --network live
```

In this command **--network live** takes the configuration from **truffle-config.js** and deploys the **AssetTracker** contract to the AWS Ethereum network. Once the deployment is successful, explore the EthStatsURL and the EthExplorerURL.

Conclusion

We have created the smart contract for the vehicle AssetTracker management application, and we have deployed this contract onto the AWS Ethereum private network. The same contract can be extended to include more details like the QRCode, IoT detail, and so on.

You have learned to write a smart contract for the AssetTracker management application. With this knowledge, you will be able to write smart contracts for other usecases like to track high-value goods (Rolex watch, gold, and so on.) and for other asset use-cases.

In the next chapter, we shall write tests for the AssetTracker smart contract, and run it through the Truffle test. We will learn to execute to the AssetTracker contract from the front end through **web3.js** library.

Points to remember

- Redesigning asset management system with blockchain has the following advantages:
  - o **Traceability and auditing:** Asset state can be traced to the origin when we store transactions in blockchain.
  - o **Consensus:** Each transaction will be validated by the participant in the network, which makes the transactions trustable.
  - o **Smart contracts:** Makes business rules and contracts programmable, automates the processes, and eliminates the wait in the life cycle.
  - o **Security:** Private blockchains mitigate much of this operational risk, eliminates fraud and data tampering.
  - o **Decentralized:** No one in the supply chain controls the data, this makes data trusted. Every participant in the network will have a copy of the ledger, which makes the system consistent, highly available, and fault-tolerant.
  - o **Auto payments:** Based on asset arrival and condition through crypto or off- chain payment system.
  - o **Eliminates middlemen:** Eliminate transfer agents, broker-dealers, and so on. Reduces operation cost.
  - o The Ganache makes the development of smart contracts faster and easier. Instead of using an alive/test blockchain network for Ethereum development, you can use Ganache to createlocal blockchain network, to deploy contracts, develop applications, and run tests.
  - o Truffle is the development framework to build the Ethereum blockchain applications. It aims to make the life of a developer easier.

Multiple-choice questions

1. `npm install -g truffle`, this command installs the Truffle:
   a. Yes
   b. No

2. web3.js is a collection of libraries that allows you to interact with a local or remote Ethereum node, using an HTTP, WebSocket or IPC connection.

   a. Yes

   b. No

Answer

1. a

2. a

Questions

1. What is Truffle framework?

2. What is Web3.js?

3. Create Healthcare supply chain system with Truffle and Web3.js.

Key Terms

1. **Asset Management:** Asset management refers to the systematic approach to the governance, and realization of value from the things that a group or entity is responsible for, over their whole life cycles.

2. **Asset**: An asset is something that has potential or actual value to an organization. An asset can be tangible or intangible. Tangible assets (anything can be touchable) include buildings, materials, vehicles, properties, and equipments, among others. On the other hand, intangible assets (assets cannot be touched physically) like copyrights, patents, software, and so on.

3. **Ganache**: Ganache makes the development of smart contracts faster and easier. Instead of using a live/test blockchain network for Ethereum development you can use Ganache to create local blockchain network to deploy contracts, develop applications, and to run tests.

4. **Truffle framework**: Truffle is the development framework to build Ethereum blockchain applications. It aims to make the life of a developer easier.

5. **Web3.js**: web3.js is a collection of libraries that allows you to interact with a local or remoteEthereum node, using an HTTP, WebSocket or IPC connection.

CHAPTER 12
Testing and Interacting with Asset Tracker on AWS

In the previous chapter, we created an Ethereum private network. We also created and deployed the AssetTracker smart contract on the AWS Ethereum private network. We executed the smart contract functions against the AWS network. We explored blocks and transactions using EthExplorer and EthStats.

In this chapter, we will build an Asset Tracker front-end application using HTML, CSS, JavaScript, and Node.js. Write tests for the AssetTracker smart contract and invoke smart contract functions using the web3.js library.

Structure

In this chapter, we will discuss the following topics:

- Writing a unit test for smart contracts
- Using web3.js to interact with smart contracts
- Invoke smart contracts through the UI
- Execute smart contracts against the AWS Ethereum private blockchain

Objectives

After studying this unit, you should be able to:

- Testing of smart contracts
- Testing of Asset Tracker blockchain application
- Design the UI for the Asset Tracker application

Pre-requisites for this chapter

In this chapter, we will write tests with the Mocha framework. Having a basic understanding of these tools/technologies will make it easy to continue with this chapter.

You need to have the following pre-requisites before we proceed with this chapter:

1. The Ethereum private network should be deployed on AWS as mentioned in *chapter 9* AWS Blockchain Template to Create Private Ethereum.
2. The AssetTracker smart contract should be deployed on the private Ethereum network on AWS as mentioned in *Chapter 11* Create and Deploy Asset Tracker Contract on AWS..

Make sure you have all the pre-requisites in place.

Unit testing of the Asset Tracker smart contract

Every unit of the code we write should be validated against the expected behavior. A unit is a small testable part of the code. Writing a unit test builds confidence in modifying the code and makes it easy to refactor and maintain.

You should write more unit tests than integration tests as per the testing pyramid guidelines. At least 70% of your tests should be unit tests in order to deliver a high-quality product.

Identify the application behavior to write test cases

Before we develop any feature for an application, we should identify the different behaviors of the application so that we can deliver the right product. Identify the different behaviors by considering the application workflow, business rules, happy/ unhappy paths, platforms, parameters, operations, and roles. The more scenarios you identify, the product quality will be high.

We have identified a few scenarios and we will write the unit tests for the AssetTracker smart contract functions to validate the following behaviors:

- Creating of manufacturer
- Creating of shipper
- Creating of dealer
- Creating of buyer
- Creating of asset
- Transferring of asset from manufacturer to buyer

We will validate all the preceding functions in the smart contract.

Creating a test file

We can write tests for solidity files in either JavaScript or Solidity, and we will write tests in JavaScript here.

Let's continue to add tests in the same project which we created in the *chapter 11* Create and Deploy Asset Tracker Contract on AWS.

Add a new test file called `TestAssetTracker.js` under the `test` folder as shown in the following screenshot:

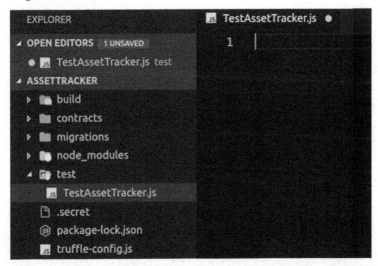

Figure 12.1: Create a test file

The naming convention of the filename starts with a test and contract name like `TestAssetTracker`.

Initializing the test file

In this section, we will add the contract reference and contract setup for the test file.

The steps to initialize the test file are as follows:

1. **Adding a contract reference**: As we need to test the AssetTracker smart contract, let's add a reference to the `AssetTracket.sol` file. Add the following code to the`TestAssetTracker.js` test file:

```
var AssetTracker =
artifacts.require("../contracts/AssetTracker.sol");
```

2. **Creating an instance of the AssetTracker contract**: We will create an instance of the AssetTracker contract with Truffle. Our test code interacts with the contract function with this instance. Add the following code to the `TestAssetTracker.js` test file:

```
var AssetTracker =
artifacts.require("../contracts/AssetTracker.sol");

contract('AssetTracker', (accounts) => {

let assetTrackerInstance;
let assetId = 0;
let owner = "";

//Initial Setup
beforeEach(async function () {
//Deploy AssetTracker contract to test
assetTrackerInstance = await AssetTracker.deployed();
});

});
```

3. Verify your code as shown in the following screenshot:

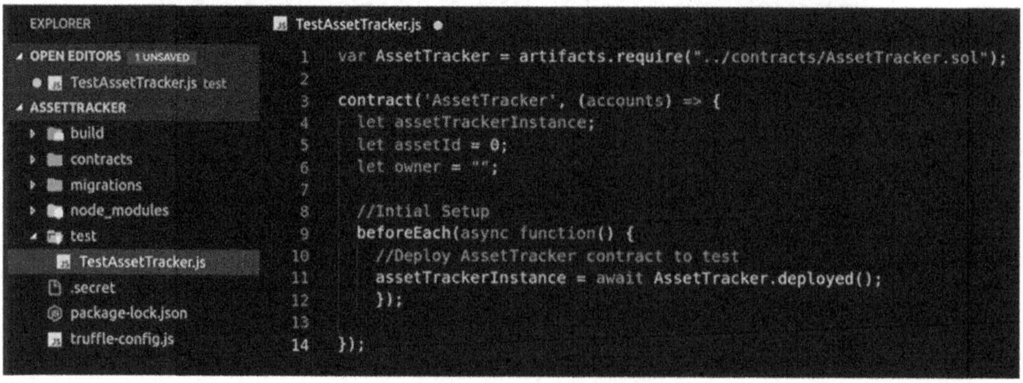

Figure 12.2: Verify your code

In the preceding code, create a global variable `assetTrackerInstance`, `assetId`, and an owner which will be used in all the tests. The `beforeEach()` function executes and attaches the contract instance to the `assetTrackerInstance` variable.

Writing tests to validate the behavior

We will write tests to check the following scenarios:

- For a newly created asset, the owner should be a manufacturer.
- An asset must be transferred only to a shipper from the manufacturer.
- An asset mustbe transferred only to a dealer from the shipper.
- An asset mustbe transferred only to a buyer from the dealer.

You can identify more scenarios like negative conditions, boundary conditions, different parameters, operations, platforms, and so on. For now, we will write tests for these four scenarios, but make sure you write more unit tests in real-life projects.

> **Note: Make sure Ganache is running as all the tests will run against Ganache, refer *chapter 11* Create and Deploy Asset Tracker Contract on AWS on how to run Ganache.**

Test 1: For a newly created asset, the owner should be a manufacturer.

Before we create an asset, we need to create all the participants (manufacturer, shipper, dealer, and buyer). Once the asset is created, the owner of the asset should be the manufacturer. Add the following code to the `TestAssetTracker.js` test file:

```
it('Create participants and asset, owner should be Manufacturer', async
()
=> {
    //Create all the Participants
    assetTrackerInstance.createManufacturer("manufacturer1", accounts[0],
"AL");
    assetTrackerInstance.createShipper("shipper1", accounts[1], "IL")
    assetTrackerInstance.createDealer("dealer1", accounts[2], "CO")
    assetTrackerInstance.createBuyer("b", accounts[3], "CA")

    //Create an Vehicle asset
    assetTrackerInstance.createAsset("Aston Martin DB11");

    //Get AssetId of the vehicle create from above statement
```

```
        assetId = await assetTrackerInstance.assetId.call();


    //Get the current owner
    owner = await
assetTrackerInstance.getCurrentOwner.call(assetId.valueOf());


    //Assert is current owner account address is Manufacturer's account
address
    //If it fails prints below message "Current owner is not the
Manufacturer"
        assert.equal(owner, accounts[0], "Manufacturer is not the owner");
});
```

Smart contract functions are invoked through the `assetTrackerInstance` variable. We need a unique Ethereum account address for each participant. We will use local Ganache accounts. We will use `accounts[0]` for the manufacturer, `accounts[1]` for the shipper, `accounts[2]` for the dealer, and `accounts[3]` for the buyer. The preceding code executes the respective function to create all the participants and an asset and verifies the owner of the asset.

Test 2: An asset can be transferred only to a shipper from the manufacturer.

Once the asset is created and the owner of the asset is the manufacturer, as per our requirement, the asset should be transferred to a shipper in our supply chain.

Execute the `TransferAsset()` function by passing the shipper's address and asset Id.

Write the second test and add the following code to the `TestAssetTracker.js` test file:

```
it('Transfer to Shipper, owner should be shipper', async () => {

//Execute transfer function to transfer Aston Martin DB11 asset to
Shipper (accounts[1])
    assetTrackerInstance.transferAsset(accounts[1], assetId.valueOf());
    owner  =  await  assetTrackerInstance.getCurrentOwner.call(assetId.
valueOf());
    assert.equal(owner, accounts[1], "Shipper is not the owner");
});
```

The preceding code transfers the `Aston Martin DB11` vehicle asset to `Shipper` and validates the transfer.

Test 3: An asset can be transferred only to a dealer from the shipper.

Now, let's transfer an asset from the shipper to the dealer, and execute the `AssetTransfer` function by passing the dealer's address and asset Id.

Write the third test and copy the following code:

```
    it('Transfer to Dealer, owner should be Dealer', async () => {

    //Transfer to dealer

    assetTrackerInstance.transferAsset(accounts[2], assetId.valueOf());

      owner = await assetTrackerInstance.getCurrentOwner.call(assetId.
valueOf());

      assert.equal(owner, accounts[2], "Dealer is not the owner");

});
```

The preceding code transfers the **Aston Martin DB11** vehicle asset to the dealer and validates the transfer.

Test 4: An asset can be transferred only to a buyer from the dealer.

Now, let's transfer the asset from the dealer to the buyer, and execute the `AssetTransfer` function by passing the buyer's address and asset Id.

Write the third test and copy the following code:

```
    it('Transfer to Buyer, owner should be Buyer', async () => {

    //Transfer to buyer

    assetTrackerInstance.transferAsset(accounts[3], assetId.valueOf());

      owner = await assetTrackerInstance.getCurrentOwner.call(assetId.
valueOf());

      assert.equal(owner, accounts[3], "Buyer is not the owner");

    });
```

The preceding code transfers the `Aston Martin DB11` vehicle asset to the buyer and validates the transfer.

Run all the tests with the Truffle test

We have written four tests to validate the smart contract behavior. In this section, let's run these tests.

Navigate to the `AssetTracker` folder and run the following command in the Terminal. The **truffle test** will run all the tests:

```
$truffle test
```

The output of running the tests will be as follows:

```
murughan@murughan-Inspiron-5570:~/projects/AssetTracker$ truffle test
Using network 'development'.


Compiling your contracts...
===============================
> Everything is up to date, there is nothing to compile.



  Contract: AssetTracker
    ✓ Create participants and asset, owner should be Manufacturer (537ms)
    ✓ Transfer to Shipper, owner should be shipper (94ms)
    ✓ Transfer to Dealer, owner should be Dealer (73ms)
    ✓ Transfer to Buyer, owner should be Buyer (72ms)


  4 passing (972ms)
```

Figure 12.3: Run all the tests

In the preceding screenshot, it shows that all the tests are passing. If your tests are failing, which means the contract is not behaving as expected, you need to fix the contract functions.

This finishes our testing of basic expectations, and you can add more tests for high quality. In the next section, we will build the UI and interact with the AWS Ethereum private network through web3.js.

web3.js

web3.js is a collection of libraries that allows you to interact with an Ethereum node using the HTTP, WebSocket, or IPC connection.

web3.js provides the following three libraries to interact with the Ethereum network:

- web-eth:This is used for the Ethereum blockchain and smart contracts.
- web3-shh: This is used for the whisper protocol to communicate p2p and broadcast.
- web3-utils: This provides a helper function to build a Decentralized Application (DApp).

Installing web3.js

We have installed web3 in the previous chapter, and if you have not installed it, as yet, please install it now.

web3.js can be installed using npm node package manager. Enter the following command inside the `AssetTracker` directory to install **web3**.

```
$ npm install web3
```

Initiating web3

To use the **web3** library, firstly you need to set up the provider. The provider is the **Ethereum** network. It can be the local **Ganache** network, **Rinkeby**, **Kovan**, **Ropsten**, **Infura**, main network, or private network.

The following code is used to connect to a local network. We will use this code in the next section:

```
Import Web3 from 'web3';

const web3 = new Web3(Web3.givenProvider || 'http://localhost:7545');
```

Enter the following command to connect to the AWS Ethereum private network:

```
const web3 = new Web3(new Web3.providers.HttpProvider('<AWS private Etherum RPC>'));
```

web3 modules and functions

web3 provides many modules and functions to interact with the network, deploy smart contracts, get details for Ethereum blocks, transactions, and so on.

The following are some of the modules and functions of web3:

- **web3.eth**: To interact with the Ethereum network
- **web3.eth.getBalance()**: To get the account balance of an account
- **web3.eth.getAccounts()**: To get the list of accounts
- **web3.eth.getCode(<address>)**: To get the code for the provided address
- **web3.eth.getBlock(<blockHashorBlockNumber>)**: To get the details of the block
- **web3.eth.getBlockTransactionCount(<blockHashOrBlockNumber>)**: To get the transaction in a block
- **web3.eth.sendTransaction({from, to, value })**: To execute a transaction
- **web3.eth.call(callObject)**: To call functions of a smart contact
- **web3.eth.contract(<ABI>)**: To create the contract object
- **web3.shh**: To interact with the whisper protocol
- **web3.net**: To interact with the network properties
- **web3.personal**: To interact with Ethereum accounts

Building the frontend application with HTML, CSS, and Node.js

In this section, we will build the frontend application with HTML, CSS, JavaScript, and Node.js. Truffle provides boxes for React, Vue.js, and Angular., You can build it with any of your preferred frameworks.

Adding UI and JavaScript files to the project

I have created these UI components and files that are available on my GitHub repository, which you can download from this URL- https://github.com/murughan1985/AssetTracker-Blockchain-AWS.

Make sure you copy all the files as shown in the following screenshot:

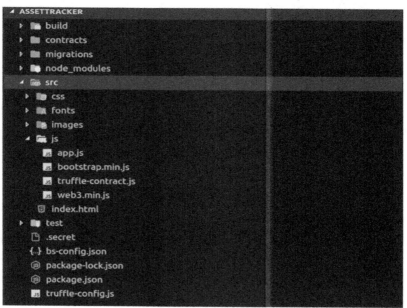

Figure 12.4: Project files

We will explore each of the files in detail in the upcoming sections.

Writing app.js to interact with the Asset Tracker contract

We have deployed our AssetTracker contract and tested the behavior in the *chapter 11* Create and Deploy Asset Tracker Contract on AWS.

In this section, we will interact with the contract through the web3.js library.

We will add the following functions to the app.js file which is under the src/js folder.

Creating the application object

We will create an application object called App to hold the variables and objects, and add the following code to the app.js file:

```
App = {
  contracts: {},
  init: async () => {
    await App.initWeb3();
    await App.initContract();
  },
}
$(() => {
  $(window).init(() => {
    App.init()
  })
})
```

In the preceding code, we have declared contracts variable to hold our AssetTracker contract. When the page starts, the web3.js provider will be initialized and an instance of the AssetTracker contract will be created withthe init() function.

Initializing the web3 provider

Here, we need to establish a connection with the local or AWS Ethereum blockchain network where we have deployed our AssetTracker contract. Metamask will be used for all the transactions. We will connect to the AWS Ethereum network which you have deployed in *Chapter 9* AWS Blockchain Template to Create Private Ethereum.

Open your AWS Ethereum private network CloudFormation template which you have deployed in the *Chapter 9* AWS Blockchain Template to Create Private Ethereum, copy the `EthJsonRPCURL detail,` and paste the following configuration in the `app.js` file:

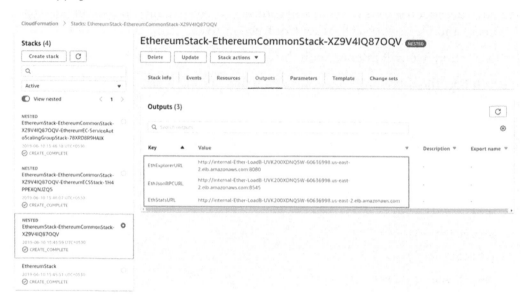

Figure 12.5: *Copy URLs from the CloudFormation output*

Add your `EthJsonRPCURL` link as follows:

```
initWeb3: async () => {
  if (typeof web3 !== 'undefined') {
    App.web3Provider = new Web3(web3.currentProvider)
  } else {
            App.web3Provider  =  new  Web3(new  Web3.providers.
HttpProvider('<EthJsonRPCURL>:8545'))
  }
},
```

This code will check whether you are using the modern DApp browser or the recent MetaMask which comes with the Ethereum provider which is injected into the window object. If you are using the older DApp browser, then we will get its provider and create a web3 object. This code will connect to the AWS Ethereum private network.

Instantiating the contract

We need to instantiate a smart contract so that web3 can interact with the AssetTracker contract. Truffle provides the `truffle-contract` library which holds the contract in sync with migrations and takes the recently migrated/deployed network.

In the same `app.js` file, add the following code:

```
initContract: async () => {
  // Create a JavaScript version of the smart contract
  const AssetTrackerArtifact = await $.getJSON('AssetTracker.json')
  App.contracts.AssetTracker = TruffleContract(AssetTrackerArtifact)
  App.contracts.AssetTracker.setProvider(App.web3Provider)
  // Hydrate the smart contract with values from the blockchain
  App.instanceAssetTracker = await App.contracts.AssetTracker.deployed()
},
```

This code retrieves `AssetTracker` ABI which was created while compiling the contract. This is a JavaScript object which has all the contract details. Using these details, `TruffleContract` will create an instance of the contract.

Now, the `AssetTracker` contract is instantiated and the `App.instance AssetTracker` variable holds the instance to our contract. In the next section, we will invoke contract functions through the `App.instanceAssetTracker` variable. Each Ethereum transaction requires gas which is the fee to be paid in Ether cryptocurrency.

Function to create a manufacturer

We will create a JavaScript function to create a manufacturer. Add the following code to the `app.js` file:

```
createManufacturer: async () => {
 await App.instanceAssetTracker.createManufacturer($('#manufacturerName').
val(), $('#manufacturerAddress').val(), $('#manufacturerLoc').val());
  },
```

This code reads the input (manufacturer account address, manufacturer location, and manufacturer name) from the UI and invokes the `createManufacturer()` function in the contract. This transaction will be mined by one of the nodes in AWS and a block in the network will be created.

Function to create a shipper

Now, we will create a JavaScript function to create a shipper. Add the following code to the app.js file:

```
createShipper: async () => {
    await App.instanceAssetTracker.createShipper($('#shipperName').val(),
$('#shipperAddress').val(), $('#shipperLoc').val());
},
```

This code reads the input (shipper account address, shipper location, and shipper name) from the UI, and invokes the createShipper() function in the contract.

Function to create a dealer

Let's now create a JavaScript function to create a dealer. Add the following code to the app.js file:

```
createDealer: async () => {
    await App.instanceAssetTracker.createDealer($('#dealerName').val(),
$('#dealerAddress').val(), $('#dealerLoc').val());
},
```

This code reads the input (dealer account address, dealer location, and dealer name) from the UIand invokes the createDealer() function in the contract.

Function to create a buyer

Now, let's create a JavaScript function to create a buyer. Add the following code to the app.js file:

```
createBuyer: async () => {
    await App.instanceAssetTracker.createBuyer($('#buyerName').val(),
$('#buyerAddress').val(), $('#buyerLoc').val());
},
```

This code reads the input (buyer account address, buyer location, and buyer name) from the UI and invokes the createBuyer() function in the contract.

Function to create an asset

We will create a JavaScript function to create an asset. Add the following code to the app.js file:

```
createAsset: async () => {
  await App.instanceAssetTracker.createAsset($('#assetName').val());
  const assetId = await App.instanceAssetTracker.assetId.call();
  alert("Asset is succesfully created with the ID of: " +
assetId.valueOf())
},
```

This code reads an asset name from the UI and invokes the `createAsset()` function in the contract. This function creates a new asset in the blockchain and maintains the unique ID (assetId) for each asset which will be used to transfer the asset and get the current owner of the asset.

Function to transfer an asset

Let's now create a JavaScript function to transfer an asset, and add the following code to the `app.js` file:

```
transferAsset: async () => {
  await App.instanceAssetTracker.transferAsset($('#toAddress').val(),
$('#asssetId').val());
    const owner = await App.instanceAssetTracker.getCurrentOwner.
call($('#asssetId').val());    alert("Current asset owner is : " + owner.
valueOf())
},
```

This code will be used to transfer the asset from one participant to another. The flow of asset as per our use case is from manufacturer ->shipper ->dealer ->buyer. Once the transfer is done, this code verifies the current owner by calling the `getCurrentOwner()` contract function.

Writing the index.html page

We have created all the required JavaScript functions to interact with the `AssetTracker` contract which is deployed on the AWS Ethereum private network. In this section, we will create an `index.html` page as our UI. We have created this page with HTML, CSS, and jQuery, but you can use any UI frameworks like Angular, React, and Vue.js as well.

Open the `index.html` file from the `src` folder and look at the following code:

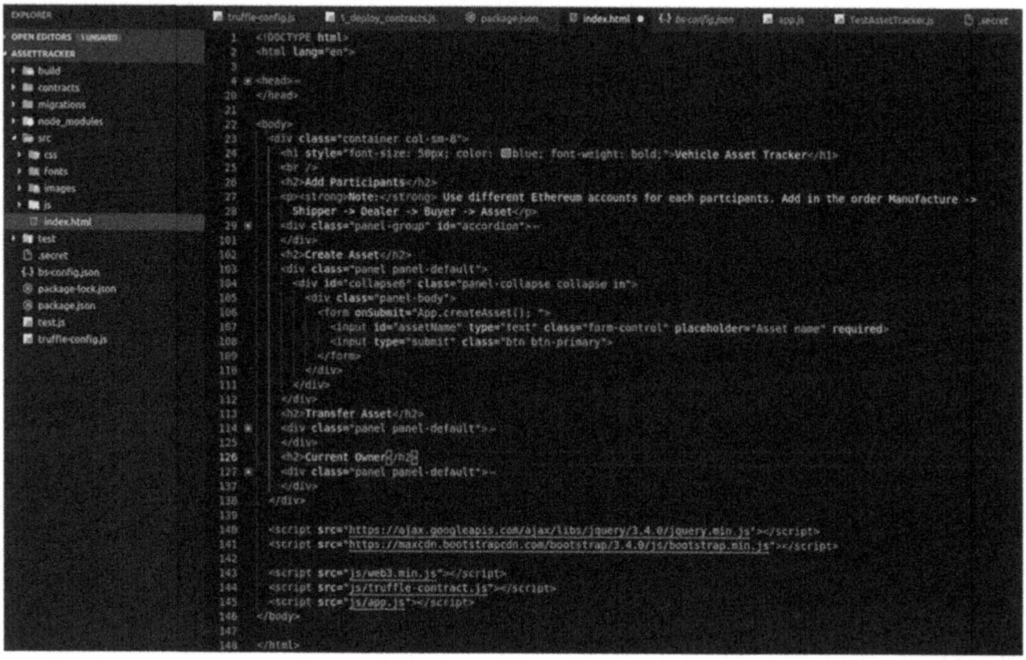

Figure 12.6: The index.html page

It's just the regular HTML and CSS, but the only difference is that we are calling all the JavaScript functions with the click of a button:

```
<form onSubmit="App.createAsset(); ">

<input id="assetName" type="text" class="form-control" placeholder="Asset name" required>

<input type="submit" class="btn btn-primary">

</form>
```

Running the application against AWS

So far, our frontend application is ready, and we have written a JavaScript code to interact with the AWS Ethereum private network. In this section, we will run the application and interact with the `AssetTracker` smart contract deployed on AWS through the UI.

The steps to run the application are as follows:

1. Configure lite-server.
2. Verify the connection to the bastion host and MetaMask which is connected to the AWS Ethereum private network.

3. Run the application.

4. Interact with the UI.

5. Monitor the AWS Ethereum private network through Ethstat and EthExplorer.

Step 1: Configure lite-server

We will usethe lite-server library to run our static files.

1. Create a file called `bs-config.json` under the project's root directory AssetTracker and add the following code. This configuration tells lite-server which files to include.

```
{
"server": {
"baseDir": ["./src", "./build/contracts"]
}
}
```

2. To run the code locally, let's add the **dev** command in the `package.json` file:

```
"scripts": {
"dev": "lite-server" },
```

Step2: Verify the connection to the bastion host and MetaMask connected to the AWS Ethereum private network.

1. Make sure you have created the AWS Ethereum private network with the AWS Blockchain template and deployed the AssetTracker smart contract as mentioned in *Chapter 9* AWS Blockchain Template to Create Private Ethereum *Chapter 11* Create and Deploy Asset Tracker Contract on AWS.

2. Verify if you can `ssh` to the bastion host as shown in the following screenshot:

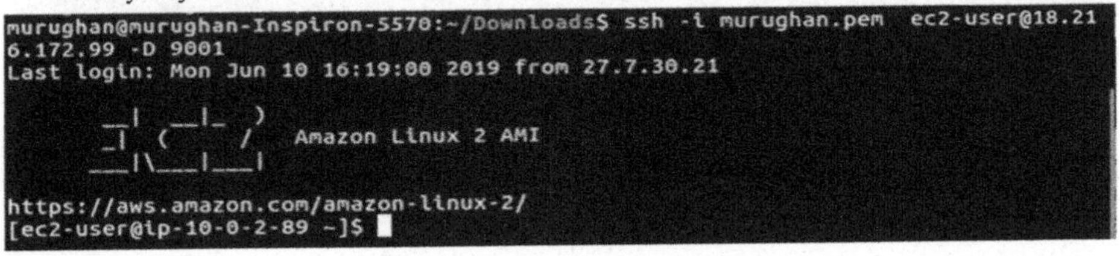

```
murughan@murughan-Inspiron-5570:~/Downloads$ ssh -i murughan.pem  ec2-user@18.21
6.172.99 -D 9001
Last login: Mon Jun 10 16:19:00 2019 from 27.7.30.21

     __|  __|_  )
     _|  (     /   Amazon Linux 2 AMI
    ___|\___|___|

https://aws.amazon.com/amazon-linux-2/
[ec2-user@ip-10-0-2-89 ~]$ 
```

Figure 12.7: ssh to the bastion host

3. Verify if you can connect to EthJsonRPCURL with MetaMask as shown in the following screenshot. If you haven't done this, please refer to *Chapter 9* AWS Blockchain Template to Create Private Ethereum.

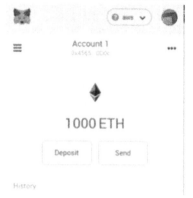

Figure 12.8: Connect to EthJsonRPCURL

Step3: Run the application and interact through the UI.

1. Navigate to the Terminal root directory of the project, and enter the following command:

```
$npm run dev
```

```
murughan@murughan-Inspiron-5570:~/projects/AssetTracker$ npm run dev

> Asset-Tracker@1.0.0 dev /home/murughan/projects/AssetTracker
> lite-server

** browser-sync config **
{ injectChanges: false,
  files: [ './**/*.{html,htm,css,js}' ],
  watchOptions: { ignored: 'node_modules' },
  server:
   { baseDir: [ './src', './build/contracts' ],
     middleware: [ [Function], [Function] ] } }
[Browsersync] Access URLs:
----------------------------------------
     Local: http://localhost:3000
  External: http://192.168.0.7:3000
```

Figure 12.9: npm run dev

2. This will open the AssetTracker UI in the browser with **http://localhost:3000/** and make sure your AWS network is selected in MetaMask:

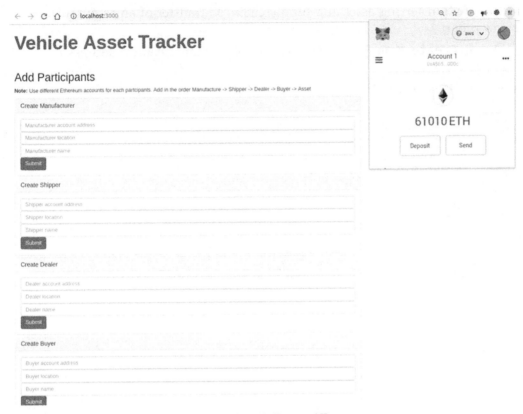

Figure 12.10: Browser UI

Step4: Interact with the UI.

Our UI is now ready. We will use a different Ethereum account address for each participant. If you have already created accounts in MetaMask, you can use them, or create the accounts as follows:

Figure 12.11: Use MetaMask account

As we are transferring asset in a supply chain, so transfer of an asset must follow below order:

1. In **Create Manufacturer**, give your Ethereum account 1 address:

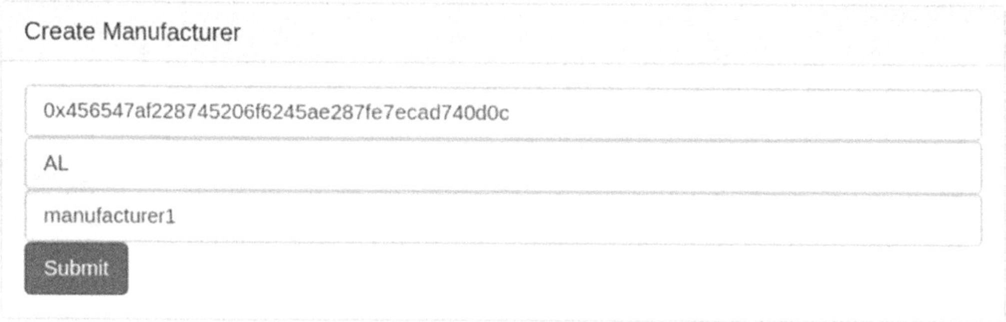

Create Manufacturer

0x456547af228745206f6245ae287fe7ecad740d0c

AL

manufacturer1

Submit

Figure 12.12: Create Manufacturer

2. In **Create Shipper**, give your Ethereum account 2 address:

Create Shipper

0x0e13d46e5E8960f597a84DfBDd435b4C329771c1

shipper1

IL

Submit

Figure 12.13: Create Shipper

3. In **Create Dealer**, give your Ethereum account 3 address:

Create Dealer

0xEc0Bc2f0137121f27A325B2487ff5ED3625FBECe

CO

dealer1

Submit

Figure 12.14: Create Dealer

4. In **Create Buyer**, give your Ethereum account 4 address:

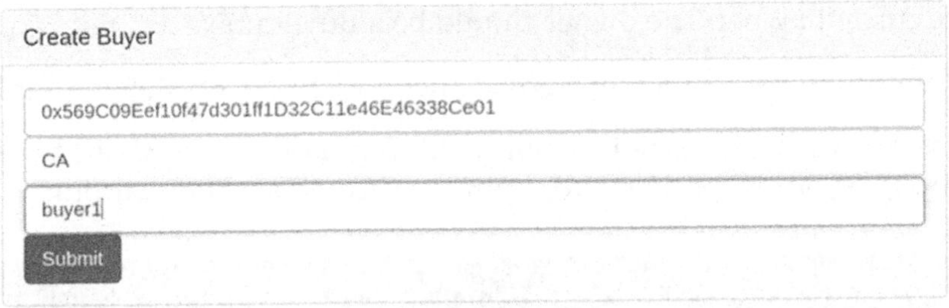

Figure 12.15: Create Buyer

5. In **Create Asset**, give any name for the vehicle asset:

Create Asset

Figure 12.16: Create Asset

6. In Transfer asset to Shipper, provide the shipper's Ethereum account address:

Transfer Asset

Figure 12.17: Transfer Asset to Shipper

7. In Transfer asset to Dealer, provide the dealer's Ethereum account address:

Transfer Asset

Figure 12.18: Transfer asset to Dealer

8. In Transfer asset to Buyer, provide thebuyer's Ethereum account address:

Transfer Asset

Figure 12.19: Transfer asset to Buyer

Check the current owner. The owner should be a Buyer now.

Step5: Monitor the AWS Ethereum private network using Ethstat and EthExplorer.

You can verify each transaction detail in **EthExplorer** as shown in the following screenshot. Use your respective URL from the CloudFormation output:

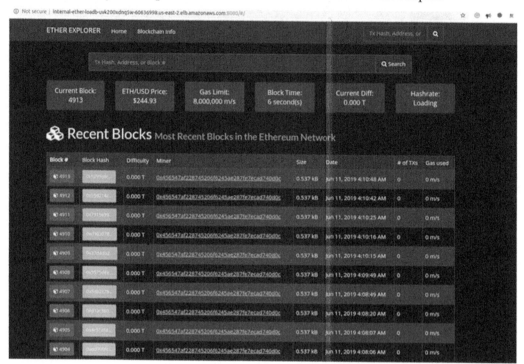

Figure 12.20: EthExplorer

You can verify each transaction detail in EthStat as shown in the following screenshot. Use your respective URL from the CloudFormation output:

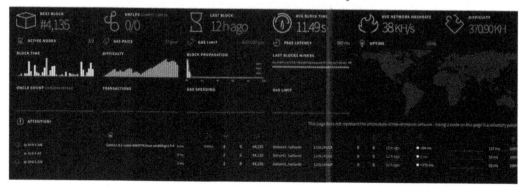

Figure 12.21: EthStat

We have successfully completed deploying AssetTracker to the AWS Ethereum private network and interacting with the contract functions through the UI.

Conclusion

We have written the unit test for multiple scenarios, and we have built a simple UI and used web3.js to interact with the AWS Ethereum private network.

We learned how to build an end-to-end application with Ethereum and host it on AWS. With this knowledge, you will be able to build any Blockchain application to interact with the Ethereum network.

Points to remember

- Every unit of the code we write should be validated against the expected behavior. A unit is a small testable part of the code. Writing a unit test builds confidence in modifying the code and makes it easy to refactor and maintain.

- Use the **truffle test** to run tests.

- Monitor the AWS Ethereum private network using **Ethstat** and **EthExplorer**.

Multiplechoice questions

1. Truffle is used to:

   a) Develop smart contracts

   b) Deploy smart contracts

   c) Test smart contracts

   d) All of the above

2. **Ethstat** and **EthExplorer** are used to monitor the Ethereum network.

   a) Yes

   b) No

Answers

1. **b**

2. **a**

Questions

1. What is a unit test?

2. Write a unit test for a healthcare smart contract.

3. Design a UI and run tests for a sample healthcare supply chain.

Key terms

1. **Truffle test:** Helps in validating a smart contract by running tests.

Index

Made in the USA
Coppell, TX
20 January 2022

71997674R00208